DEEPENING
INTIMACY IN
PSYCHOTHERAPY

DEEPENING INTIMACY IN PSYCHOTHERAPY

Using the Erotic Transference and Countertransference

Florence W. Rosiello, Ph.D.

JASON ARONSON INC.
Northvale, New Jersey
London

This book was set in 11 pt. Berkeley by Alpha Graphics of Pittsfield, NH and printed and bound by Book-mart Press, Inc. of North Bergen, NJ.

Library of Congress Cataloging-in-Publication Data

Rosiello, Florence.
    Deepening intimacy in psychotherapy : using the erotic transference and countertransference / Florence Rosiello.
        p. cm.
    Includes index.
    ISBN 0-7657-0265-7
    1. Psychotherapy—Erotic aspects. 2. Transference (Psychology) 3. Countertransference (Psychology) I. Title.

RC489.E75 R67 2000
616.89'14—dc21   99-089270

Printed in the United States of America on acid-free paper. For information and catalog write to Jason Aronson Inc., 230 Livingston Street, Northvale, NJ 07647-1726, or visit our website: www.aronson.com

To my niece,

Lauren F. Henry

Contents

Acknowledgments

I would like to express my gratitude to my husband, James, for his support and encouragement, and especially for his ability to find curious references in unusual places. I would like to thank Jason Aronson, M.D., and his editorial staff for their help and assistance. Particularly, my gratitude goes to Jeffrey Seinfeld, Ph.D., who read my papers on erotic transference, at the request of Gary Jacobson, CSW, and liked them enough to help move them toward publication in this book. It was Dr. Seinfeld's suggestion that I send my writings to Dr. Aronson with hopes of publication. Dr. Seinfeld's readings of each chapter, sent to him piecemeal over a year, elicited his enthusiasm and support and for this I am indebted.

My inspiration in writing this book was derived from a Study Group that I have been attending for the last twelve years. This group, led by Emmanuel Kaftal, Ph.D., created the opportunity to struggle with theory, clinical material, and unformulated ideas in a challenging, stimulating environment. I would like to thank the Study Group members, who always managed to find time in their schedules to read developing papers in a critical manner, spurring me on to think more about a therapeutic notion or to support an idea that was forming. Their input has been crucial to the development of my thoughts and to my writing. Thank you to Gilbert Cole, CSW, Leslie Goldstein, CSW, and Rosanna Murry, CSW, who make up the Study Group. A special thank you to Dana Lerner, CSW, who wrote of her experience as my supervisee in a companion paper to Chapter 8.

Much of my writing and clinical work has been mentored by Emmanuel Kaftal, Ph.D., who has been a constant source of scholarship, clinical expertise, and friendship. His influence on my writing began when I was in psychoanalytic training where, as my teacher, he suggested I write a clinical paper on a patient I was treating, "just for the experience of writing." Dr. Kaftal has guided the development of my style of writing and, through his encouraging insight on my work, helped me give form to concepts and ideas.

Lastly, I would like to thank my dance instructor Mark Poucher, who taught me how to tango and led to my writing Chapter 7, on "The Tango, Female Fetish, and Phobia." Thanks also to Melissa Caspary, whose computer skills and organizational direction kept me moving ahead at times when portions of the manuscript were lost in cyberspace. Her retrieval abilities were crucial to the production of the manuscript.

Introduction

I have never considered myself a writer. My colleagues say I must update this attitude since having written a book typically means a person actually has become an author. Instead, I think of myself as a good storyteller, a recorder of other people's narratives that create form and fantasy in my mind. This book is a collection of stories of clinical experiences with patients who have developed an erotic transference and about a therapist who has struggled with erotic countertransference issues in response. I have not written a prescriptive text on treating individuals who are subject to erotic transference developments, although some readers may perceive it that way; rather this is a clinical account of relational strife around sexuality. I have struggled to provide a different insight into mind–body configurations within a particular patient population. In discussing these patients' sexualized stories, as well as my own in response, I found that the process of writing down our experiences became a way of understanding and recognizing what we were creating or constructing together.

This foray into writing began over a decade ago, originating in a desire to better know my own emotional experience with a group of gay men with AIDS that I was treating. Their response to the method of psychotherapy I practiced then was outrage and a demand for more of my own emotional involvement in the group process. When I began treating this AIDS group, I was working from a one-person self psychology perspective, a classical Kohutian stance based on the analyst as mirrored screen of the patient's subjective experiences and selfobject transferences. This type of self psychology has an analogous connection to the blank screen of the traditional therapists who practice abstinence in relation to the patient's neurotic transference.

The AIDS group I was leading insisted I take as large an emotional risk as they did, in order for the group process to develop in an emotionally honest manner for all participants. In other words, if the group members wanted my emotional reaction to something that was said, they didn't just want an empathic response, or an interpretation, or an insight—they wanted my real emotional reaction in recognition of their own. That reaction could be followed up with an empathic response, with a genetic or transference interpretation, or an insight, but somewhere in the intersubjective mix, the group wanted the therapist to relate as an emotional and real being.

At the time, the group members' demand for my being emotionally present and forthcoming felt quite risky. How much was too much emotion to give? How much was just enough? On my part, thinking these thoughts made me feel manipulative, because it meant I was thinking, just how much could I give and manage to wiggle out of, or get away with, and still have the group members provide their emotion anyway? I then realized I would be guilty of their charge, which was that I wasn't being as emotionally present as they were.

Some people might say that therapists do not, or don't have to emote in the way the patient does. It's not the therapist's treatment, it's the patient's treatment. These individuals would contend the therapeutic relationship is asymmetrical, with the therapist in control of the process, and I agree. Treatment is not equal; the roles and responsibilities of patient and therapist are different. The patient does not mirror the therapist's feelings or provide interpretations, nor does the therapist self-disclose personal histories or discuss day-to-day real life events at the therapeutic expense of the patient.

Contemporary therapists, particularly the Relational Approach therapists, among whom I include myself, would agree that the therapeutic relationship is indeed asymmetrical, but would also add that the relationship is, more importantly, mutual. Mutuality means emotional reciprocity between patient and therapist, unity through similarity of shared emotions (rarely self-disclosed by the therapist to the patient), and acceptance of difference or autonomy, all as a way to deepen intimacy, to know the self, to know an other, or to tolerate the unknown self–other creation. In the Relational Approach, mutuality finds a delicate balance of self-regulation and autonomy; it highlights the difference between a one-person and a two-person therapy. The struggle to determine the extent of the therapist's involvement has its roots in the theoretical dialectics between Sigmund Freud and Sandor Ferenczi, each considered the father of one- or two-person psychology, respectively (Aron 1996).

While the one-person perspective assigns the therapist an all-knowing, superior understanding of the patient's internal and external life, the two-person perspective assigns mutuality to knowing self and other. What this means is that both patient and therapist mutually create the meaning of what is experienced in, or what motivates other and self. The therapist's interpretations are constantly subject to multiple meanings constructed by both therapist and patient in the effort to negotiate and mutually create both what is known and what is unknown about the patient's self.

Did the AIDS group members ask for mutuality when they wanted my honest emotions and real reactions to their group plight? Actually, I think they wanted more than mutuality. At the time, it felt as if they were asking for a response that contained an emotional risk on my part. Perhaps they wanted a more powerful response because they were dealing with life-and-death issues that felt more immediate, more desperate, more demanding, more controlling than the rest of us have in our usual life experiences. Frequently, they felt they didn't have time to negotiate or co-create a mutual therapeutic process and wanted emotional gratification first, then analysis. I didn't agree then, nor do I now—analysis of a patient's inner dynamic or interaction comes first, since the therapist's actuality or reality may dilute the patient's real response, the patient's own experience or fantasy.

Still, even though I didn't agree with the group's need for my response first, and my analyses second, they had a point—they said it would work better for them. This began a mutual negotiation of sorts, in that they would take a risk and be as honest and emotionally intimate as they could be in their last years of life if I could take a similar emotional and therapeutic risk, and then we would analyze together what was co-constructed. If the members on the other team have the ball and say they won't play if you don't consider their rules, then you have to wonder where you put your own balls. I decided to risk being at risk.

But what do I mean by risk? The dictionary defines risk as the act of committing danger to one's life. Certainly, therapeutic change could be considered dangerous to one's inner life; it is a destruction of sorts of defenses that no longer help the individual. For instance, we ask our patients to take emotional risks and experience something new each time we treat them. The mutual journey that the therapist and patient make into the patient's internality suggests that as therapists we partner our patients in taking emotional risks in the clinical process; this is one understanding of risks the therapist takes. Another occurs as we ride tandem on the patient's journey and risk an emotional vulnerability of our own unknown intimacies to ourselves. By this I don't mean self-disclosing our intimate experiences or our emotions to the patient; instead, I mean surrendering our vulnerabilities to our self, and altering the self paradigm with its inherent securities as we encourage patients to alter their own safety in struggling with who they are. I also don't mean a self-analysis of the therapist during the patient's session. Rather, I mean the therapist's openness to new and unknown countertransference reactions, sexual or nonsexual fantasies, mind–body experiences that create the potential for better understanding the patient's meaning and motivation in life.

Why would an emotional risk be useful for the therapist? William James said in "The Will to Believe" (1896), "It is only by risking our persons from one hour to another that we live at all. And often enough[,] our faith beforehand in an uncertified result is the only thing that makes the result come true" (p. 25). Some therapists hold this notion true enough when considering the patient's progress in and out of the treatment hour. Still, it is important to have the same criteria for ourselves in the patient's treatment, and to risk our own emotional safety.

I will explain the notion of the therapist taking emotional risks in the patient's treatment through clinical example. When I first realized a patient of mine had developed an erotic transference I remember feeling worried about his erotic wanderings during the session. What were the limits and boundaries, who created them, he or I, who led, who followed, who evoked and who provoked the eroticism? At the time, I felt it was important to create a safe-enough environment for the patient to express what he felt, and that meant verbally conveying that erotic feelings could not and would not be enacted. This verbal frame or parameter felt false and I felt that something in its falseness created false treatment. Would I tell a patient who was angry with me that expressing anger was safe? I wouldn't. I would let the patient's anger have full emotional freedom without verbalizing that I would keep her safe.

When we say to a patient that a specific emotional expression is safe, we set up an artificial boundary around exploration and recognition of the patient's fantasy or psyche or body experience. In a mutual treatment, this artificial frame of safety also limits the therapist's fantasy or psyche or body experience in understanding or recognizing the patient. The therapist is not exempt from her own subjective experiences outside the patient's analysis, and if the patient is to take emotional risks, so can the therapist.

> Intersubjectivity refers to the capacity of the mind to directly register the responses of the other. It is affected by whether the other recognizes what we have done and is likewise charged with recognizing the other's acts. Above all intersubjectivity refers to our capacity to recognize the other as an independent subject. In the mutual exchange (or denial) of recognition, each self is transformed, [and] this transformation is a condition of each subject's expression (or denial) of her or his own capacities. Whatever breakdowns in recognition occur, as they inevitably do, the primary intersubjective condition of erotic life is that of "experiencing the dizziness together." [Benjamin 1995, p. 183]

Experiencing the dizziness together, as Benjamin states, is found in the process of recognition of the other and in mutual exchange. Mutuality—defined as shared but different emotional experience, reciprocation and unity between individuals—is a neat goal in any relationship, but it is the striving for this goal that creates a mutual-enough environment in which treatment can take place. It's two people trying to be mutual that counts, not actually achieving mutuality—a merged nirvana—between two people. Absolute sharing and sameness doesn't exist between any two or more individuals, mutuality in treatment does not include equality. This notion of mutuality as an intersubjective goal and not as an attainable intersubjective state is an important consideration in therapy—one that presents the therapist with risks.

How do therapists know when they have been mutual enough? Do we wait for the patient to be mutual first, or do we determine the degree of mutuality we are willing to create with the patient? Typically, both patient and therapist co-create their specific level of mutuality in the unfolding of intimacy in their relationship. But, what about those of us who have patients with little experience of being in a mutual relationship?

In the last chapter of this book, I discuss treatment with a man who did not speak for the first six months of therapy. The relationship existed because there were two bodies present in one room at the same time, "relationship" being relative in this sense. Our association to each other only began to take on recognizable aspects of a relationship when I began discussing and analyzing characters in the books I saw he was reading. Essentially, I created monologues two sessions a week for months as he played with his fingers or his rings or his glasses, not looking at me and not verbally responding. It was a risk (it was certainly grandiose on my part) to critique classical literature as a means of developing some obvious communication between us. While this was a therapeutic risk, it was fairly safe because so much was withheld from the therapist that there was little to lose. But what about a therapeutic risk that creates more emotional chance-taking for the therapist, including chances that realign the therapist's own boundaries like Lego parts, snapping into place here or there depending on what is being constructed? The metaphor of Lego parts that snap into and out of place to create structures and boundaries unknown to the builder (except in hindsight) captures the uncertainty the therapist feels when treating patients who develop erotic transference or transference love, as one works with the power and control inherent in sexual issues between people.

Then is this book just a history of sexual self-indulgence and exhibitionism on my part? I don't think that it's self-indulgent or exhibitionistic, because both treating patients who develop erotic transferences and working with one's own erotic countertransference create treatment and professional vulnerabilities for the therapist. Surrendering to the verbalized sexuality of patients and those sexual feelings within our self during therapeutic exploration creates opportunity for personal self-reproach. Publishing such cases opens the door for professional criticism. Still, discussing sexual or loving feelings in therapy when these feelings are directed at the therapist, and working with erotic emotions without eliminating them, can deepen or create an emotional intimacy that no other aspect of human relatedness can accomplish. Some of us just speak in a sexualized manner, as a method of communicating, a deeply felt inner language, just as for some of us sexuality is the origin of intimate feelings.

If this book is indeed a history of sexual self-indulgence in treatment, then maybe that's not such a bad thing. If it is self-indulgent, what is nevertheless described is a particular means of relating for some people, the sexual motivation for relatedness, a striving for sexuality through mutuality, or for meaning through sexuality.

I have found in writing this book that each chapter seemed to promote the development of the book. With the completion of one chapter, I felt the desire to include other patients or other dynamics in the next. Consequently, this book is an attempt to contribute to the clinical illustration of relational theorizing about erotic transference–countertransference.

In the first chapter, "Transference Love, Eros, and Attachment," I provide a brief review of the historical recognition of and the bias against the erotic transference in psychoanalytic literature. In addition, I use a variety of clinical examples to express my early experience with patients who developed erotic transference. The AIDS psychotherapy group I led for a few years was included in this chapter because that experience made such a powerful impact on me, as well as on the group members. From this experience, I altered my understanding and clinical use of erotic dynamics between patient and therapist and began to view sexuality from a theoretical perspective that focused more on mutuality, including mutual emotional risk between patient and therapist.

I also begin writing about a patient named June in the first chapter. June is a young woman who identifies as lesbian, and who has been as influential as the AIDS group members in changing my understanding of sexuality, the erotic transference–countertransference matrix, and in continuing the mutual struggle to explore previously unknown feelings, both within the self and with another.

It is interesting that although June finds it difficult to attain her own emotional and professional standards, her inner struggle and her journey to know her self through our work has had an enormous impact on me. Her questioning of her thoughts and feelings, whether in sessions or positioned in letters or e-mails to me, her desire to think creatively, and her ambition for emotional growth have left me wondering about my own affective input in her treatment. In other words, what emotional risks was I willing to take to help her in treatment? Could I be as mutually engaged and intimate as she wanted to be with me? Was I as willing to risk what I know and feel as she was in her treatment? June's psychic development in her therapy is chronologically presented in this book, culminating in the chapter entitled "The Tango, Female Fetish, and Phobia."

In Chapter 2, "Varieties of Erotic Transference and Countertransference," the three clinical illustrations focus on erotic transference–countertransference created by male patients with a female therapist. This chapter also highlights mutuality in treatment and discusses "who goes first" in developing reciprocity between therapist and patient. The chapter is subdivided into three sections. The first concerns the therapist's unconscious erotic countertransference with a patient, Benjamin, where erotic transference–countertransference issues were illuminated by the therapist's dream about this patient. The second section is about the therapist's response to the patient's conscious erotic transference. In this section the erotic transference is complicated by Michael's personal history of sexual abuse during his childhood, as well as by sexual abuse from his previous male therapist. The third section concerns the patient's response to the therapist's conscious transference. This section focuses on a patient, Peter, who has compulsive sex with women. He began treatment desiring the therapist's help in stopping his sexual compulsion, as well as with a desire to add me to his list.

Chapter 3 is titled "Homoerotic Transference and Countertransference between a Female Analyst and Female Patients." This essay grew from my frustration at failed attempts to find psychoanalytic literature on same-sex desire between heterosexuals. While some writing does exist, papers on this topic make up little more than a handful of essays.

This chapter focuses on three women, one who identified as bisexual, another as heterosexual, and one as lesbian. All three developed an erotic transference, and—in varying degrees, as with the three male patients in the previous chapter—I experienced erotic countertransference. In the first case, with Pauline, the patient who identifies as bisexual, the treatment focused on the patient's desire for the analyst as sexual subject–object, in the patient's exploration of herself as sexual subject. The second clinical example addresses homoerotic feelings of a heterosexual woman, Simone, and those counter-homoerotic feelings that developed in me, as well. This section details a phase of treatment where both women struggled with unknown erotic feelings within themselves as intimacy between them intensified. The question of "What makes sex, sex?" is posed in this section. In the last clinical illustration, with June, lustful feelings develop into loathing as her desires for my surrender to her emotional deadness locked us into a fierce battle for survival.

Chapter 4, titled, "Impasse as an Expression of Erotic Countertransference," was the most difficult chapter to write because it discusses a failed treatment that was never resolved. This chapter focuses on a female patient's desire for self-differentiation through her masquerade of two different types of clothing, one set of clothing performed her identification with her mother, and the other set of clothing performed her identification with me. This essay also addresses how a patient can masquerade changes in her outside life and appear to reflect changes motivated by inner-world alterations. My own erotic countertransference in this treatment masqueraded as awareness as well as desire, and it masked my not seeing what I thought I saw, and not knowing what I knew was, in this treatment and in the patient, an unfulfilled desire.

In Chapter 5, "Gender Performance: Possibility or Regret?" I discuss two clinical examples. One example is a biological man who identifies as "lesbian," a transgender male-to-female (MTF), whose sexual object choice is women. The second clinical example is of a gay man who performed drag at nightclubs. This chapter on transgenderism had its origins with June, who began one of her own sessions questioning my sexual identification and ended up wondering about my biological gender. Her questions only highlighted my own internal dialogue on my work with MTF patients.

In this chapter I also discuss masquerade, not as a mask of things hidden as in Chapter 4, but rather a masquerade of what exists, of emotions that perform gender, of presentation of self, of gender as an illustrated preference. The theme of this chapter on transgenderism is regret; for my transgendered patients it is the regret felt at not being in the biological body they desire, and for me in treating transgendered individuals, it is the regret that "anything is *not* possible."

"The Sacrificed Sister," Chapter 6, is the most personally revealing in that it originated in a real-life event in which I was "found" by an adult half-sister who hadn't known I existed. My thoughts about this experience and the effect it had on me prompted questions about my patients who had similar dynamics with their sisters. This chapter presents two clinical examples, as well as my own personal example of self and other sacrifice. The dynamics inherent in same-sex sibling relationships with a mother who is excessively available and who desires merger with one child, create the potential for a sacrificed sibling, who may allow the other sibling to escape emotional sacrifice . . . or not.

In Chapter 7, "The Tango, Female Fetish, and Phobia," I discuss another phase of treatment with June—who, after years of therapy, told me of a long-held secret sexual fetish. Its origins were described in relation to the origins of her pigeon phobia, which she had told me about when she began treatment. Listening to narratives on a phobia, however, is quite different than listening to descriptions of a sexual fetish that I found emotionally upsetting. In my desire to know June's inner life and to tolerate stories about her fetish, I found that my fantasy of dancing the tango played a major part in mutating my countertransference disgust. My inner-world fantasy created an opportunity to tolerate and listen to an other's inner fantasy, a flexibility which until then had been unavailable to me.

Chapter 8, "Supervision of the Erotic Transference," is about the process of surrendering to another as a means of altering the self. Although the notion of a patient surrendering in treatment as an aspect of object usage or being known by an other is an idea accepted by quite a few therapists, surrender as part of the supervisory process is not considered a necessary development. A basic assumption in therapy is that each patient has different needs and therapists modify responses to best fit each patient. Perhaps this assumption needs to be generalized to supervision for those supervisors who use experience-near instruction with supervisees.

This chapter is about my work with one particular female therapist whom I supervised for a year. She was treating a young man who developed an erotic transference. Dana came to supervision for help in working with the patient's transference as well as to explore her own erotic countertransference. Her personal experience in supervision is included as a companion essay at the end of this chapter.

Chapter 8 also includes a second look at my AIDS group experience. In a sense, this book comes full circle regarding clinical examples, as the first chapter included this same AIDS group therapy experience but from the perspective of aggression in erotic transference. In this chapter, however, I explore the notion of mutual surrender, first in the AIDS group, in the desire to know and recognize self and other, and then in the mutual risk between therapist and patient in being emotionally honest in intimacy. Such a process means that the therapist constructs emotional responses with the patient that are real and intimate, rather than offering a presentation of emotionally distant, intellectual interpretations. Intrapsychic and interpersonal motivations and meanings are not ignored. Instead, they are presented in the emotional moment, at more personal cost to the therapist's involvement.

Chapter 9, "The Treatment of an Asexual Man," is a clinical illustration of therapy with a male patient who presents as having no understanding or experience of love or sexuality. He feels he is destined to live out an isolated existence as punishment for the crime of being born to parents who did not want him and who physically abused him. Classical literature created an opening into this patient's story, and classical literature is the structure this patient uses to understand life around him. This chapter opens with Dostoevsky's *Crime and Punishment* and Mario's identification with Dostoevsky's main character, Raskolnikov, in that they both live as tortured souls relegated to piteous lives for a crime against humanity.

I have chosen to end the book with this chapter because here the importance of sexuality is highlighted through its absence. The chapter is about an asexual man who has structured his life to never experience another's touch or desire of him. Sex is nonexistent for this patient and because it is "nowhere" in the consulting room; its absence creates an enormous presence of regret—a regret for sex. In this last chapter, I have returned to the notion of regret as sorrow and remorse and loss as in Chapter 5, but here regret is also meant as a polite refusal of another's invitation for involvement in a function: a refusal to function as a human with potential for ever being sexual.

CONCLUSION

This book is about making meaning through sexuality in psychoanalysis and psychotherapy. I have written essays that highlight challenges, emotional risks taken by both patients and therapist, and treatment successes and failures, all of which focus on sexuality or the eclipse of sexuality. The therapeutic work we perform with patients builds new realities and some patients build these realities in a sexualized manner. At first, in my work with such patients, I attempted to deny my own sexual nature. I interpreted transference love as resistance, analyzed my countertransference outside the treatment room, and kept sexuality as limited as possible. With hindsight, I was putting my patients and myself into a mold that, while it was psychoanalytic, it did not encourage self-honesty or trust of another, and to me it is the latter that is the foundation of psychoanalysis and therapeutic action. Later, I realized that who I am creates the instrument I use in treatment, and that it was important to be as authentic as possible in helping my patients achieve their own authenticity.

I realize what I have written is not right for all patients and therapists. Some patients feel threatened by their own sexual feelings, as do some therapists, and for those individuals, my work may conjure a fear of unbridled countertransference, or feelings of being burdened by an alien way of relating. For others, it may seem that I have taken my own character into account, used a theoretical perspective that allows for both analyst's and patient's subjective experience and mutual exploration in treatment, and work with patients who are also predisposed to relating to another in a sexualized manner. Still, I am not promoting "a way of working" with patients, but rather "another way of treating some patients"— and this may be useful.

Transference Love, Eros, and Attachment[1]

In one of the last sessions of Anna O's treatment with Josef Breuer in 1882, she revealed she was pregnant with his child (Freud 1932). One account of this day suggested that Breuer abruptly terminated the treatment, another stated it was Anna O, but nevertheless, Breuer learned that same evening his patient was in the throes of a hysterical pregnancy. The next day, Breuer left Vienna with his wife for a second honeymoon.

Later (Jones 1953) Freud wrote about Breuer's trauma to his own wife, Martha, who hoped this phenomenon would not happen to her husband. Freud admonished Martha for her vanity in thinking other women would fall in love with her husband, and denied that his patients would ever fall in love with him. Martha, on the other hand, had intuitively understood the universal nature of the problem. A short time later, Freud learned that Anna O's reaction to Breuer was more the rule than the exception—the "talking cure" in psychoanalysis inherently facilitated the development of erotic feelings (Person 1993).

---

1. This chapter was originally published in Tosone and Aiello (1999).

It is my assertion that the erotic transference[2] can serve a facilitating function toward therapeutic "cure" in the sense of its being a special love or symbol of intimacy with the analyst. I am referring to patients who are able to immerse themselves in their own inner life through the development of transference love. The patient experiences this love as creating a very special intimacy that allows exploration of the self in relation to (an)other.

The unfolding of transference love in such patients is developed by their having a particular *symbolic attitude* (Deri 1984). This implies a paired stance vis-à-vis experience, in which the patient feels an interpenetrating alteration of the *symbolic* with the *real* or actual. This way of thinking, conceived by Deri (1984), differs from Freud's thoughts on the nature of the mind. Freud (1923) envisioned the mind as a mental apparatus always at odds with itself. He gave the example of the horse as the id struggling with the rider, the ego. Deri (1984) argued that the mind could develop symbolic structures that functioned to unify conflict. She used the example of the *centaur* (p. 292) rather than the horse and rider to represent the different dimensions of the mind, as not merely a condensation as Freud would have considered it, but as a new structure that unified the conflict between ego and id—in other words, the mind as a complex whole rather than two antagonistic and conflicting parts.

I would like to use Deri's metaphor of the centaur to illustrate the symbolic along with the real or actual quality of transference love. The *symbolic* is the patient's fear and resistance against an emergence of incestuous wishes (represented by the horse), and the *real* or actual quality is the patient's wish to enact his or her love toward the analyst (represented as the rider). These two inimical representations make up—in the reorganization of the mind—a third entity, neither horse nor rider but centaur, that is, transference love.

---

2. For the purpose of this book, the term *erotic transference* is used interchangeably with the term *transference love*, in keeping with analytic literature on the subject. Transference love refers to a combination of sexual and tender feelings that a patient develops in relation to his or her analyst. This phenomenon can also encompass demands for physical and sexual relations, assaultive antagonisms, demands for approval, and dependent fears of object loss (Person 1985).

In my experience, this capacity on the part of some patients only partially overlaps with what is usually called *ego strength*. Yet there are so-called borderline patients who seem very able to work with a transference that is experienced as real, while there are so-called neurotic patients who, like Freud's rider on the horse, seem to need a clear distinction between transference fantasy and transference reality (Kaftal 1991).

But the patient does not function alone in transference love. The reparative effect of transference love matures in the analyst's receptivity and participation in a unique mutuality of affect in the therapeutic relationship. It is not only the patient but also the analyst who shares in the responsibility and development of transference love, and therefore transference love is a two-person system (Gill 1993). It is within this intimate, erotic transference that there can be an integration of self and environment, experienced by the self as a part of its own wholeness. Thus, the erotic transference is not merely a resistance to the emergence of incestuous wishes, not just a sign of a structural deficit, not simply a real or unreal treatment phenomenon, not just a confusion between satisfactions or securities. The erotic transference is also an intimate facilitator of therapeutic action.

Our attitude about transference love should be guided by the theory of therapeutic action. Freud's main concept of therapeutic action was the analysis of resistance in order to bring unconscious needs into consciousness. Yet Freud continually vacillated on this concept with regard to the phenomenon of transference love. In his postscript to "Fragment of an Analysis of a Case of Hysteria" (1905b), while he attributed the breakdown of Dora's treatment to his failure to interpret the transference, he also seems to wonder whether he could have kept Dora in treatment if he had exaggerated how important she was to him, in a sense actually providing her with a substitute for the affection she desired (Eickhoff 1993).

Another, perhaps more emphatic, comment on transference love is found in Freud's (1907) paper on Jensen's *Gradiva*: "The process of cure is accomplished in a relapse into love, if we combine all the many components of the sexual instinct under the term 'love'; and such a relapse is indispensable, for [if] the symptoms on account of which the treatment has been undertaken are nothing other than precipitates of earlier struggles connected with repression or the return of the repressed, . . . [then] they can only be resolved and washed away by a fresh high tide of the same passions" (p. 90). I will repeat this part, because in it Freud addressed a crucial struggle for the analyst working with the erotic transference. In essence, he said, "The process of cure is accomplished in a relapse into love [which] . . . can only be resolved and washed away by a fresh high tide of the same passions."

In both these early papers, Freud presented the importance of the patient's perceiving the analyst as a "substitute" object. But what is the therapeutic action that creates or allows passionate unconscious currents to develop within the transference? Freud alluded to transference love as creating a reparative or facilitating opportunity to perceive the analyst in a particular manner where the patient's perception of the analyst can serve a distinct psychic function in moving toward cure. Unfortunately, Freud did not elaborate on this notion of reparation through a passionate love for an all-powerful substitute. Yet these early papers set a precedent for a continued analytic controversy—a controversy that the erotic transference highlights—regarding whether analysis is a one- or two-person psychology. In a one-person psychology, the analysand's endogenous fantasies are the predominant concern in treatment. In the two-person perspective, the patient's fantasies are seen as one part of the focus, and the analyst's experiences and influences on the patient make up an additional focus. Freud often took one perspective and sometimes the other in the same paper (see Freud [1915a], "Observations on Transference Love").

Freud (1915) did allow for a two-person system, particularly in regard to his original interest in the seduction theory, with its focus on memories of interpersonal consequences, but his theoretical work focused on the analyst as a blank screen, with treatment carried out in abstinence. Freud considered abstinence the driving power of therapeutic action in uncovering and bringing instinctual motivations of unconscious processes into consciousness. Freud stated that the analyst could not offer the patient anything other than a "substitute" object, who gratified her wishes and needs without eliminating inner conflict and motivations to change. Freud's theory of abstinence as a driving therapeutic action affirmed a primarily one-person psychology. It wasn't until Ferenczi's (1933) paper on the actuality of children being traumatized by adult misreading of what they meant, that the concept of a two-person psychology was introduced—a concept that has been gaining the favor of contemporary analysts.

In continuing to look at Freud's early conflict between transference love as a facilitator and the analysis of transference love as a resistance, we come to Freud's 1912 paper on technique, "The Dynamics of Transference," in which he noted that if the individual's need for love does not find satisfaction in reality, when he meets new people he continues to maintain hopeful conscious and unconscious libidinal ideas. Freud asserted that, in treatment, it was normal and expected that the unsatisfied libidinal cathexis would be held ready in anticipation and should be directed to the figure of the analyst. The libidinal cathexis resorts to prototypes already in the patient's psychic structure as the patient introduces the analyst into already existing "psychical 'series'" (Freud 1912, p. 100). Freud argued that if the analyst did not stay distant, the early origin of conflict would not be recognized. He said that when the analysis uncovers the hiding place of the libido, a struggle develops that is imbued with all the forces that had caused the libido to regress. These forces rise up as resistances in order to preserve the patient's psychic homeostasis. Transference, then, appears as a weapon of resistance. "The mechanism of transference is dealt with when we have traced it back to the state of readiness of libido, which has remained in possession of infantile images; but the part transference plays in the treatment can only be explained if we enter into its relations with resistance" (p. 104). In other words, the transference develops as a mean of resistance (not as a means of direct reparation, but as an indirect, thwarted, albeit generative yet facilitating process) as it allows the patient to express or resist early wishful impulses with regard to the person of the analyst, to whom the impulse now appears to relate.

Freud (1912) maintained that the patient does not want to remember the painful unconscious impulses but wants "to reproduce them in accordance with the timelessness of the unconscious" (p. 108). The patient regards his unconscious impulses as real and attempts to put his feelings into action. The analyst puts these emotional impulses to intellectual consideration to understand their psychical value. There is a battle between analyst and patient, intellect and instinctual life, and understanding and enactment in the transference situation as the patient attempts to hide his forgotten erotic impulses. Freud's theory moved away from the idea of the analyst "playing a part" in the transference, and more and more he saw analysis as an intellectual process. In so doing, Freud further distanced himself from his wife's emotional intuition about the special love inherent in the talking cure.

I have been involved in a reading and study group for many years, and during one of those years we read literature pertaining to the erotic transference. My own clinical experience seemed quite different from that described in most of the articles I read, which focused on the erotic transference as a treatment resistance. There is a possibility that the notion of transference love as a facilitator of treatment was forced on me by my work with patients, since it is an essential part of my clinical experience. Certainly I was influential and evocative in the erotic transference development through my receptivity of the patient's loving and sexual feelings. In addition, transference love was not just evoked by the analytic situation, but was also influenced by my character and persona. Did this mean it was all countertransference?

The idea of the analyst being evocative of and receptive to the erotic transference places emphasis on the analyst's part in treatment development. The analyst's countertransference was not traditionally a focus of analytic theory; instead, the literature highlighted the patient's transference. Searles (1959) was one of the few exceptions, in his classic paper "Oedipal Love in the Countertransference," where he said it was "only the rare [analyst] who [publicly] acknowledged the presence of [erotic and romantic countertransference feelings] in himself" (p. 285). Certainly, public acknowledgment of erotic countertransference can often evoke professional criticism. Self-criticisms, however, are perhaps more damning, in that the analyst typically fears being a seductive, victimizing, powerful, incestuous parent. When the analyst is behind closed doors with a patient who is talking about erotic feelings, it seems safer and more theoretically familiar to genetically interpret the erotic transference as resistance, as negative therapeutic reaction, or as solely the patient's development of unreal love, than to freely move within a mutual transference–countertransference exploration.

The diversity between traditional and contemporary perspectives in handling erotic material was brought home to me when I attended a conference on transference love. During one of the workshops, I presented material on one of my patients to illustrate a mutually sexually stimulating transference and countertransference development. Sean was a very handsome man, blond, Irish, blue eyes, maybe 6 feet, 4 inches tall, with a terrific body, and in his early forties. He quickly fell in love in the treatment and asked if he could take me for a walk through the park, since he wanted to point out his favorite places. He added that he hoped we would end up, bodies intertwined, making love in a secluded spot. This was quite moving—countertransferentially—in that I felt very emotionally and sexually stimulated by his passions.

In the conference workshop, the group discussion of this material focused largely on the question of interpretation—What should or could I have said about Sean's fantasy? The workshop participants largely agreed to the need to interpret Sean's wishes as infantile longings and unconscious needs. Despite my colleagues' insistence on interpretations, I stated that my experience with Sean had shown that efforts to make genetic interpretations were felt by him as the verbal building of a restrictive emotional frame around his freedom. Sean responded to genetic interpretations as though I were constructing walls between us, and felt narcissistically wounded and emotionally abandoned if I discussed an early incestuous wish or fear in relation to his transference love. Interpretations of this kind are a hallmark of the blank-screen analyst who considers abstinence as motivating therapeutic action. Sean was powerfully immersed in his feelings toward me and his immersion could be traumatized by my emotional abstinence. This clinical material clearly poses the question of therapeutic action. Is therapeutic action facilitated by Sean's knowing the information that would make up my interpretation, or is therapeutic action facilitated by Sean's emotional experience in the erotic transference?

The reaction I experienced in this workshop is fairly typical of the larger analytic community, where most analysts perceive the erotic transference as a resistance to bringing unconscious material into consciousness, as an unreal phenomenon, and/or as a transitional phase in treatment. I believe there are valid understandings of the erotic transference, but I also feel transference love can be understood as a facilitator of a deeper analytic intimacy.

A second problem with the traditional approach to understanding the erotic transference as a treatment obstacle rests with Freud's theory of narcissism. Freud's perception of the therapeutic value of the analyst as love-object, which is still adhered to by the traditional analysts I just mentioned, is inconsequential in the light of his interpretation of the role of narcissism in the configuration of libido (Canestri 1993). In "On Narcissism: An Introduction" (1914) Freud said:

> He [the patient] then seeks a way back to narcissism from his prodigal expenditure of libido upon objects, by choosing a sexual ideal after the narcissistic type which possesses the excellences to which he cannot attain. This is the cure by love, which he generally prefers to cure by analysis. Indeed, he cannot believe in any other mechanism of cure; he usually brings expectations of this sort with him to treatment and directs them toward the person of the physician. The patient's incapacity for love resulting from his extensive repressions naturally stands in the way of a therapeutic plan of this kind [p. 101].

A central part of the traditional concept of therapeutic action was that "cure by love" did not work because it was so narcissistic and different from real love. But Freud realized it was not so different from real love and yet was confused about the difference between real love and transference love.

Finally, in Freud's 1915 paper, "Observations on Transference Love," he suggested that an analysis of the complexities and vicissitudes of the transference neurosis can encourage the development of intense erotic transferences, which manifest as demands for love and gratification: "The patient, whose sexual repression is of course not yet removed but merely pushed into the background, will then feel safe enough to allow all her preconditions for loving, all the phantasies springing from her sexual desires, all the detailed characteristics of her state of being in love, to come to light; and from these she will herself open the way to the infantile roots of her love" (1915a, p. 166).

Freud was now saying that psychoanalysis enabled the ego to grow within and from transference love into a mature capacity to love. Also in this paper, Freud took a one-person perspective, that the transference was the patient's doing, as well as alluding to a two-person perspective. ". . . [the analyst] has evoked this love by instituting analytic treatment . . ." (pp. 168–169).

There is a vagueness in Freud's discussion on the distinction between "genuine love" and transference love. He characterized all transference love as unreal and suggested it was always overly intensified by the analytic situation, and then added that the emotional features of erotic love are different from other inner or outer manifestation within the analytic situation. Therefore, Freud implied, the analyst saw only the patient's primitive, narcissistic love, and the analyst differentiated this from the genuine love the analyst experienced in his or her own personal life. Yet, in erotic transferences, patients do experience their own love as authentic and, equally important, they have come to analysis because of their difficulties in loving. It would seem that the erotic transference offers a rather pristine opportunity and not just an expression of narcissistic pathology.

Throughout most of his 1915 paper Freud considered transference love as an impersonal treatment resistance that arose in response to the patient's emotional defense against painful repressed memory. But if we read the last few pages, we again hear Freud's struggle with the paradoxical vicissitudes inherent in transference love. He commented:

> I think we have told the patient the truth, but not the whole truth regardless of the consequences. The part played by resistance in transference-love is unquestionable and very considerable. Nevertheless the resistance did not, after all, create this love; it finds it ready at hand, makes use of it and aggravates its manifestations. Nor is the genuineness of the phenomenon disproved by the resistance. It is true that the love consists of new editions of old traits and that it repeats infantile reactions. . . . Transference-love has perhaps a degree less of freedom than the love which appears in ordinary life and is called normal; it displays its dependence on the infantile pattern more clearly and is less adaptable and capable of modification; but that is all, and not what is essential. [p. 168]

In this quote, Freud breaks from his earlier stated conviction that transference love is merely a form of resistance. It is in these last few pages that Freud gives transference love the rank of a specific type of love.

The ego psychologists had an understanding of therapeutic action similar to Freud's, that is, of its making the unconscious conscious. But the ego psychologists did not have to speculate on the analyst's role, while Freud clearly did. By this time, the ego psychologists' notion of the detached analyst had become dogma. Ego psychologists argued against "cure by love" or cure through a corrective emotional experience. The erotic transference was considered a treatment resistance that replaced a workable transference neurosis.

In the erotization of the transference, the breakdown of the distinction between the analyst and patient meant that the patient had an impairment of ego function, reality testing, and critical judgment (Blitsten, personal communication, in Rappaport [1956], p. 515). The successful erotization was a sequence of narcissistic, borderline, or psychotic functioning (Blum 1973, Gitelson 1952, Rappaport 1956, 1959). Ego psychologists handled the erotic transference in a harsh way. The analyst was not to engage in the patient's distortions or to duplicate the qualities of either the pathogenic parent or the desired one. According to Rappaport (1956), these patients "should be told that they are playing a cheap burlesque and that their behavior is delusive . . . their delusional omnipotence [should be] . . . carefully undermined [and] they can be encouraged to learn something they had never known before, namely self-respect and self-esteem" (p. 527). Ferenczi's experiments with the analytic role were, according to Rappaport (1956), considered a function of the analyst's inability to control his own narcissism, leading to an unsuccessful treatment.

The shortcomings of this ego psychological, one-person perspective on erotic transference truncated an understanding of its vicissitudes and clinical implications, since a one-person psychology contends that only the analyst holds a true perception of the analytic relationship and that the patient holds a distorted view. In conceptualizing the transference as a distortion, the analyst has used her own construction of psychic reality. Yet, since the analyst already has a

sexualized view of human development, at least from institute training in psychoanalysis, we must wonder about a bias in the construct
of the analyst's psychic reality.

The two-person perspective is an innovative approach to cure, as it
tends to emphasize the influence of both analyst and patient operating
in a new relational experience, and the fact that the relational experience is the primary vehicle of the therapeutic action. The erotic transference is part of this new relational experience (and therefore a transference vehicle) in that it moves or allows the patient to have a different
attitude than he formerly had. What was once considered too personally intimate for analytic consideration is now made public and acces-
sible within the therapeutic relationship.

Most of the traditional literature on transference love prior to the
1970s was written by male analysts about female patients. Those articles
that were written by female analysts said their male patients did not develop
erotic transferences, with the exception of Bibring-Lehner's case example
in 1936 where an "eroticized" transference was discussed toward a female
analyst. Lester (1985) stated there were almost no references in the literature in which male patients were reported to have developed intense
erotic transferences toward their female analysts. In general, erotic transferences from male patients toward female analysts were considered to
be less overt, unconsciously experienced or dreamt, short-lived, or
muted, or were merely enacted triangulated wishes and were expressed
as a wish for sex rather than a longing for love (Person 1985).

Within the last decade, however, contemporary female analysts, influenced by the current feminist perspective on sexuality, have begun
writing about their male patients' erotic transferences (Davies 1994,
Goldberger and Holmes 1993, Karme 1993, Kulish and Mayman 1993,
Lester 1993, Marcus 1993, and Wrye 1993). Not surprisingly, some of
the female authors were the same therapists who had written differently
on the subject prior to the acceptance of feminist thought in psychoanalysis. Certainly, the patients' pathology hasn't changed; however, society's
attitudes on women's sexuality have greatly altered both gender role expectations and receptivity to sexual expression in the last few decades.

As women become more in possession of their own sexuality and
feel less guilty about playing an active sexual role in the world, it is im-

portant to consider if female analysts, or analysts in general, feel more able analytically as well as more receptive to evoking an erotic transference in their patients. Of course, a great deal of work needs to be done to distinguish an analytic evocation of an erotic transference from the analyst's being sexually seductive. If we accept the importance of the analyst's person and gender as influential in treatment, we are again returned to the concept of a two-person psychology.

A very salient influence on therapeutic action and on the new relational approach to treatment was Kohut's (1971) psychology of the self, since it led to major revisions in analytic attitudes in the 1970s. While Kohut felt his clinical observations altered his perception of the drives, he no longer saw sexuality as a motivator of human interrelatedness (Kaftal 1983); rather, he saw development as stemming from the psychic need for self-cohesion. Kohut also understood (1971, 1977) that one person uses an aspect of another's personality as an essential, functional component of the self—this is his concept of the relationship of the self to the selfobject. He wrote (Kohut 1984) that the "I–You" experience had a selfobject frame of reference, as well as a mutual influence frame of "two intertwining sets of experience" (pp. 52–53), and he added, ". . . object love strengthens the self . . . [and] a strong self enables us to experience love and desire more intensively" (p. 53).

For many years, I used a classical Kohutian perspective. I found it very helpful, particularly with narcissistic patients. I believe it provided an opportunity to understand my patients in a very different and very real way, as the analyst steps into the shoes of the patient and responds empathically. This means not just using empathy, which all perspectives use, but rather using empathy as "vicarious introspection" (Kohut 1959), which means the capacity to think and feel the inner life of another person.

Kohut's (1984) theory addressed the analytic battle of whether psychoanalysis could have elements of a "cure by love" as opposed to its being a "cure through love" (p. 102). Both notions are often associated with cultism by the scientific community. Still, Kohut's concept of empathy encompassed the elements of the "special love" that Freud had previously addressed as a factor in therapeutic action.

Self psychologists are currently struggling with a change in the concept of the nature of the relationship between self and objects, brought about, perhaps, by Kohut's own ambiguities on the concept of cure (1977, 1984). In his last book, *How Does Analysis Cure?* (1984), Kohut stated that empathy or vicarious introspection was not in itself curative, and that therapeutic action was also facilitated through a phase of understanding, followed by a phase of explanation or interpretation. This understanding phase, and particularly the interpretive phase, creates a need for "negotiation" between the two psychic realities of the two participants (Goldberg 1988). Did Kohut's theory of the self only temporarily accept the patient's experience, with the eventuality of including it in a reciprocal relationship between the self and object? Was Kohut struggling with the notion of therapeutic action facilitated by a mutually reciprocal relationship? I believe, and many will disagree, that Kohut, as did Freud, moved between one- and two-person psychologies.

THE VICISSITUDES OF AN EROTIC TRANSFERENCE: AN ILLUSTRATION

The erotic transference is not just simply a love relationship between two people; it can also encompass profound feelings of hatred and anger between . . . a few people. This was made very clear to me when I ran an AIDS psychotherapy group for gay men. In this group, I experienced the erotic transference as an aggressive penetration of hateful rage. When therapists work with extremes, such as patients who are dying or those who are sexually demanding, there can be an elevation of passions in everyone involved. In group work, these passions can arise between individual group members, as well as between the therapist and particular group members. I found that this intimate group relationship, with its focus on life, death, and sex, placed a demand on me, as the analyst, to be receptive to—and to reciprocate—intense, passionate feelings. An analyst who remained an "outsider" would only exacerbate to an intolerable level the real future of isolation, abandonment, loss, and death in these individuals.

In the AIDS group, the emotional demands to relate on a mutual level were instantly powerful. I was expected to find a similarity with them or be "killed off" by their rejection of my differences. For instance, in the first session one of the group members began to eliminate all "different" group members, those who were too ill, those who were not analytically insightful, those who would not disclose their intimate emotions, and so on, as well as the one very different, straight, healthy, uninfected female therapist. This one particular group member, John, a social worker who ran AIDS groups in a hospital setting, quickly developed a rageful narcissistic transference, which I realized was exacerbated by my early interpretations of the psychic motivations for his behavior. For instance, I interpreted that he was angry at being infected and that exerting control in the group meant feeling powerful against the virus. With hindsight, I wonder if I could have worked with my awareness of being attracted to him.

My countertransference feelings were an indicator of an empathic resonance or attunement to John's innermost, secret feelings toward me. I thought he was attracted to me because he would often stare at me and study my mannerisms while he preened and stroked his body. He identified with me professionally, and I felt he was also furious about being attracted to me. And he was rageful that I was more powerful in the group and in better health. I addressed his anger—it was overwhelming—and for a long time it covered his wish for my love and approval.

In addition, the other group members were in full support of John's rage, perhaps also in defense of their loving feelings. John served as the group's "ego ideal" (Freud 1921), something that occurs when individuals in a group identify themselves with a chosen subject whom they imbue with special abilities and allow to express the group's forbidden wishes.

The group now seemed to want to kill me and to infect me with the hate they felt about their having contracted the HIV virus. They were aware of a group wish to murder me and so validate their power in life and over life. When John, early on, stated he wanted to have sex with me, he said he wanted a murderous experience. Later when he said he wanted sex it felt like he wanted my life encased within his skin, or wanted to have me in his life in another way. Within these emotional requests, the group demanded a mutuality in the treatment that changed my work, and that, more importantly, was integral in the alteration of the rageful transference into an erotic one. The group needed a mutual flow of affect among all of us, and I found this reciprocal relationship began to encourage insights. But it was not just insight that made the group experience more intimate; it was not just the group members' feeling understood within the context of an empathic milieu. The therapeutic action hinged, in my view, on our mutual interaction and how we shaped each other in the treatment. We understood the psychic reality of the other—the group members needed to feel and provide love—and this emotional experience far outweighed insight and empathy in bringing about change. As I openly struggled to alter my analytic attitude to a more emotionally reciprocal one, the group members likened my struggle to theirs and we experienced a shared bond that felt passionately reparative. I remember that upon nearing the end of this struggle, John aggressively asked me to have sex with him—and this time I replied that I knew I sexually aroused him. I told him I knew it because I had experienced his penetration when he looked at me and felt both his anger and love . . . my experience highlighted his.

It was at this point and within the erotic transference that these group members reached a pinnacle in the intimacy of loving desires and wishes among each other and with me. I took an intense journey into the emotional experiences of these men that led to passionate material. My receptivity created a group intimacy that they said allowed them a sense of cohesion, often to their last moments alive. This experience made me a little fearless about working with patients' profound transference reactions, and helped bring the realization that I could tolerate difficult, passionate countertransference emotions. The construction I made from this group experience was that therapeutic action was facilitated from passionate feelings—both by my patients, who experienced their emotions as intimate and reparative, and by me in my receptivity and evocation of the transference.

A number of analysts have delineated the erotic transference as serving a reparative purpose. Goldberg (1975), Stolorow and Atwood (1984, 1992), Stolorow and Lachmann (1979), and Stolorow and colleagues (1987) are intersubjectivists (a theoretical branch of classical self psychology that incorporates a two-person perspective) who describe the function of sexuality in the transference as restoring a precarious sense of self. The erotic transference is conceptualized as a reaction to an empathic break in the self-sustaining relationship with the analyst. In other words, the erotic transference served as the patient's reparative attempt if the patient felt the analyst had created a narcissistic injury. The erotic transference is the patient's attempt to repair a fragmenting self through loving feelings that replace an unsteady selfobject experience (Gould 1994, Stolorow 1986, Tropp 1988), that is, it is a therapeutic action originating from the reparative selfobject function.

   This view of erotic transference as facilitating therapeutic action in being restorative and self-enhancing, yet still having resistant aspects as a line of interpretation, is derived from Ferenczi (1933). Ferenczi's concept of mutual analysis highlighted particular issues that are now being discussed by contemporary psychoanalysis—specifically that countertransference reaction plays a critical part in treatment, that the analyst must be comfortable with countertransference and analyze it, and that there needs to be a creative, therapeutic way to express countertransference with the patient. Ferenczi took his "active technique" of psychoanalysis, which included relaxation experiments as well as exchanging physical embraces that were symbolic of the mother–child relationship, and attempted to repair his patient through love (Aron and Harris 1993). He experimented with his technique in the hope that his investigation would lead to theoretical revision, believing that "analytic technique has never been, nor is it now, something finally settled" (Ferenczi 1931, p. 135). Ferenczi (1913) made the first and most important shift in psychoanalytic theory from a one-person model to a two-person model. He felt that transference developed within the framework of countertransference, and that resistance arose in response to the analyst's empathic failures.

AN EROTIC TRANSFERENCE–COUNTERTRANSFERENCE CLINICAL ILLUSTRATION

When I first interviewed June a little over a year ago, I thought, "She's mine." My countertransference was immediate, in that I felt there was a very early powerful bond between us. In our first few sessions, I felt she was sexually attracted to me in the way she studied my appearance and smiled seductively as she did so. For myself, I was receptive to what I felt was an early development of an erotic transference. It is important to wonder what part my countertransference feelings played in evoking June's early transference development, and vice versa. It was also significant to consider if her erotic transference was an initial resistance to the treatment. A month into the treatment June wrote the first of many letters to me; it read:

"I feel better already. I think I express more of my sexual feelings toward you in letters than in person. The reasons are obvious. I probably do want to control you. I don't think my past therapists could possibly have evoked all of this sexual stuff. Why? Well, we'll speak about it in detail when I see you."

In this short letter, June made a meaningful point—she felt I had evoked "all this sexual stuff." She later defined this, saying she was attracted to my personal presentation, my manner of dressing, and my humor—all of which can have a sexual edge. Certainly, my countertransference played a part in evoking her sexual feelings, since I must have been responsive and given receptive nonverbal clues that further evoked her sexual material and relatedness. In addition, I was very encouraging of her sexual comments about her self and her lovers, as well as her remarks about my person. I decided not to provide oedipal interpretations of her sexual material, but rather allowed the transference to unfold by encouraging her to discuss her sexual wishes and desires in the hopes of deepening the eroticism. This is not to say that I did not discuss her feelings about her mother or father, but rather that I did not use genetic material to explain her sexual attraction to others since this seemed to shame her. I found June's comments about her sexual wishes facilitated therapeutic action as they led her to discuss her inner experiences and intimacies. For instance, after great hesitation, she let me know about her daily sobbing spells where she ended up in a fetal position under her sink for protection. Her need for protection, in a womb-like environment, involved her fears and wishes of merger with women, which led her to express a long-held shameful secret wish to have sex with her mother.

One day she said, "I had three dreams about you. I don't remember two of them, but in the third dream I'm sucking on your breast. I've also been fantasizing about you, you know, sexually. It's not easy to talk about this stuff, but since I think about it all the time and I think about you all the time—sexually—then it seems like I would need to talk about this. I never mentioned this stuff in my other therapies, you know, I just told them what I did between sessions. They might have asked, but . . . you know . . . I didn't 'have' to tell them because I could distract them and we'd go off on other topics. Anyway, the last time I fantasized I was thinking about your body. How do your breasts look, you know . . . I wondered how you looked naked. (she paused) Oh, do I really have to tell you more?"

Her question was understood as asking permission to tell more, rather than as an appeal to stop. I asked if she felt I was torturing her to get this fantasy. She laughed and said I wasn't torturing her—she was torturing herself.

She continued to let me in to her illusion, "Okay, the fantasy I have takes place in here, in your office. I fantasize you're standing at your desk, right in front of it and you've bent over the desk and I touch you, sexually. I also have the fantasy of watching you have sex with someone else." I did not interpret her comment as a resistance regarding infantile incestuous longings because I believed it would truncate and concretize her answer. Instead, I wondered aloud if that didn't make her feel left out. "No," she answered. "It makes me feel more like I'm part of the couple. I wish I had been able to see my parents have sex." This was the infantile wish I might have interpreted, but instead I focused on her sexual feelings as the vehicle toward further insights.

June quietly admitted to feeling ashamed of her wish to watch her parents have sex. I was not sure, however, if she was ashamed of her wish or ashamed to admit it. Since this was a long-held secret fantasy, I decided her conflict around its existence must have been mutated over the years or else she would have worked against its continued creation. From her vantage point, her wish was titillating, and I therefore pursued it as such, asking her what she experienced in her sexual fantasy about her parents. June then described the placement of bodies, and how her fantasy included an observation of her own masturbation while she watched her mother sexually climax. She seemed surprised she was telling me these secrets since they were never mentioned in her earlier treatments.

June's erotic narrative of her innermost fantasy developed in relation to my erotic countertransference. Our experience created a special intimacy in which she felt cohesive in the expression of her deepest secret wishes. This was different than it had been in her previous treatments, and different than it was in her life, where she mostly felt fragile and fragmented through loss of others and loss of self in relation. Over time, experience like this is reparative, in that the sexualized and loving bond matures through a special mutuality of affect and receptivity of innermost feelings.

I then asked about her wish to merge using a shared sensuality as the vehicle for insights. I said, "You have an exquisite means of getting in, don't you?" She answered that she was like a puppeteer—not the kind on a string, but hand puppets. "I make the bodies perform the way I want. It's all my show." I responded, "Am I one of the puppets you're manipulating in your fantasy of bending me over the desk? Are you verbally masturbating me when you tell your sexual fantasies?" "That's how I function," she said. "I'm always thinking about everyone in a sexual way. I want to be in people. And you let me into you when you let me say what I want sexually."

June's sexual feelings toward me now facilitated her discussion about her other relationships. I then learned about her desires with her current lover. She spoke about being aroused by the scars on her lover's skin and how she saw the scars as vulnerable junctures and opportunities to enter her lover. She would masturbate on the scars and feel infused by her lover. Then, she said, her lover didn't even need to participate. She associated the experience with her lover to her thoughts about her mother's self-preoccupations and obsessions.

I asked if June felt she was required to participate in her mother's obsessions. "Do you enter or merge with your mother when she is most vulnerable and preoccupied in her obsessions? Do you manipulate her with mutual obsessions and then feel close to her?" "Yes," June answered. "Are mutual obsessions the only means of relating to your mother? Do you ever feel penetrated by your mother's needs and manipulations? Is your mother the ultimate puppeteer?"

June responded, "Oh, definitely. You'd be talking to her and she'd be off in her own world. You know what being with her was like . . . she spent half her time rearranging furniture. I'd go to school and when I came home the house would look entirely different when I got there. But you couldn't say anything because she would feel criticized and rearrange it again." "Do you worry that one day I'll move the couch?" I asked.

June said, "I'm worried that you'll be like my mother and you'll get fed up with me and leave me behind. That's what I fear you'll do. But the fact that you let me write to you and call you and you call me back, and that you're here every time I come here, and you listen to me...well, that's very different from my mother. So, the difference between you and my mother is that I kind of know that you're not going to leave me. You even seem okay with my secret sexual thoughts . . . nobody else knows that stuff. I actually feel pretty dependent on you and it happened pretty quick, too. I didn't feel this dependent on my other shrinks. How did I get to the point of feeling almost entirely dependent on you?"

What appears most clearly in this excerpt is that June's loving and sexual feelings created an intimacy that allowed the therapist to enter a treatment level that might not have been achieved had June's sexual feelings been interpreted as a defensive maneuver. Rather, my receptivity allowed June to move freely, using her sexual feelings to deepen the emotional intensity. There was no attempt to create an oedipal interpretation about June's feelings for the analyst as infantile longings, no attempt made to address them as unreal phenomena, or as transferred oedipal feelings. The intimacy June and I attained through the erotic transference led to more analytic work in areas that might not have been discovered had I heard her erotic material as resistance. This relational concept of therapeutic action means that a new kind of relationship makes insight possible. June and I formed a cohesive mutual bond in our first session that allowed the development of an erotic transference. Was this just projective identification? If it was, then I believe my receptive response to her would have been problematic and the treatment would have been different. We see in her treatment that mutuality in the erotic transference was more than a resistance.

SUMMARY

As it cuts across oedipal and preoedipal boundaries, the erotic transference facilitates and gives form to the development of the analytic relationship, in that it need not be treated as purely real or unreal, and that it is not merely a resistance or defense against decompensation or self-fragmentation. The erotic transference can serve a facilitating function toward therapeutic cure when it is perceived as being a special love or a symbol of intimacy with the analyst. The reparative effect of transference love develops in the analyst's evocation, receptivity, and participation in a distinctive mutuality of affect in the therapeutic relationship. It is within the intimate, erotic transference that there can be a synthesis of self through sensitive, erotic, and loving communication within an intimate environment, which is experienced by the self as part of its own completeness. And the struggle for self-completeness is the purpose of therapeutic action.

Varieties of Erotic Transference and Countertransference

In the session, a dream was recalled from the previous night: "The dreamer, a woman, is lying in the middle of a bed. On her right is a young boy with blond hair. He is fast asleep and faceless. A man begins to get into bed on the side where the boy is sleeping and repeatedly kisses the woman. The man wants to get closer to the woman and walks around the bed to the other side. They begin to kiss and the dreamer feels frightened they'll go too far. In a moment, they are seated on a bench and the woman says, "We can't do this. I'm your analyst."

This was my own dream about a man who has been an analytic patient for many years. Early on in his treatment he developed an erotic transference that consisted of a variety of emotions such as loving feelings with expressions of intimacy, warmth and tenderness; feelings of sexual desire that sometimes physically aroused him as he lay on the couch; and also hostile and aggressive outbursts that developed sporadically when his desires felt especially intense.

My dream expressed an experience of a treatment development that was until this particular session unavailable to me. The dream occurred the night before I began writing this essay, and I have come to regard it as an unconscious erotic countertransference reaction. Here, I will focus on the analyst's unconscious and conscious erotic countertransference responses, as well as on the patient's erotic transferences, in an effort to illustrate difficulties that arise in treatments complicated by erotic longings such as sexual stimulation, feelings of love and tenderness, and aggressive defenses.

In regard to the notion of countertransference, I am referring to Kernberg's (1965) "totalistic" perspective, in that it is a reflection of all the analyst's unconscious and conscious fantasies and emotional responses to the patient. The totalistic approach to countertransference supersedes the classical notion that it is a hindrance to treatment. In addition, I am referring to the contemporary analytic literature on the uses of countertransference that takes exception to the belief that the analyst's experience is purely reactive. Instead, I understand countertransference as a subjective experience of an ongoing mutual influence in which both patient and analyst are affected. Countertransference is considered the genuine, responsive, necessary correlative to the patient's manner of relating, and to the patient's transference reactions (Epstein and Feiner 1979). This latter relational perspective has theoretical elements derived from Ferenczi's theory of mutuality between therapist and patient. Ferenczi was the first analyst to seriously consider the impact of the analyst's subjectivity within the analytic situation (Dupont 1988).

THE EROTIC TRANSFERENCE–COUNTERTRANSFERENCE MATRIX

Sensually loving and sexually stimulating feelings are complex phenomena that can create fearful and wishful desires in the patient, as well as in the analyst. In his paper "Observations on Transference Love" Freud 1915a, presented a moral warning on the development of love in psychoanalysis. Freud thought that the patient's love for the analyst arose in response to her emotional defense against painful repressed memory, an impersonal treatment resistance. The focus of psychoanalysis was to uncover the instinctual motivations of unconscious processes to make them conscious. Freud adhered to the view that the analyst's abstinence was a technical requirement of therapeutic action. As a consequence, both the analyst's countertransference and the patient's erotic transference were hindrances that impeded treatment.

Early analytic literature, particularly that of the ego psychologists of the 1950s and 1960s, shared Freud's understanding of therapeutic action of psychoanalysis, making the unconscious conscious. It was the male analysts of this era who typically wrote about their female patients who developed erotic transferences. They contended that these patients were playing cheap tricks that masked delusional behavior and omnipotence (Rappaport 1959). The erotic transference was interpreted as the female patient's preoedipal longings transferred to the male analyst in a defense against complex early childhood aggressive feelings (Blum 1973, 1994, Menninger 1958, Swartz 1967). In addition, many analysts were then entrenched in the notion of the analyst's abstinence as the motivator of therapeutic action. Erotic countertransference was to be masked or eliminated under the analyst's neutrality. The analyst was expected to refer the patient to another treatment, or return to his own analyst if the erotic transference–countertransference matrix was not ended. Annie Reich's 1951 paper on countertransference added that it was rare for an analyst to really fall in love with a patient (p. 26). And Hartmann's (1958) "average expectable environment" theory contended that all analysts could behave equally neutrally since the patient's transference was fantasy.

Analysts of this period often felt they held the true perception of the analytic relationship and that patients held a distorted view. Yet, in conceptualizing the transference as a distortion, such analysts used their own construction of psychic reality. Because the therapist already had a sexualized view of human development (at least from institute training in psychoanalysis), one must wonder about an inherent bias in the construct of the analyst's psychological stance. It comes as no surprise that during this era, Ferenczi's experiments with the analytic role were considered by Freud to be a function of Ferenczi's inability to control his own narcissism, ultimately leading to unsuccessful treatments.

It is interesting that analytic literature from the early object relations theorists had already begun focusing on countertransference as an inevitable interpersonal phenomenon. Yet the popularity of ego psychology in this country, as well as the influence of neoclassical theory, resulted in a rather strict adherence to the traditional notion that the patient misinterprets the analytic relationship while the analyst correctly interprets or prohibits his own emotions. Meanwhile, Klein's (1946) notion of projective identification was already being widened by Heimann (1950), who stated that countertransference and projective identification were the patient's real and actual influences in treatment that caused the analyst to identify with the patient's self and/or object representations. Heimann contended that countertransference should be defined as being both realistic and distorted feelings of the analyst in response to the patient. Yet, even though these beliefs were evolving, countertransference was still considered an obstacle to be overcome.

Erotic feelings in the countertransference were not written about until long after Freud's 1915 ethical alarm. Tower's 1956 paper, and Searles's (1959) "Oedipal Love in the Countertransference" were the first. In Searles's paper, the (erotic) interactions between the patient's transferences and the analyst's countertransference were highlighted as a means of creating interpersonal experience for analytic investigation. Specifically, he wrote about his countertransference love toward many of his patients and considered his feelings an important criterion for determining the patient's emotional growth. The analytic community, still steeped in Freud's notion of abstinence, responded to Searles with negative rumors about a deterioration of his mental health. It wasn't until ten years later, when Racker (1968) wrote a classic paper on countertransference issues arising in response to patients' transference love, that the analytic attitude seemed more receptive.

In the 1960s, the use of the analyst's empathy became an important element in the therapist's relationship with the patient (Greenson 1960, Kohut 1959, and Schafer 1959). Grinberg (1962) proposed "projective counteridentification" as an aspect of countertransference that could provide the analyst with an even greater empathic understanding of the patient.

Still, and although some people may disagree, it was Kohut (1959, 1968, 1971) who arrived at a unique approach to understanding the importance of the analyst's subjective experience in therapeutic action. Surprisingly, no one before Kohut had placed importance on the analyst's vicarious introspection as a means of empathic attunement with the patient's innermost feelings—which are the basis of a self psychological treatment. While empathy is an important ingredient in all analytic theories, Kohut (1959) added the clinical nuance that the therapist must immerse herself in the patient's experience as it serves the function of ". . . maintenance of the patient's narcissistic equilibrium" (p. 294). Kohut's contributions to psychoanalysis have had an impact on the way contemporary analysts clinically respond to their patients, as the analyst's empathic resonance with the patient's feelings is increasingly identified as an aspect of countertransference. For instance, Wolf (1988) understands transference–countertransference dynamics as a *"dialectic of subjectivities"* (p. 137). Stolorow and colleagues (1987) state that ". . . transference and countertransference together form an intersubjective system of reciprocal mutual influence" (p. 42).

Many self psychologists don't emphasize the importance of countertransference and some even take a very traditional view. However, Kohut himself had a very particular understanding of the relational matrix. For example, it was Kohut (1971, 1977) who understood that one person uses an aspect of another's personality as an essential, functional component of the self—this is his concept of the relationship of the self to the selfobject. He wrote that the "I–You" experience had a selfobject frame of reference, as well as a mutual influence frame of "two intertwining sets of experience" (Kohut 1984, pp. 52–53). Empathy becomes the emotional provision that one person makes for the other person in order to understand the other's subjective experience.

It was not until the mid 1980s and 1990s that female analysts began writing about sustained erotic transferences by male patients who desired sex and/or love from the analyst, Goldberger and Evans Holmes 1985, 1993, Gould 1994, Karme 1993, Kulish and Mayman 1993, Lester 1985, 1993, Marcus 1993, McDougall 1995, Wrye 1993, and Wrye and Wells 1994, are examples. Certainly this could be due to the influence of feminist thinking on analytic theory, as well as evolving notions of the binary structure of gender, and the reevaluations of traditional social and cultural expectations in treatment. The latest contributions to the literature on erotic feelings have been in the countertransference arena (Bergmann 1994, Gabbard 1994, Hirsch 1994, Hoffer 1993, Karme 1993, Kernberg

1992, Kumin 1985, Russ 1993, Tansey 1994, Welles and Wrye 1991, 1994, Wrye 1993). What is interesting here is that the articles and recent books on erotic countertransference that are creating a stir in the analytic community are by women (Davies 1944, Wrye and Welles 1994). Finally, there is also a lack of analytic literature on homoerotic transference–countertransference, either when both patient and analyst have heterosexual identities, or between gay patients and gay analysts—perhaps due to the perceived professional repercussions of coming out.

The notion of allowing oneself to engage in an erotic analytic milieu was addressed by Wrye and Welles (1994), who hypothesized that the problem may be less one of behaving oneself than of allowing oneself to participate (p. 63). In an erotic transference, language can feel insufficient when the patient is wanting the analyst to "really know" the patient through body contact. Often both patients and analysts long to physically merge into each other's bodies, and both participants must organize and struggle with these desires.

Yet, if, by virtue of a professional prohibition against it, we are unable to consider an erotic feeling toward a patient, there may be unintentional though inevitable consequences. We may find ourselves acting out by becoming tired and inattentive, or interpreting the oedipal desires, or actually becoming maternal with overly empathic or sympathetic responses, or we may sit dumbfounded with nothing to say to the patient. It is unfortunate when erotic countertransference remains unconscious, since this can freeze, sidetrack, or prematurely terminate a treatment—but it is not much easier if such feelings are conscious (Wrye and Welles 1994). Davies (1994) gives a graphic example of an erotic transference–countertransference struggle in which she felt "enraged, seduced, misled. . . . sick to my stomach, [with] an experience of dread that became physically palpable and frightening" (p. 164). Still, such contemporary analytic literature suggests that erotic material for both patient and analyst needs to be worked through to allow an unfolding of erotic feelings for the analysis.

A while ago, I gave an address on the nature of the erotic transference. The reactions afterward were quite interesting in that many of the participants said they had not had patients who developed erotic transferences, typically the first step in the erotic transference–countertransference matrix. In other words, not only were they not working with it, they were not recognizing its early signs, such as the patient providing more sexual material or eliminating it from his narrative. Why does this occur? One reason may be that both parties are embarrassed by feeling sexually aroused or ashamed that they may experience love for a patient or a therapist.

The focus of treatment has changed greatly from Freud's "rule of abstinence" with the therapist's suppression of self, to the contemporary relational analyst's viewing herself as a mutually related participant who can use her emotional responsiveness to deepen intimacy in the analytic process. It is this contemporary relational approach to treatment that utilizes (1) the object relations idea of countertransference as an inevitable interpersonal phenomenon that includes all the analyst's feelings toward a patient, (2) Kohut's concept of empathy as the analyst's attunement with the patient's inner experience, and (3) Ferenczi's notion of mutuality between analyst and patient—to arrive at the concept that transference develops within the framework of countertransference. In other words, both analyst and patient become consciously and unconsciously attuned to the other's inner experience, both may struggle to understand the other's experience consciously and unconsciously, and one may unconsciously present the other's unconscious experience as their own, particularly when one person's feelings are disavowed.

I am, therefore, operating within a two-person psychology in which both parties' subjective experiences can be equally influential, although not necessarily symmetrical. The question now becomes, how, as analysts, can we let an erotic transference–countertransference do its work and not defend against its arousal? And, how can we work with our subjective feelings without minimally enacting them in the treatment (Carpy 1989, Wrye and Welles 1994)?

THE THERAPIST'S UNCONSCIOUS EROTIC COUNTERTRANSFERENCE

In the opening paragraph of this chapter, I said that the dream was recalled from the previous night's sleep. I remembered my dream a moment after Benjamin presented his. His dream was, "I remember walking up the street with my girlfriend Karen. There was a young blond boy with her and I was upset that we weren't alone. I didn't know who the boy was in the dream. As we walked up the street, we started getting harassed by a homeless man. I guided the two of them into a bodega for safety. Karen and the boy seemed oblivious to the homeless man who I warded off by standing in the doorway of the bodega. But Karen and the boy slipped out the door, right past me and the homeless man, and started walking up the street without me and without looking back. There I stood, face to face with this homeless man until the dream ended."

It seemed that Benjamin and I had similar dreams. Both of us dreamt about a young blond boy, maybe a youthful idealized version of Ben, and perhaps symbolic of the preadolescent behavior he often presented when frustrated by people he perceived as omnipotent. In both our dreams, the boy was an obstacle to Benjamin's attaining the woman. He interpreted that his girlfriend's presence in the dream symbolically represented the analyst. In Benjamin's dream he faces off with a homeless man, embodying a recent lament that he sees himself as emotionally homeless. Benjamin is trying to protect Karen and the boy from the homeless man's invasion, and in my dream I am trying to protect the innocent, pristine self from penetration or merger, as well. Both dreams have an element of potency, domination, and control.

Benjamin understood his dream in relation to his analysis. He thought a part of the dream was about Karen's recently leaving him for another man she had been dating. He thought this arose from his feeling that he could never chose a woman who would take him away from me. Ben had had a string of sexual and emotionally merged relationships with unavailable women that typically ended after a year. He repeatedly said they were unfulfilling since I was his true love and he could not leave me. I remember saying to him that he was a classical analyst's delight and I quoted Freud's 1910 paper, "A Special Type of Choice of Object Made by Men," where Freud stated that a precondition for loving a particular object is the presence of a third party. Some men can never choose as a love object a woman who is disengaged but only one who is unattainable, typically due to the involvement of another man or obstacle—or the oedipal complex.

Benjamin's transference has been eroticized for many years. He was initially unconscious of his loving feelings and the first glimpse of the transference appeared when he told of an affair he had had with a therapist who was my age. I wondered aloud about the similarity. He was taken aback, apologetic and felt shame for the professional breach. I expressed surprise at his surprise: "Don't all relationships have sex as an element in them?" In the ensuing discussions, he told of feeling intimately accepted by the therapist he dated and how he was having a similar experience in treatment with me. This early dialogue created a sense of permission for Benjamin to communicate in a loving and sexualized way in order to express his inner life experiences.

Soon thereafter, Benjamin began seeing another woman, again my age, a massage therapist who he felt worked on his body while I worked on his mind. Ben was now consciously aware of his feelings about this woman and his similar feelings and transference reaction toward me. He said I was free to interpret that the women he dated were substitutes for his feelings toward me. I was reminded of Freud's 1915 paper on transference love, in which he said the analyst could not offer the patient anything other than being a substitute love object and that gratification of the patient's longings would eliminate inner conflict and motivations to change. Benjamin, however, was experiencing his erotic feelings in the treatment as an opportunity to express his innermost emotions to the analyst and about the analyst. He thought the women he dated were substitutes for the analyst.

While Ben was dating his most recent girlfriend, his narratives became full of sensual exploits, erotic positions, and details of manipulations with sexual toys. He spoke of a newfound freedom in being allowed to tell formerly forbidden stories to me, a receptive woman. He would look up from the couch and gaze lovingly, saying he had never felt so safe in expressing his emotions and experiences and how lucky he was that he had me. This treatment facet culminated when he turned onto his stomach and asked me to come lie beside him as he slowly played with the fringe on the carpet a few inches from my feet.

I was engaged, mesmerized, and erotically stimulated. During this period, Ben became my favorite patient. I could barely wait for him to enter my office so I could fantasize about him while he spoke about his sexual exploits. I nearly basked in his regret when he wished I was in his bed and of his fantasy of spending the day having sex. At the end of his sessions, he would sit on the couch and remind me that his relationships with women were in lieu of our dating, and he would often end with declarations of love and desire.

While I was consciously aware that Benjamin was nourishing my narcissism, I did not feel lost in my countertransference. I responded to him in what seemed to me to be an appropriate analytic manner. For instance, we discussed his ability to express his intimate feelings, talked about his feeling understood and how this helped him to feel recognized and validated, and spoke about his experiencing how he was able to talk about parts of himself that had previously been unavailable. In addition, I interpreted possible infantile longings and resistances to other transference developments that might exist.

I also wondered throughout this phase of treatment if Benjamin was only reflecting my narcissism or if I was only unconsciously mirroring and resonating his. For instance, he had often felt like a social misfit with women, as if he were unable to date anyone of the best kind, settling instead for women other men did not desire. Yet now, in the transference, Benjamin assumed that I was single, albeit with a steady partner, but thought he was preferred. He felt loved and in love with a professional woman whom he experienced as his intellectual equal. He praised my comfort with sexuality and he imagined I liked to sexually experiment as did he. He insisted he could please me if only I would come to bed with him.

After I began writing about my work on erotic transferences and countertransference, I started to worry that I would only be able to produce half an essay. I could write about the patient's love and sexual desire for the analyst and I could write about the analyst's sexual arousal to the patient's erotic material. But I really couldn't write about falling in love with the patient. For me, it was just a sexual arousal. I reminded myself of an adolescent boy, "It's just testosterone." I must admit that this was a secret I had kept for a while, at first unconscious but eventually conscious as I settled into the notion that an erotic countertransference need only be a sexualized response.

I did not feel love for the patient. I began to worry that maybe there was something wrong with me and maybe I just could not feel this type of love because of some old oedipal issue. Maybe I just needed to return to treatment, I thought. On the other hand, I had spent most of my adult life in analysis and if I hadn't worked through my feelings about loving people, then maybe I wasn't fixable and should just accept being broken.

Finally I thought, "It's ridiculous to think I have never been in love with a patient." It was that night, thank goodness, that I dreamt about desiring Benjamin and finding a way to love him in the dream, all the while keeping in mind that I was his analyst. (I'm sure the dream has other meanings, but that would be another paper.) What had kept me in the dark for so long? What was my unconscious fear of feeling love for this patient? Why was I only comfortable with my sexual feelings and not with my sense of feeling love? I believe a part of the answer has to do with our sense of surrender to a patient. I felt comfortable when Ben was mirroring my narcissism; I was idealized, and in that idealization I was in charge. While he talked about being directive in bed with his girlfriends, in a sense I was in control of his new ability to attain and perform with these more sophisticated "substitute" women. On the one hand, I was treating the patient in a contemporary relational manner— by creating a milieu for a mutually experienced eroticism in the analysis, albeit a sexual eroticism—which then led to intimacies as well as an expression of the patient's innermost thoughts. And on the other hand, I was adhering to Freud's notion of abstinence when it came to experiencing my own feelings of love for the patient.

The day after my dream, I greeted Benjamin and felt embarrassed at how flirtatious I wanted to be with him. He looked so attractive and was so attentive to me that I felt quite shaken. I believe he felt my altered (subjective) experience of him because it was in this session that he said, "You have something with me that you don't have with anyone else. I know I'm your favorite patient. You like the others, but you don't feel the same about them as you do toward me. You share something profound with me that you don't have in the same way with anyone else." This time, I felt his words in a way I never had previously, I felt a mutual love between us. I said nothing in affirmation and just felt his tender words.

As I mentioned earlier, Benjamin's erotic transference was conscious to both of us fairly early in the treatment. While I knew that he could often sensually arouse me by caressing the carpet or by relating sexual exploits, I was fully aware of not being in love with him even though he often spoke of his love and commitment to me. I felt I always maintained an analytic attitude and used my countertransference effectively in the treatment, and therefore did not enact my feelings or experience them too intensively. These were typical feelings I had experienced toward all my patients who developed erotic transferences. I felt close to them, treatment was exceptionally intimate, I listened and was moved by their inner experiences, but I did not fall in love or emotionally lose myself to my countertransference. With hindsight, I believe my disavowed feelings were my erotic countertransference, and I believe Benjamin's erotic transference was a mirrored reflection or manifestation arising from my dissociated feelings. In other words, Benjamin unconsciously experienced something about me that was out of my awareness and he unknowingly enacted it as a means of communicating his experience of my feelings—and as a consequence, his emotional resonance with my subjective experience influenced his erotic transference development.

THE THERAPIST'S RESPONSE TO THE PATIENT'S CONSCIOUS EROTIC TRANSFERENCE

Another example of the erotic countertransference can be found in the analyst's response to the patient's conscious erotic transference. A few years ago, a young man in his twenties requested psychoanalysis. He had been in treatment previously with a male therapist who had seduced him while continuing his treatment. The therapist claimed he wanted to know all of Michael and that meant sex in conjunction with therapy. Michael and the therapist maintained this complex, cultish relationship for a year. Michael eventually ended their relationship because he felt he was continually losing contact with his sense of self—he felt increasingly more dissociated.

A week into his treatment, he gave me two videos that he insisted I watch in order that I know "all about him," or all of him. In the first video, I watched a group therapy session where I actually saw Michael's therapist proposition him in front of the group. It was under the guise of an aggressive enactment where the therapist was teaching the group members how to handle difficult encounters. Michael said the group did not know about his affair with the therapist and with hindsight he recognized the therapist's aggression.

The second video was a short film Michael had starred in for a film school project. In the final scene of the film, Michael lay nude in a tub as the camera panned back to reveal all of him. I was fully aware of my emotions watching the video since I felt embarrassed, seduced, angry, controlled, and also sexually stimulated by Michael. My subjective experience was of being physically manipulated and emotionally masturbated by him. Interestingly, in treatment neither Michael nor I seemed to relate emotionally to his narratives or to the discussions about the videos afterward. We both felt angry with each other in beginning his treatment, he for having to begin again in treatment with the covert desire to have sex with yet another therapist, and me for feeling sexually aroused and fantasy-laden by his video. When I asked if he was trying to seduce me, he provided a flat "yes." He theorized that sex with a female therapist would create a "yin-yang bisexual balance" equalizing sex with his male therapist. A sexual symmetry to his inner universe.

In this instance, I understood Michael's erotic reactions as an aggressive resistance to treatment. As he related his history, I learned that his actions were a resistance against other affects, particularly a fear of and wish for merger reminiscent of his relationship with his mother. The clue to defining Michael's erotic transference as resistance was my subjective experience and emotional resonance with his dissociated aggression. My reaction to Michael's stories of his being attracted to me and his desire to develop a May–September relationship left me with a sense of being emotionally raped by him. I had the horrible sense that I was both victimized by his desires and a willing participant. My reactions reminded me of an experience a female adolescent patient related when she was raped at knifepoint at age 11. She wondered for years why she had been aroused by the attack even though she detested the man who raped her.

Michael's father was killed when he was 6 when a large rock fell through the windshield of the car he was driving. His mother never remarried, but housed a series of men whom Michael referred to as losers. His mother never worked and interested herself in shamanism, tarot cards, smoking pot, sporadic alcohol binges, and long, manipulative, guilt-producing letters to her two sons. Whenever she left their house, Michael and his brother were put in the care of a man who sexually abused them. This ended after a year when Michael finally informed his mother, who then found a new sitter, though she never confronted the abuser. Did Michael unconsciously want me to report his first therapist for having sex with him? He didn't think so. What was the mutual fear and greed that we shared in the treatment? We seemed to both desire more from the other although neither of us knew what exactly.

One narrative Michael told about his mother addressed this conflict through its depiction of seduction, merger, and aggression. It took place at his high school graduation party. His mother invited the neighbors and his friends over to celebrate and began the event by asking them to stand circling him. She said he had to cast off his old self and tell what negative feelings he harbored about her. Then he had to express his feelings through a dance as everyone watched. This body experience was intended to be a secondary expression of anger. He ended his dance writhing on the ground sobbing uncontrollably, after which his mother pronounced him an adult.

While I was aware that I found Michael attractive, I felt my initial experience seemed to mirror his description of his trips to hip-hop dance clubs. In these clubs there is a dance space called a "mosh pit" where mostly young men aggressively dance by kicking and punching the air, slamming themselves into pillars and each other, and sometimes jumping up to land on the upwardly extended hands of other dancers who then pass them along. In other words, the music might have had a great beat, but the emotion that prompts the dancing is meant to repel, defend against, and yet seduce the dancer–other. This inner conflict reflected Michael's erotic transference and my countertransference, as well as his genetic history. For instance, I was aware that I found him sexually attractive when he stretched himself on the couch. He was a great-looking bodybuilder. Every so often, when he would recount his sexual encounters with men or women he would become erect. I found myself feeling a bit perverted looking to see how much of him was involved in his story. I then felt seduced and repelled by my feelings all in the same moment.

Michael was conscious of wishing to seduce me; he said so, and he knew when he stretched or became sexually aroused that I was engaged. Throughout this period of treatment, we discussed mutual feelings of emotional and sexual stimulation in session. In addition, I mirrored his narcissistic needs through empathic responses, as well as provided oedipal interpretations such as his wish for and fear of having mother after father's death, and preoedipal interpretations of his desire to devour the other so that only he might live. We discussed the vicissitudes of his infantile longings, and of course there were many interpretations about his wishes and fears regarding treatment resistance, which lay under his erotic behavior. Michael felt sex with the therapist was inevitable, as nearly all his relationships were sexual on some level.

At about that time I had just purchased a new answering machine and was not accustomed to all its technical details, such as turning down the volume on incoming messages. In one particular session, Michael was lying on the couch with his arm stretched up toward me stroking his arm while he discussed feelings of desire. At that moment, a voice on my answering machine penetrated the session and I sprang from my chair to turn down the volume. Michael, being further away from the machine than I was, didn't really hear the voice, he only saw me leap into the air. He bolted upright, shouting "What are you doing? What's happening? Why are you standing?"

At that moment, I had the perverse countertransference fantasy of standing over him saying, "Oh yeah, what's all this malarkey about your wanting me to come to the couch!" Instead, I returned to my chair and said, "You thought I was finally coming to you and you were frightened." He lay there motionless with his hand over his heart trying to calm himself and answered that he would rethink his desire for me. I quietly told him he wouldn't lose me, no matter whether he desired me or not. While I had expressed this many times before, with hindsight it now seemed to me that he needed illusion to be separated from actuality in a very real way. He needed to experience my boundaries and personal limits in order to define his own, owing to his fear of merger and abandonment with his mother, as well as due to his early sexual abuse—as sexual abuse frequently blurs fantasy into reality.

Soon after, Michael began talking about his younger brother who he felt his mother had abandoned when she moved out west. This was the first time in the treatment that I experienced emotion in Michael's narratives. As the passion in the room evolved from erotic suffering to suffering from abandonment, he was finally expressing the angry feelings I had been containing for him.

THE PATIENT'S RESPONSE TO THE THERAPIST'S CONSCIOUS TRANSFERENCE

About two years ago, I conducted an initial consultation with a young man in his late twenties. I was not very impressed with him and found his presentation to be emotionally lacking and deadened. I referred him to a colleague and that was that. A month later, I received a phone call from Peter saying he didn't like the therapist and would I see him. I told him to discuss his feelings with the therapist and if it didn't work out, I would find him someone else. He called back a few months later saying he had quit therapy and wanted to start treatment with me. I told him to call me in a few months, because I wasn't able to take him as a patient at that time.

A month later, while leaving Starbuck's, I saw him standing on the sidewalk waiting for me. He walked me to my office, all the while saying he wanted to begin treatment. I kept wondering how did he know I was in Starbuck's? Was he following me? Had he followed me before? I felt quite frightened. I asked him what had gone wrong with the first therapist, and he explained, adding that he would only go into therapy with me. Then he said I reminded him of the therapist in *The Prince of Tides* (1991) and he thought that was important. I felt insulted that Peter must think I look like Barbra Streisand, who starred in the movie. Still, I told him I would think about it because I wasn't sure how to get away from him without saying "I would think about it," and because by now I was feeling even more frightened and couldn't really think of anything else to say. Later that evening, Peter found a way of bypassing the security code to my office, entered the suite, moved a chair to the middle of the waiting room and left a long note on the chair that said he had to come to therapy with me.

I began to think that I should at least talk to Peter and let him know he was frightening me. I also wanted to know what I was up against. Was he sociopathic or obsessive-compulsive or manic or psychotic? I informed the two rather physically impressive male analysts in the suite that if they heard me yell between 7:30 and 8:15 on Thursday that they should burst into my office and save me.

When Peter arrived for his session, I was quite taken aback. He had on an Armani suit, his jet-black hair was slicked back, accenting his dark Mediterranean skin, and he stared at me intently as he slipped off his Italian shoes to get comfortable. He then told me that he needed to talk about his obsessions with women and sex. He felt he was falling into an abyss of sexual exploits and thought I had seemed comfortable and open with him during our consultation when he mentioned he frequently experimented with sex.

At this point, I was frantically trying to remember the end of the movie *The Prince of Tides* (1991) and kept getting it confused with the film *Fatal Attraction* (1987). Would I end up like the bunny in the soup? Yet, as Peter continued to talk I found myself feeling more comfortable as I watched him. He was strikingly handsome. I'd missed that before. He wasn't frightening. I realized this was projective identification, in that he was both frightened that I wouldn't work with him and frightened that he could not stop his involvements with women. I found myself smiling and looking into his deep-set, dark brown eyes. Melville said in his book *Pierre* (1852) that "a smile is the chosen vehicle for all ambiguities." I was consciously aware of feeling suspicious and flattered at having been pursued, and by the end of the session, I agreed to work with him, twice a week.

Peter then began relating his exploits. A few times a week, he went for a massage at the Russian Steam Baths, a legitimate massage salon. He picked women who he said were not prostitutes, who would massage him and later perform oral sex. He spoke about how he could analyze a woman to see if she was amenable, slowly begin to stroke her face, move delicately toward her body, and within twenty minutes have completely seduced her. Afterward, he would go to a sex club. Some he could enter alone; at others he needed a woman to be admitted, and he would convince a prostitute to accompany him unpaid. He spoke about finding the most attractive woman in the club, creatively pursuing her, and then performing exhibitionist sex. He was frequently drawn to group sex and felt himself the main performer. Peter also told stories about seducing beautiful women on the subways into sex, often performed in the space between the subway cars. Sometimes he would approach women on the street, talk to them and end up fondling or having sex with them in doorways. To make many long stories very short, Peter had sex anywhere, from two to four times a day, typically with different women. In addition, he dated two to three women who he considered devout Catholic virgins who he would never touch sexually because they were the kind of women he wanted to marry. He said, "If I don't stop having sex with every woman who moves, I'm going to lose my mind. You have to help me stop." I tried to remember if Don Juan had ever been stopped in his exploits. Or was this like the tale of Scheherazade who escaped the death that was the usual fate of King Shahrigar's wives by telling the tales of the *Arabian Nights*, interrupting them at interesting points or postponing the continuation until the next night? Was Peter afraid that if he stopped his obsessional sex something about him would die?

My countertransference was clearly in collusion with his obsessions, as well as resonating with them, as I was both engaged by his stories and attracted by his appearance. I was reminded of Pauline Réage (1965), who, during the 1950s, wrote *The Story of O* in an attempt to further engage her lover, a well-known French literary figure. She was afraid he might end their long affair and her story was conceived to ensnare a very sophisticated man, which it did. In a *New Yorker* interview (de St. Jorre 1994), I believe Réage spoke to the notion of domination and surrender inherent in both storytelling and love when she said, "we are all jailers, and all in prison, in that there is always someone within us whom we enchain, whom we imprison, whom we silence" (p. 46).

Peter's obsessional use of sex and seduction indicates an emotional emptiness that I may never fully understand or reach in his treatment. To date, he typically rebuffs any attempt to discuss his childhood or family experiences. He also rebukes any and all interpretations as pop psychology and often will beat me to the punch, making both traditional and contemporary interpretations of his sexual behavior. What I have found most effective with Peter is immersing myself both consciously and unconsciously in the wonderment, narcissism, and grandiosity of the subjective experience of his stories. Slowly, he seems to be finding a more stable equilibrium and within the last few months he has slightly decreased his womanizing.

In this treatment, the analyst's experiencing of the countertransference is a crucial requirement and opportunity for the patient to remain in treatment. Peter needs to feel his influence on the analyst as well as on all his women in order to claim his existence. Is this merely repetition or will the analyst's long-term involvement create an opportunity for a different relationship? Khan (1979) states that for those individuals who engage in sexual obsessions or perversions, sexual enactments enable at least a fundamental manner of communication with an external object—a retreat from deadness and isolation that create an inner world. "Acting out though the technique of [sexual] intimacy breaks down [a] . . . sense of isolation and establishes contact with an object, and through an object with the self" (p. 29). In Peter's treatment, the erotic transference–countertransference phenomenon may be the requirement of a corresponding involvement, a necessary reciprocal level of interest by the analyst who mirrors the patient's manner of relating, transference reactions, and sense of an existing self. Peter's treatment may eventually lead to intense levels of dissociation, perhaps even a psychotic regression as he struggles to reach authenticity.

CONCLUSION

In this chapter, I have discussed a particular intersubjective transference–countertransference experience that operated in a similar way within three clinical examples—that of mirrored or reflected narcissism. In a sense, each patient needed my narcissistic involvement. They seemed to sense a necessity in me and produced the kind of transference that played into my need for mirroring, an action that resulted in my immediate engagement in the process. Is this dynamic a universal counter-transference reaction? In the way that analysts develop the transference by evoking, mirroring, and reflecting the patient's inner experiences, do patients subjectively experience and unknowingly reflect the analyst's character issues and inner experiences and bring the analyst's unconscious needs into the transference–countertransference mix? As Aron (1996) suggests, "The patient–analyst relationship . . . [is an] ongoing mutual influence in which both parties systematically affect, and are affected by, each other. A communication process is established between patient and analyst in which influence flows in both directions" (p. 77).

The erotic transference–countertransference performs a wide variety of functions. Some patients, such as those presented in this chapter, experience the erotic transference as creating a unique intimacy that helps them explore their sense of self, as well as unfold an experience of self in relation to another. The mutually created erotic transference–countertransference matrix can help the patient as well as the analyst to become aware of defended and dissociated feelings. It can also provide a means for both participants to express aggression, as well as be an opportunity for the patient and analyst to immerse themselves in their own and the other's internality. These co-constructed feelings and the functions they provide could never be brought out by the analyst's use of abstinence.

In 1959, Searles made a departure from the accepted analytic response to transference love when he wrote about countertransference love toward his patients as a possible litmus test for the patient's maturation in the analysis (p. 291). While contemporary analytic literature on erotic transference–countertransference now largely accepts this view, a discrepancy still exists—visible in current analytic literature that seems to focus on sexual feelings rather than on loving feelings toward patients. Are sexual feelings more available to us? Perhaps sexual feelings are a necessary precursor for feelings of love. Or are they defensive versions of loving feelings? I wonder if, as analysts, we have become so expert at governing our emotions that controlling our love for a patient comes easier than controlling our sexual or body reactions. Could this be a lingering remnant of Freud's notion of abstinence?

Homoerotic Transference and Countertransference between a Female Analyst and Female Patients

There are certain analytic axioms that influence psychoanalytic treatment. One is the notion that only women can understand other women (Freud 1920), and in particular that only women should analyze lesbians. With unintentional volition, we often make a referral after speculating if the patient will work better with a male or female colleague. Still, most of us in the psychoanalytic community hold to the belief that the analyst's gender makes no difference in treatment. Feminist influence has left us with the notion that difference as well as sameness exists between all patients and all analysts and that these must be appreciated without pathologizing. The current trend in psychoanalysis has to do with understanding that our differences can mean an openness to managing our own body experience as well as our defensive constellations. When we work with patients, these experiences and defenses are typically tinted by both culturally and biologically based gender considerations. This makes a great deal of sense to me, since I have always wondered if male analysts really understand the emotional swing and bloated body experience created by female hormones and the intense need to rip off any restricting clothing and eat whatever the hell you want when estrogen is low.

Some very different issues arise when the female patient is in treatment with a female analyst. I am speaking about the particular dynamics that arise between same-sex gender dyads that may be nearly impossible to create in a male–female analytic frame. In this chapter, I will discuss specific homoerotic transference–countertransference issues that arise between female patients and a female analyst.

In the past decade, increasing attention has been paid by relational analysts to the development and clinical implications of the erotic transference–countertransference in psychoanalytic treatment. For the purpose of this chapter, erotic feelings are defined as all the patient's loving, sensual, and sexual desires toward the analyst, as well as aggressive resistances that defend against erotic feelings. Of course, in looking at the erotic transference from a position of mutuality, the analyst considers and makes therapeutic use of countertransference feelings aroused in her by her patients, as well as the analyst's own emotions and subjective experiences. In this chapter, I will present clinical material on the erotic transference of three female patients, one who identifies as bisexual, another as heterosexual, and a third as lesbian. The focus here, however, will be on the analyst's erotic countertransference, since it is in the arena of the erotic countertransference that the erotic transference often gets bogged down or eliminated.

Lately, it appears that psychoanalytic literature on the erotic transference–countertransference has been written by female analysts, and they have mostly concentrated on erotic feelings between female analysts and male patients. There are fewer papers on erotic longings between female analysts with lesbian patients (Davies 1994, Elise 1991, McDougall 1986, 1995, McWilliams 1996, O'Connor and Ryan 1993, Siegel 1988, Wrye and Welles 1994). And there is an unfortunate lack of analytic literature on homoerotic transference–countertransference when both patient and analyst are heterosexual. McDougall (1986, 1995) seems to be one of the very few exceptions. Let me give an example of what the literature contains. In McDougall's 1995 book, *The Many Faces of Eros*, she discusses homoerotic longings within a transference–countertransference enactment in which she had an emotional deafness toward the patient's erotic material. McDougall thought this deafness defended her own repressed homosexual fantasies. During the analysis, McDougall had what she calls a "homosexual dream" (p. 25). On waking, she began a self-analysis around her perception of denied erotic feelings toward her own mother. McDougall seems to understand her countertransference as a development related to the patient's projective identification and when she next meets her patient she interprets the patient's conflict about feeling loved by her mother.

McDougall's writings are a good example and a rare clinical illustration of homoerotic transference–countertransference in the analytic literature. Still, she tends to focus on transference, and when she does discuss the erotic countertransference, her erotic countertransference feelings are revealed through dreams or are masked or eliminated before she returns to the consulting room. In other words, countertransference is subsumed under varying degrees of analytic neutrality. I have a feeling that this is very representative of the way many traditional and contemporary analysts work with their erotic countertransference, whether it is with same-sex or opposite-sex patients. How does this process work in a more relational treatment where there is a mutual affective participation?

To my mind, Davies's paper (1994) stands out as one of the few exceptions, as Davies describes mutual discussion of erotic transference–countertransference feelings (albeit toward a male patient) as her countertransference developed in the consulting room. I understand such countertransference feelings or enactments to be an expected part of the analytic process. Countertransference enactments manifest as the analyst participates in collecting data about the patient's life. These enactments are co-created by both patient and analyst in the living out of emotional experience within the boundaries of the analytic frame. Levenson (1992), in discussing how the analyst reveals herself in the process of gathering data about the internal workings of the patient, believes that all dialogue the therapist participates in is a metamessage about who the analyst is— that is, comments, interpretations, nearly anything and everything the analyst says. "The ultimate issue . . . is not only what the patient says about his/her life to the therapist, nor is it only what the therapist says to the patient about the patient's life: but also, what they say about themselves—however inadvertently—to each other" (p. 562). In this way, the notion of enactments places countertransference closer to the notion of transference (Hirsch 1994). But how do we know when we've co-created this erotic transference–countertransference material particularly when it can be so well defended against by the patient and/or the analyst?

Bollas (1994) states, and I disagree with him, that the "erotic transference is restricted to the analytic partnership that splits the sexes . . ." (p. 581). He elaborates that there is a displaced manifestation of the erotic transference in heterosexual same-sex analyses, one that could perhaps best be described as a form of "rhapsodic identification" (p. 581). In this particular relationship with the analyst, the patient falls in love with both real or imagined aspects of the analyst's character and perceived life, such as how the analyst expresses ideas, his mannerisms, or his sensitivities. "The patient develops an intense inner relation to the object of identification that gains its rhapsodic character from the analyst's . . . presence" (p. 581), a type of idealized love. In the heterosexual analytic dyad, the patient becomes immersed in a fantasized involvement, perhaps a voyeuristic preoccupation with the analysts' life. "The rhapsodic identification displaces erotic states of mind even though the erotic transfer [is what] organizes affective experiences . . ." (p. 581). Is Bollas suggesting that there aren't any homoerotic transference–countertransference developments between heterosexuals that the analyst can work with? It seems to me that his "rhapsodic identification" is an early phase of a developing or budding same-sex erotic transference, not an end in itself. It is more likely that Bollas is expressing his own discomfort with homoerotic transference–countertransference material.

So then how in the world does the analyst work with this unconscious or consciously held defense against the erotic transference in the same-sex analytic dyad? Wrye and Welles (1994) contend it is their experience that patients who develop erotic transferences evoke in the analyst powerful feelings and defenses that may include "manic, depressive, obsessional, schizoid, or paranoid elements" (p. 62). They suggest that such emotions are difficult for the analyst to contain, and that as analysts, we often cannot permit ourselves to participate in the erotic dynamic. Feelings of merger and desire between the analytic couple, along with mutual penetration wishes, may create both longing and fear in both participants.

Intolerance of erotic countertransference in ourselves may result in enactments of it through mothering responses or in arrested feelings

that are kept out of awareness, bringing about an altered analytic process. The most powerful erotic countertransference feelings are those
fused with aggression, because these inhibit the analysts' experience and
can completely change the course of the analysis (Wrye and Welles
1994). It is unfortunate that Wrye and Welles focus on the analyst's
aggressive countertransference reactions to the patient. Are they agree-
ing with Bollas (1994) that analysts are fighting the odds or at least
working against nature's elements when they work with the erotic transference–countertransference relationship? Wrye and Welles do give good
clinical examples of a heterosexual female patient's erotic transference
but they understand the patient's narrative as "coalescing around issues
of fusion, schizoid or obsessional distancing, and grandiose or manic
treatment agendas" (p. 64). They add that the female patient was experienced by the female analyst as a "toxic, parasitic infant who seemed
bent on, and capable of, dismantling and devouring" the analyst (p. 76).
Why is the erotic countertransference so slippery when the patient is
heterosexual? Is it different when the patient is gay?

Frommer (1995) began his paper on "Countertransference Obscurity in the Psychoanalytic Treatment of Homosexual Patients" by noting that within the psychoanalytic literature there is an absence of discussion of the analyst's countertransference in the treatment of same-sex
patients where there is sexual desire. Frommer's essay is an important
theoretical contribution to the literature on the treatment of gays, but
unfortunately he provides no clinical illustrations of erotic transference–
countertransference.

There are a few recent publications in which a smattering of authors come close to discussing erotic countertransference to same-sex
and/or lesbian patients, but more often the attention is on the erotic transference (Elise 1991, McWilliams 1996, O'Connor and Ryan 1993, Siegel
1988, Wrye and Welles 1994). For instance, one author says she took
her countertransference to an authority (I assume her analyst or supervisor) who understood and accepted her conflicted feelings of sexual
longing toward her patient. Again, this is the rather traditional response
to working with erotic countertransference feelings, in which the analyst
returns to the consulting room with her own emotions intact. In addition, the analyst felt it was important that her patient not feel an erotic

indifference and interpreted that her patient's "sexual interests were stimulating, delightful, precious, poignant, and safe" (McWilliams 1996, p. 218). Why was it necessary to qualify that erotic feelings in treatment are safe? Doesn't saying something is safe in treatment mean to the patient "Don't worry, all this material we're discussing is unreal. It's just verbal dry humping—there's no chance of really getting affectively pregnant, because I won't penetrate you by taking any emotional risks." As it turned out, the patient started focusing on images of a future loving relationship with the analyst and wanted to leave treatment before analyzing it, to really "have" the analyst. Does this mean the erotic fantasy broke down? Did it become stuck on the patient's actually loving the analyst with her hopes of the treatment ending?

In a presentation by Muriel Dimen in 1997 titled "Bodies, Acts and Sex: Thinking Through the Relational" she spoke about an erotic transference–countertransference development in which she felt a female patient was about to unconsciously enact the analyst's erotic feelings by developing a destructive relationship outside the treatment. In this particular analysis, the patient had a history of cultivating disastrous relationships with men when the erotic transference–countertransference manifested in treatment. Dimen interpreted this to the patient in the hopes of stopping the patient's acting out. In other words, Dimen told the patient she had sexual feelings about her and said she thought the patient had in the past unconsciously enacted the erotic transference–countertransference feelings in destructive relationships with men. To my knowledge, this is the only paper where homoerotic feelings were disclosed by the analyst to the patient in the hopes of developing treatment.

With the exception of Dimen's unpublished paper, analytic literature indicates that the erotic transference and countertransference feelings are altered through the analyst's interpretations into a more workable or sexually neutered transference alliance, or that treatment is ended either by the patient or the analyst, which is what Freud originally suggested in his 1915 paper on transference love.

Kaftal (1994) in an unpublished paper on treating gay men, suggests that the heterosexual analyst subtly signals ambivalent feelings about homoerotic fantasy. He warns that transferential fantasies need to be opened up and expanded before understanding and interpretation can begin because "A simple push to move more quickly to the interpretive phase is more than enough to suggest [to the patient] that emotional expression and erotic phantasy are not entirely welcome" (p. 9). This treatment warning differs from that of the traditional analytic stance, in that Kaftal is saying be careful about using interpretation to dilute the erotic transference–countertransference into nothing but unreal or real feelings and fantasies, or to head too quickly into discussions on infantile longings, since this may lead to a premature ending of the erotic transference or of the treatment itself, in order to be with the analyst sexually.

So why is the erotic countertransference so difficult to work with, especially within the same-sex heterosexual dyad? Butler (1995) wrote an important paper on "Melancholy Gender—Refused Identification" in which she spoke of "the foreclosed status of homosexual love that never was" (p. 169). In order for the female child to transfer love from her father to a substitute object, she must first renounce her love for mother in such a complete way that the aim and object of her love are foreclosed in her renunciation. It is not the female child's transferring homosexual love to a substitute feminine figure, but instead it is a matter of "renouncing the possibility of homosexual attachment itself" (p. 169). Only in this transfer can heterosexual aims become secured as sexual orientation. It is on this condition of foreclosed homosexuality that the stage is now set where the father, and all future substitutes for him, become the female child's objects of desire—it is mother who now becomes the unsettled arena of identification.

Butler (1995) uses the word "foreclosed" to mean a "preemptive loss, a mourning for unlived possibilities; for if this is a love that is from the start out of the question, then it cannot happen and, if it does, it certainly did not; if it does [anyway], it happens only under the official sign of its prohibition and disavowal" (p. 171). The heterosexual then disavows a constitutive relationship to homosexuality. And then, if this is so, what does it mean to erotic transference–countertransference feelings within the heterosexual analyst and same-sex patient dyad?

I have never struggled with the beginnings of a paper in the way I have with this one. I felt all over the place, way too fluid. I couldn't come up with an outline to save my life. I put off writing it for months because I was "thinking." I told nearly everyone who would listen that I was writing it, almost to the point that I would introduce myself and within moments launch into the struggles I was having with the piece. Then I realized, by writing about homoeroticism in heterosexuality it's like I'm "coming out." Do lesbian and gay analysts professionally present themselves as such or do we all have sexuality secrets? Are there professional or personal risks? Isay (1996) has suggested that gay therapists should acknowledge being homosexual when patients ask. Not disclosing compromises the truthfulness of the analytic relationship. However, Isay adds that such disclosure is complicated by shame. Is this just true about the analyst's sexual identity, or does shame relate to most sexual issues and feelings that arises in psychoanalysis?

Lately, I have been giving some thought as to whether or not we as analysts put our own emotions at risk when we treat our patients. We ask our patients to question what they feel, to analyze their experiences, and to let us guide them—and may this not also be an emotional risk to or seduction of unknown parts of the patient's self? How can we do that if we aren't prepared to take a similar sort of risk? This got me to thinking about the risks I have taken in psychoanalysis and the risks I haven't. To my mind, taking a risk as an analyst means putting one's own emotions on the line, risking the disclosure of one's own feelings at times, and thus stretching the boundaries of the analytic playground through emotional risk without being out of control.

Recently, in a class I was teaching at an analytic institute, I found myself discussing my intimate feelings about my work with patients, as well as my subjective experiences and countertransference. I was pleased at the innermost quality of the responses the candidates returned about their work and themselves. In this last meeting of the semester, in a discussion of our thoughts about the readings, one of the candidates said she loved the class because it made her question her work and herself. Then she added she also hated me for having made her do that, meaning she hadn't intended to give so much of herself emotionally in and to the class. My having taken risks with my own feelings allowed her to feel a desire to respond in kind. She was able to meet me at the threshold.

CLINICAL ILLUSTRATION OF A FEMALE BISEXUAL PATIENT

Pauline came to analysis to discuss her conflict about her sexuality. She has only been in heterosexual relationships, yet she believes she is bisexual and would like to fulfill her desires with a woman. She was one of six children from a Catholic family. A female child, born dead eighteen months before Pauline, had also been named Pauline. When she was 5, Pauline and an older brother experimented with mutual masturbation without penetration. She feels this was disgusting, and sex as an adult, with men, has retained a vulgar edge for her. Pauline's longest relationship, of seven years, was with a verbally abusive man who shared her alcoholism. Since becoming sober nine years ago she has only had "crushes" on women.

Pauline related an interesting memory about her mother. She remembered being about 6 years old, riding alone with her mother in their car. She said it was one of the few memories she had of being alone with her mother without the other children. Pauline stared at her mother as she drove in an attempt to get her to respond in some way to a multitude of stories and questions she was asking. Her mother was preoccupied and eventually told Pauline to be quiet and they drove on in silence with Pauline feeling humiliated at her mother's rejection and obliviousness to her desire. It's not surprising that as an adult Pauline is rather isolated and emotionally withdrawn.

In an early session with her, she talked about the lack of any sex in her life. I asked if she masturbated. She didn't, saying it took too long and she got too tired before climaxing. "Don't you use a vibrator?" I asked. She giggled with discomfort and titillation and seemed thrilled at our topic. In the next session, she announced that she had gone to the Pleasure Chest Shop in Greenwich Village and purchased a large dildo, not a vibrator, that had all sorts of special features and had used it the night before our session. She felt pleased I'd given her permission to have this sexual experience. I realized that I was somehow involved in her fantasy, either as overseer, voyeur, participant, or maybe as the prey, and she agreed.

At this point, she became intensively curious about my life. What did I do on weekends? Who were my friends? Was I married? She thought not and hoped I had female lovers. Monday morning sessions were full of her questions about my weekend. I considered Pauline's fascination with my life to be an example of Bollas's (1994) "rhapsodic identification." However, a patient's preoccupation need not stop at this level if the analyst can allow or tolerate a further unfolding of the erotic transference, as it can organize affect and create intimate experiences.

Pauline became increasingly flirtatious in the successive sessions. Adam Phillips (1994) declared that "Flirtation keeps things in play, and by doing so lets us get to know . . . [people] in different ways." "[Flirtation] plays with, or rather flirts with, the idea of surprise . . . [it] confirms the connection between excitement and uncertainty, and how we make uncertainty possible by making it exciting" (p. xii). Pauline took her flirtation to courtship and started bringing small presents from the store where she worked: she also began writing letters and calling between sessions. When I asked if she was trying to emotionally seduce me, she responded that she thought so, and punctuated this session with a long letter. "To answer your question from Friday," she said, "the feelings I have for you are sexual, which scares the hell out of me to tell you that. I fear that it will disgust you to know my attraction is sexual."

I am certainly not disgusted by Pauline's sexual desire and have told her so. She appeared less humiliated on hearing that. Perhaps she has learned that I can be engaged through her presentation of erotic material. Through my work over many years, I have slowly come to the realization that I speak a very passionate language. Words that to me feel warm and intimate are sometimes experienced as seductive, enticing, and alluring by others. Patients quickly learn their analyst's language and seem to know what topics spark our interests, whether it's narratives about aggression, separation-individuation, sex, or whatever, and often patients will consciously or unconsciously engage the analyst by evoking such topics—and of course, vice versa. Pauline's engagement of my attention is a different experience than the one she had riding in her mother's car as a child. I feel quite comfortable with Pauline's sexual wishes and fantasies. She came to treatment with a longing to be with a woman and, for now, I have become the object of her desire. I assume her sexual longings will become more and more explicit as we continue to work together, and that I will feel attracted to her in the erotic transference–countertransference matrix. What concerns me is the possibility of the patient's unconscious enactment of the erotic transference–countertransference outside the treatment, as in Dimen's clinical illustration. If Pauline develops a relationship with a man or a woman, is this an erotic transference–countertransference enactment, or an expression of the patient's maturation, or is it a regression?

What I find curious in treating Pauline is the lack of conflict I experience regarding my erotic countertransference. Perhaps it is because her sexuality is so conflicted for her that I am left with only a sense of calm, the antithesis of conflict. My tranquility may also be a maternal erotic countertransference (Wrye and Welles 1994), a resistance to an even more threatening homoerotic feeling, or perhaps my emotional peace is an aspect of a maternal countertransference. Still, our work has an intimate, warm quality, in that I feel very emotionally engaged and related to her stories and memories. Pauline's sexual desires and my caretaking of them, as well as of her, are parts of our mutual relationship that allow for an unfolding of both the patient's and the therapist's creativity and that open opportunities for even more emotional intensity. Pauline has desires for women, as do my lesbian and heterosexual male patients, and as a woman I am, therefore an object of her desire—as well as the sexual subject she desires to be.

CLINICAL ILLUSTRATION OF A FEMALE
HETEROSEXUAL PATIENT

Simone began treatment eight years ago after she found out that her husband had had a brief affair. Years passed with the two of us struggling with her failed career as an interior designer in relation to her husband's business success. Treatment was uneventful—easy, I thought—and Simone was funny and entertaining and I enjoyed her visits. She was also quite beautiful, with large saucer eyes, blonde hair, and a lovely smile. This was a psychotherapy case and the transference was rather calm and maternal for many years, much as she had described her life in Kansas as a child. Her mother sang in the church, her father was a teacher, and her only sister was her closest friend.

About four years into the treatment, Simone decided to take a temporary assignment as a secretary at a construction company. She had never been exposed to an environment of this kind. Her boss cursed up a blue streak and screamed at clients. The receptionist was openly having an affair with the boss's partner, who videotaped their sex and showed it to the men at the office. Mobsters showed up for private meetings with the boss, and sexual harassment in the office was expected and casually accepted—or elicited—and on and on. It was as though squeaky-clean, churchgoing Dorothy from Kansas had stumbled into a licentious den of iniquity.

Simone was fascinated, frightened, and mesmerized by their behavior. Sessions became a weekly recounting of unusual relations between coworkers, which she told in a hilarious way. The two of us would roar with laughter as she described feeling like Michelle Pfeiffer in the movie *Married to the Mob* (1988). She then began talking more specifically about her boss, Tony. He was a big, gruff, burly, but good-looking Italian guy who was becoming charmed by Simone's innocence, appearance, and humor. They began having lunches together and then drinks after dinner and finally he told her he was falling for her.

At the same time, Simone was very busy being the corporate wife in her husband's career. His boss began inviting them to the Hamptons for weekends and after one evening meal, Simone found herself followed into a bedroom by her husband's boss. He professed a sexual desire as he pulled her on the bed and attempted to seduce her. At that point she knew that something sexual was in the air, kismet or karma, and she told him she wasn't interested in an affair. A few days later she told Tony she was.

In her treatment, Simone's stories had heated up. I anticipated the coming attractions of her narratives and found myself musing and fantasizing about the upcoming events outside the hour. When Tony finally propositioned her, she came to the session and asked what to do. I wondered if she wanted my consent to have an affair and she said yes. After an exploration of her desires and fears, and after discussing how she would be living a secret life, she decided to have an affair with Tony and asked if I would help her through it. I told her I would always help her and she interpreted this as permission. At this time, I wondered about the homoeroticism inherent in triangulations, specifically about those in Simone's decision. Certainly, when Simone went to bed with her lover, she took along her thoughts about his wife. In a sense, theirs would be a very full bed and I assumed I would be present in some form, as well.

Simone began a very passionate affair with Tony and her relationship with me became equally steamy. It often felt like we were mutually watching porno flicks as she narrated weekly events with her boss. We were both becoming sexually aroused by her stories. In Benjamin's book *The Bonds of Love* (1988), in the chapter entitled "Woman's Desire," she writes that the developing child wants more than a plain satisfaction of need. Instead, each specific "want" is an expression of the child's desire to be recognized as a subject. "What is really wanted is a recognition of one's desire; what is wanted is a recognition that one is a subject, an agent who can will things and make them happen" (p. 102). Desire is often framed by gender—women are frequently the objects of desire, in that someone else, the subject (often the man, in heterosexual relations) gets pleasure, and the object of desire (usually the woman) gets sexual enjoyment from pleasing the subject. Being the subject of desire, however, would mean that a woman would have her own wants.

My own fantasy about how I am perceived is that I have my own wants. This is conveyed in the way I dress, my manner, sensitivities, how I use language, and my attitudes—all of these have a sexual component or edge. Benjamin (1988) suggests that the "'real' solution to the dilemma of woman's desire must include a mother who is articulated as a sexual subject, one who expresses her own desires" (p. 114). This was true of my relationship with my mother, and now it was in my relationship with Simone, as she began to identify with a female analyst who has her own desires.

Simone wanted to be able to want. She wanted sex, she wanted to be sexual, and she wanted to have an affair. She was the subject of desire, and through my recognition of her desire, I became a co-conspirator. Yet, because I facilitated her becoming a subject, the real affair was with me, since I had also facilitated her subjectivity. It was the same for me, since this facilitation was outside the realm of men and their objectifying selves.

Benjamin (1988) suggests that it is "recognition of the other that is the decisive aspect of differentiation" (p. 126). In recognition there is a sense of self and other that evolves through an awareness of shared feelings and experience, as well as the sensation that the other is external and dissimilar. It is a mutual recognition that provides a point of self-differentiation. When we have erotic feelings toward another person, we desire, want, and experience the other as being inside and outside us. It is as though our mind and body are made up of aspects of the other, and this often gives us a sense of wholeness as well as a differentiation of self in relation to the other. The erotic transference can be a powerful arena that can help many patients differentiate.

In erotic unions between men and women, it has been my experience that while men may desire a loss of self in an erotic relationship, they are least likely to tolerate too much of it. It is more usually women who can merge with the other temporarily. Yet merger is a core issue in lesbian relationships and often results in sexual bed-death: a merged relationship defuses the shared, mutual power of two individuals engaged in the erotic fantasy of being swept away by each other, and the "lack of longing" in merged relationships often results in a lessening of erotic feelings.

Very soon after the beginning of the affair, Simone's boss arranged an apartment for the two of them and let her decorate it. They would meet there frequently during the week and perform an unusual sexual interaction. Tony did not undress himself, nor did he entirely undress Simone, but he would instead perform oral sex on her. This is rather different from the typical outcome of a heterosexual affair, in which the woman performs oral sex or the man penetrates the woman. She was happy with the arrangement and so was he. To my mind, it was Tony who was objectified by this woman's desire.

Still, was Simone in more control than I knew, both outside and in the treatment? Were her stories of their meetings meant to seduce, dominate, control, and/or objectify me? Was Tony performing my part in his surrender to her as the subject? Simone wasn't sure, but said I was definitely in the room when they were together. I remember feeling uneasy when she said this. Just how large was my part? How much was I colluding or not colluding? I felt caught up in the events at this time and I couldn't seem to interpret the transference successfully. Yet what kind of reality would an interpretation of this enactment have? More and more, I felt like a participant in her stories and as though I were being masturbated in the sessions. Or, was I manipulating her, like Svengali? Who was Simone having sex with?

As she shared her sexual fantasies with Tony in the office, and with me in the sessions, she spoke about an experience she had as an adolescent. She and a very close girlfriend had taken to spending time talking as they lay on her friend's bed. As they shared intimacies and secrets they found themselves fantasizing and telling the other of their sexual as well as nonsexual desires. She said they both began to feel aroused and eventually began affectionately touching each other. In a short while, their thinking and talking about sex had become action as they progressed to kissing and then sexual exploration and eventually mutual masturbation. She then confessed to recently having masturbated to the fantasy of two women together and when I asked if she meant us, she said yes.

In Simone's mind, she was imagining having sex with me. On the one hand, I could consider her feelings to be an unreal erotic transference experience. We weren't really having sex and we weren't going to, and one way I could choose to understand her reactions would be to attribute them to infantile longings. And, while I didn't rule out such an interpretation, I also didn't feel it was specific enough in my relationship to Simone. Our affiliation seemed more complex, more mutual, more intimate, and the sexual stimulation that we both felt in relation to her narratives was very real. As long as we didn't engage in the action of sex, did that mean there was no sex between us?

What constitutes a sexual relationship? Is actually having sex real sex? Or, is imagined sex real sex, too? The notion of what is "real" between people is a powerful aspect of shared intimacy. In an unpublished paper, Kaftal posed the question, "What makes sex, sex?" I feel this question relates very much to my experience with Simone. For instance, is sex in transitional relating, such as in the analytic relationship, different than imagining having sex with someone? Is imagining having sex the same as really having sex? Some people might answer "yes" and others might say "no" to that question. But the next query might be: Is phone sex sex? Many of us have an immediate answer to that question, and to my mind, phone sex *is* sex. And if that is so, then how does phone sex differ from imagined sex if imagined sex is *not* sex? Where do we draw the line, and what makes something "sex?"

The answer has to do with the intention of the people involved. If we believe that imagined sex is helpful in dealing with the patient's other issues in treatment—for example, when a patient's sexual feelings are defending against other nonsexual feelings, such as aggression or intimacy—then sexual feelings between analyst and patient are diffused. In other words, the sexual feelings between both individuals are imagined and unreal. However, what about the experience of two individuals in the same room, bedroom or backroom, who are jerking off together? Isn't that sex? If the room is a consulting room and one of the individuals is a sex surrogate, and if there is a clinical reason for the other person to jerk off or masturbate, is it sex? Or is it the same as just jerking off?

In psychoanalysis or therapy, a whole different rule exists for physical actions. In psychoanalysis, our actions are verbal and we think about the intentions of both the patient and the therapist, and then how we read these intentions. What constitutes sex is not fixed in any certain way. At this moment in our current society and culture, what really matters to us is what we really do or feel—not just what we intend to do. For instance, when someone asks "Do you really love me?" while what you say does matter, what you feel and do matters more. This is the way we understand what sex means, and it is the meaning system we use to understand sex that matters. In my mind, there is a certain kind of mutuality in what constitutes sex. For instance, sex need only be a sharing of similar sexual stimulation, a mutual sexual feeling that is experienced at the same time. For me, what occurred between Simone and me was sex, and it is my interpretation that it was sex for Simone too. Simone and I co-constructed or created our sexual feelings for each other, with each other. It's not because I uncovered a clandestine closet that was full of secret fantasies that she'd always had and psychotherapy brought it to the surface—rather we created these sexual feelings together, and maybe I started them.

Certainly, my experience with Simone felt this way when she talked about her affair and about her sexual fantasy to be with me. We weren't really having sex, but sexuality had become the theater for getting the point across between us, and we were definitely sharing emotional intimacies. Our mutual recognition, the encounter of our separate selves, had become the context for desire in knowing an other and in knowing the self.

I then told her that I had wondered for a long time about the extent of her sexual fantasies about me, particularly since I had recently become aware of mine about her. I then went on to say that we were involved with each other in many ways and levels, and that our relationship felt deeply intimate, sexual, and loving. Simone and I had developed and shared a mutuality of affect and a sense of the other as entirely engaged and saturated. Mitchell (1988) remarked "There is perhaps nothing better suited for experiencing and deepening the drama of search and discovery than the mutual arousal, [and] sustaining, [of] . . . sexual desire" (p. 108). Our intimate feelings climaxed and were maintained after my disclosure of this particular countertransference vulnerability. Benjamin (1988) states that "Women make use of the space in-between that is created by shared feeling and discovery. The dance of mutual recognition, the meeting of separate selves, is the context for their desire" (p. 130).

Tony showered Simone with gifts and she delighted in showing me all of them. On her birthday, he gave her beautiful pale pink roses that she brought to the session and left with me, saying she could not take them home because of her husband. Interestingly, around this time, her husband began pressuring her to have a child. He began a subtle seduction by spending more time with her. He bought her a sexy teddy, and began dominating her in bed, and penetrating her in the way Tony did not. (Simone and her husband had a history of satisfying sex until he became overinvolved in this new job.) While she felt seduced back into his bed, Simone thought her husband could not possibly raise a child because he had been so isolated in his own childhood, but she let herself be swept away and immediately became pregnant. Tony promptly fired her.

Throughout the pregnancy, Simone was very interested in finding a way to raise the baby without having her husband be too involved. She thought he had no experience with children and she wasn't too sure about her own abilities. She decided I would help her raise the baby by telling her what to read and catching her if she did something wrong. In a way, the erotic transference was facilitating Simone's sense of herself as powerful and she experienced my penetrating qualities as offering her a new intersubjective perspective on what she could want or desire. She wanted an inner space into which her interior self could emerge. She missed her session one week, called me from the hospital, and brought the newborn baby in the next week. He was colicky and she was having trouble nursing, which she showed me during the session. I realized that as soon as the baby fussed she pulled him off her breast and stopped feeding. I also realized that I was seeing Simone's exposed breast. Next week, the baby looked horrible and she complained he cried all the time. I told her not to take him off the breast entirely, but to let him breathe a little and feed him until he was full. The following week he was much better and she sobbed, saying she had been starving him—and I think she had been. I was now deemed an official parent. Each week for the next year, she brought the baby into the session and nursed him at some point. At the end of the session, she would hand him over to me while she went to the restroom and he and I would play together for a bit. In a way, we were married in our transference–countertransference enactment. We had a child, and, like some couples with children, the sexual tension was somewhat reduced as we focused on the baby. In hindsight, the baby was the next male Simone used to get closer to me—her husband, Tony, and now the baby were offerings of her love.

Some people might say that the erotic transference had just become maternal. I don't think so, because there was still such a powerful erotic component in our relationship. In sessions, we discussed the emotional closeness we felt with each other, and Simone told of an ongoing internal dialogue in which she imagined telling me her feelings about everything that happened or everything she wished would happen to her. At times she questioned her heterosexual identity and wondered if she might be bisexual, saying a woman had more emotional potential with another woman than with a man. In a footnote, Benjamin (1988) says, "Ideally, in the psychoanalytic process, analysand and analyst create a transitional space, in which the line between fantasy and reality blurs and the analysand can explore her own insides. The analytic relationship then becomes a version of the space within which desire can emerge freely, can be felt not as borrowed through identification but as authentically one's own" (p. 127). In this treatment, Simone and I were maintained in our subject-to-subject space. In our relationship there was a recognition between self and other self that originated in the desire to be known and to know an other.

CLINICAL ILLUSTRATION OF A LESBIAN PATIENT

June has been in psychoanalysis for four years now and the transference has until recently been lustfully erotic. I receive multiple letters per week from her, many of them with drawings of the naked torso of a woman who she says is me. Often she speaks about her wish to watch me have sex with a man and/or a woman while she looks on and masturbates. She frequently fantasizes about parts of my body and tells me details of how she will arouse me sexually. June often wistfully looks up from the couch, stroking her sternum as she relates her sexual desires. Recently she told me the following joke: "'Doctor, Doctor please kiss me.'" The doctor, she said, answered "No, no, I can't." "Please Doctor kiss me." The doctor replies, "I can't kiss you, I shouldn't even be lying on the couch with you."

June was quipping about her awareness of our mutual erotic transference–countertransference relationship. I have repeatedly asked her what meaning she makes of sexually arousing me, and she has interpreted that our mutual sexual stimulation is akin to actually having sex.

June doesn't believe in making love, rather she takes pride in "fucking like a man." She recounts affairs where she has seduced a woman, usually one who identifies as heterosexual and married, has sex with her, and leaves while the woman is still naked in bed. Is this an analogy of our relationship, I asked her. She thought so and said it expressed her desire to control me—an enacted triumph over her fear of abandonment, and of her wishes for merger in achievement of intimacy through sexuality.

A few months ago, June's transference turned from lust to loathing. June had been obsessing about getting a new job and was feeling very out of control. Concurrently, I began experiencing a deadness in the treatment, a countertransference reaction I had successfully interpreted in the past. This time, however, the more she obsessed, the more I felt sleepy and angry at her for making me struggle to stay awake. Sessions seemed to drag on and even though I tried to interpret the emptiness in the hour, in her, and in me, how her obsessions were burying and also defending her—nothing brought the dead back to life. Finally after a few weeks, I just couldn't tolerate it or her any longer and, grappling with my grogginess, I angrily told her to stop it. I said, "I hate your obsessionalism, I hate feeling sleepy, and I hate being controlled. You're treating me exactly the way your mother treats you—killing me with deadness and obsessionalism. You're trying to make it impossible for me to work." In a fury, she called me a "fucking cunt" or variations on that theme for the remainder of the session. Throughout the day, June called my office leaving additional messages about my being a "fucking cunt," and threatened to take a break from treatment. I called her back, told her she had to come back, that she was in psychoanalysis and not finishing school and she couldn't take a break. She kept cursing at me, but agreed to return—maybe in her mind she wanted an opportunity to berate me to my face.

In the subsequent sessions, my name seemed forever linked to "fucking cunt." Had the erotic transference just been a defense for an underlying aggression waiting to erupt? Or had we both created a mutual narcissistic injury in the other and were both seeking revenge? June had wounded and obliterated me through her obsessionalism, which made me feel unnecessary. And I had not contained or successfully interpreted June's underlying feelings about envy, control, and abandonment.

Mitchell asserts (1988, 1993) that sexuality is an essential human experience because it is a powerful vehicle for developing and maintaining relational dynamics—and adds that the same is true of aggression. "Aggression, like sexuality, often provides the juice that potentiates and embellishes experience" (1993, p. 165). Both aggression and sexuality can be fundamental organizing elements among multiple self-organizations. "It is universal to hate, contemplate revenge against, and want to destroy those very caregivers we also love" (1993, p. 170).

In the next few sessions, my subjective experience and countertransference was of hating June for hating me. I wanted the return of her sexual attention and love. I wanted her to stop her aggressive feelings just as I had previously wanted her to stop her obsessionalism. Who was dominating whom, who was exploiting whom, who was possessing whom?

Then, June wrote in a letter, "Give me ambition. Real ambition. I don't wanna be sent off to track down a piece of cheese in a labyrinth. I'm scared of you because you're in the world and I think you like it. How do you know where I am?" June envied me for my place in the world and in her life, and I felt envy about her skill in controlling me. I told her this and added that I really did not know exactly "where she was" and that I should have been much kinder to her. I then asked if our mutual aggression felt comforting to her—I wondered aloud if we had both taken sanctuary in the other's powerful involvement. With hindsight, it seems that our aggressive feelings deepened our relationship in that we each now knew the other could not be easily frightened off when we showed our worst side.

She then wrote a note that said: "As time goes by, as time will do, we get closer, not further apart. So it fucking only makes sense that I'd wanna stay with you. That's the fucking nature of a relationship. The more you do the more you want to do. A relationship wouldn't be pleasurable if all you had to do was push a button. The downside of a human relationship is that you just can't eat a person, smoke, inject, or snort them. I wish I could just come in there with a lighter and a pipe and by god, I'd like to smoke you. But when I tried that you nearly died in the process when you felt clouded over by my obsessions. I think a relationship is like breakfast cereal in that it sort of satisfies the desire to smoke or eat people."

In the transference–countertransference matrix, June and I enacted her early relationship to her mother. In a sense, I became a participant in the reenactment of an early trauma and became June's abuser. It is within such disruptions and the ensuing repairs that relationships and analysis progress. In *The Clinical Diary of Sandor Ferenczi*, Ferenczi (1995) wrote, "I have finally come to realize that it is an unavoidable task of the analyst: although he may behave as he will, he may take kindness and relaxation as far as he possibly can, the time will come when he will have to repeat with his own hands the act of murder previously perpetrated against the patient" (p. 52). He added that the deepening of any relationship is promoted when the analyst acknowledges his own mistakes and limitations—because this aids in mutual forgiveness. Ferenczi was one of the first analysts to realize that the patient observes and reacts to the analyst's countertransference, as the analyst enacts a role framed by his own character traits in response to the patient's resistance. In so doing, the analyst becomes a distinct and real person whom the patient genuinely affects and is affected by.

In one of June's most recent notes, she wrote: "It fascinates me that there is no gun at my head, yet I return day after day, week after week to you."

4

Impasse as an Expression of Erotic Countertransference

The e-mail message read: "This is to let you know that I have quit therapy. Thank you for all your help over the last five years. I will not be needing your services any longer. Sincerely, Jackie." E-mail messages are usually gathered without haste. I have a certain relaxed feeling about logging on and retrieving messages from friends and colleagues as well as from computer-oriented patients who often want to reschedule their sessions. No one before Jackie or since has ever startled me by quitting therapy on e-mail. I typed a reply, "Why don't you come in for a final session so we can talk about what happened. I know you're angry, but I see no reason why we can't mend or at least talk about what went on. Think about it and let me know." There has never again been any communication between us.

Freud (1918, 1923, 1937) wrote about "negative therapeutic reactions" in regard to a patient's dissenting response to the analyst's well-meant interpretations. Essentially, the origins of therapeutic disruption stem from the patient's infantile longings, formerly concealed in her unconscious and now revealed by the analyst's interpretation. The traditional psychoanalytic literature on negative therapeutic reactions held to Freud's notion that disjunctions in treatment were due to the patient's malignant superego resistance, or to character disorders (particularly narcissism), sadomasochism, depression, and/or unconscious guilt and envy (Abraham 1919, Eidelberg 1948, Fenichel 1941, 1945, Freud 1926, Glover 1955, Horney 1936, Klein 1957, Lewin 1950, Reich 1933, Sullivan 1953). An additional conception of unmanageability of the negative therapeutic reaction was that "the analyst had become infected with the patient's negativistic rejection" (Olinick 1964, p. 495).

Reich (1933) was perhaps the first to suggest that the negative therapeutic reaction may result from the analyst's mismanagement of the patient–therapist relationship, or from the analyst's poor technique in working with latent negative transference. Still, while the analyst may make mistakes, the problem in such treatments meant that it was the patient who needed to tolerate the analyst's interpretations. It is unfortunate that Ferenczi's (1933) notion of the therapist admitting his mistakes to the patient met with disapproval from most of the analytic community with the exception of Sullivan, Fromm-Reichmann, and Thompson (Thompson 1956). Contemporary analysts who are influenced by Ferenczi's advocacy of mutuality in psychoanalysis acknowledge the therapist's participation in the analytic situation, as well as the constant impact of the analyst's emotional reactions on the therapeutic process. In essence, this notion of the analyst's experience emphasizes the constitutive interplay of two subjectivities—those of the patient's and analyst's inner and external worlds.

Stolorow and Trop (1992), in a chapter entitled, "Varieties of Therapeutic Impasse" write about ruptures in analysis as stemming from the "intersubjective disjunction" (p. 103) that occurs when the therapist's response alters or reconfigures the patient's experience and therefore what the patient meant. Impasses are expected in treatment and can either facilitate or disrupt the progress of therapy, but a disruption often illuminates a subjective disparity between the patient's and the analyst's emotional world. These authors note that when disjunctions "are recognized, [they] may . . . assist the therapist's ongoing efforts to understand the patient . . . [since the therapist's] . . . own emotional reactions can serve as potential intersubjective indices of the configurations actually structuring the patient's experiences" (p. 104).

When I first started reviewing the analytic literature on impasse, negative therapeutic reactions, ruptures, mismatches, and failures, at first glance it appeared that all the papers on this subject presented impasse as something to be worked through and resolved. A second, less anxious and more thorough investigation of the literature showed both successes and failures of treatments. So I then thought about all the impasses I'd had with patients where I'd been successful, and mused that I might write about those and portray the decent job I did with some difficult patients. Yet it seems to me that it is the unresolved problems, the failures in analysis that need more attention. Failures, as well as successes, represent intersubjective experiences particular to given therapeutic dyads (Ringstrom 1998) and highlight the vicissitudes of treatment, of ourselves as analysts, and of the intricate experience of otherness (Kaftal, personal communication). And, finally, in my mind I've had a failure that I can't seem to release and hoped to better understand by putting the experience in writing.

I believe that what's most important in treatment is for the patient to take emotional risks with his analyst and to explore parts of himself, fantasized or real, that he fears or doesn't know about in an authentic way, within an intimate, warm relationship with the analyst. In taking this a step further, I also believe it's important for the analyst to take risks in allowing the creation of inner fantasies that fuel emotional intimacies, as well as exploring realities of self-in-relation. I will take up the issue of therapeutic risk again in Chapter 8. In this chapter I'm going to take a different risk—a professional risk—in order to illustrate a treatment failure that masqueraded for five years as a developing treatment.

Jackie was in her mid-twenties. She was cute and petite, very articulate, and intellectually interested in treatment. What was odd about her was a very slight smile—the corners of her mouth turned up ever so gently—and her smile never altered, except when she was angry, which was exceptionally rarely and then only momentarily apparent. Actually, I only saw her angry twice. The first time, about a year or so into treatment, was when I asked if she would mind filling in her name and address on her insurance forms. She became immediately enraged, gritted her teeth, and snarled up at me that I should have told her that long ago.

I was taken aback at having created a narcissistic injury and was surprised I had no previous awareness of the existence of her "Janus face" until this moment. More importantly, I remember feeling frightened by her anger—her bared teeth scared me—as it was such a contrast from her small smile that, within another second, quickly covered her rage again. I remember trying to analyze her experience of my request, including the degree to which she had become enraged, as well as what had masked this other part of her for so long, and also what made her anger disappear so quickly. She calmly denied feeling mad and told me she was just caught off guard. She added that she was not aware she always smiled and thought it was just the way her mouth went. Maybe I didn't see what I thought I saw, or maybe I shouldn't know what I saw behind her smile. Did Jackie's smile masquerade a chaotic, fragmented inner world? I realized from this experience of Jackie's anger that her rage was a flash, a warning—not an opportunity.

What I was beginning to see in this therapy were the varying levels of masquerade that existed between us and within both of us, internally as well as externally. Many years ago, I remember listening to two female analysts discussing the care they took in choosing what to wear in their sessions so as not to elicit the erotic transference. One woman said she made sure not to dress too seductively, meaning no short skirts or scoop-neck blouses, because these clothes could be a catalyst for erotic feelings. Only just recently, a supervisee with long curly hair told me she always pulls it back when she is with patients, afraid they will feel seduced by seeing her hair down or envious of its beauty.

I know that my own physical presentation has a sexual quality. My clothing tends to highlight the better parts of my body. I dress in a style that I enjoy and therefore work with the erotic consequences that develop with some patients, who I believe would develop erotic transferences no matter what, anyway.

For some women, dressing in a sexually distinctive manner is a sign of collusion with a masculine society, as it often creates or presents women as sexual objects. For instance, an old saying is that men have sex in order to satisfy a sexual desire, while women offer themselves sexually in order to be desired. As sexual objects, women are expected to dress in a way that reveals potential engagement or creates longing in the other, or to offer a promise yet to be redeemed or possibilities that at once hold back some ultimate, unknown, and unattainable quality even in disclosing it. Yet, to my mind, when sexuality is displayed through clothing, it can present an untapped potentiality—as ornament expressing secrets of the woman within. Our clothing temporarily elaborates an expression of our internal life.

Women struggle to be subjects of their own desire and to be assertive about their sexuality. For instance, popular culture assumes that the woman in the four-inch stiletto heels is assertive as well as submissive. Certainly, she is a woman who is an object of desire, but she may also be a subject of desire—her clothing expressing her own desires. Benjamin (1988) has stated that recognition of the other and self-assertion together constitute a new mode of relating called "differentiation." Differentiation occurs at the point in an individual's development when a self becomes aware of its distinctness from others. Feelings, intentions, and actions of the self are made meaningful through the other's recognition of our experiences, as we concurrently recognize the other person's responses as being from their own agency and authorship. This struggle to be recognized by an other, and thus to confirm our selves, forms the matrix of relationships. Recognition of the other is the definitive feature of differentiation, in that someone who is different and external is also known to have or acknowledges similar feelings in attunement to ours. In erotic relationship, this attunement between self and other can construct a sense of being both inside and outside each other, creating a sense of wholeness.

In 1964, Grunberger wrote a paper titled, "Outline for a Study of Narcissism in Female Sexuality," in which he said, "Influenced by the trend in society . . . a woman may seek the same sexual freedom as men, but then will be unable to invest her love life other than narcissistically. Her body self will become increasingly important, extending from her body to her clothes and accessories to her [interior] 'home' . . ." (p. 70). Grunberger (1971) uses the word narcissism to mean an experience of completeness through gratification (p. xii). And in his offering of a revised look at feminine narcissism, he theorized that a woman's subjectivity and differentiation could be expressed physically through adornment (Apter 1991).

When I first began treating Jackie, I remember the discussions we had about her clothing. She didn't have much money and so she wore her mother's hand-me-downs, which were too large for her petite frame and far too matronly for her youthfulness. She was buttoned up to the neck and her skirts were only inches away from the Nike sneakers she walked to work in. Her black hair was cut in blunt bangs and chopped off in the back. She wore no makeup, no jewelry, and she carried a tattered tote bag loaded with newspapers and office memos. Jackie lived with two roommates (whom she disliked) in a dangerous section of Brooklyn where she felt frightened to come home alone after work.

Jackie was pretty talented at working with computers and we discussed a way that she could arrange for her company to pay for computer classes. They did and within a year she was promoted with more money and responsibility. Her promotion created a period of anxiety about becoming successful, but we analyzed and interpreted her fears of competition, envy, and guilt, and within the next year she found a new job. She now made even more money and had more responsibility, and we discussed a way for the new company to pay for a masters degree in computer science. By the end of Jackie's five years of therapy, she had her own apartment in Tribeca, was taking Club Med vacations, had developed friendships with men and women, had a long-term relationship with a man, and was certainly dressing differently—most of the time.

Jackie was becoming more self confident, much more resourceful, less socially isolated, less involved with her family and more capable of being emotionally intimate with her boyfriend. In addition, I felt there were periods where she seemed to want more intimacy with me and she said as much, too. These periods were marked by her desire for more sessions and a greater interest in exploring my insights, as well as her own. Do such changes over a five-year period indicate alterations in the patient's sense of self? Not really, but at the time such changes mask certain realities. I thought that her self-assertiveness and her idealized transference were modest indications of treatment progressing. Some people would agree, while others would question such superficial changes. But at the time, in the moment (and as I became more taken in by the mask) my experience was that her therapy was moving along.

Jackie went through clothes phases that mirrored both the transference–countertransference and our intersubjective experiences, although with hindsight, I now know I didn't really understand what was going on or being communicated or who was holding whom. What was obvious was her idealization of me, in that her clothing began to look like mine. She began wearing short dresses, high heels, and sometimes she upped the ante when she wore stockings with a garter belt that showed when she crossed her legs. She had her hair styled into a cute little pixie cut and she wore makeup, bright red lipstick, and sexy earrings.

During these phases, which lasted for weeks or months and sometimes for a year, the room felt quite full of emotions. She was lively, vivacious, told stories about relationships and spoke *about* her feelings in great detail. I felt engaged and animated in return, but I now think I was seduced into a type of giddy hysteria or mania that filled the room and penetrated me. Whenever I questioned her about actually "being emotional in the room with me" rather than telling "about" her feelings, or whenever I asked her about the change in her style of clothing, or commented on how her outfit looked similar to mine, she was not able to add anything and she didn't know why she couldn't. She accepted what I said, all my comments and interpretations, with a thoughtful smile. Was I to assume that the changes in her outside life and her new style of clothing were the expressed alterations of her self? Was she in potential space? She wasn't, but at the time, she looked as if she were.

There are many people in our culture who feel that when a woman dresses in a sexually assertive manner she is denying being like a castrated person. In a classic essay on female sexuality, Riviere (1929) stated that "Womanliness . . . could be assumed and worn as a mask, both to hide the possession of masculinity and to avert the reprisals expected if she was found to possess it" (p. 38). Riviere thought that some women wanted recognition of their fantasy of "supremacy in having the penis to give back" [to the father/male other], and that if this supremacy was not recognized, a rivalry might ensue, releasing an oral-sadistic fury (p. 41). The mask of womanliness veiled a castrated woman who had taken on a masculine identity. Yet, Riviere complicated her notion of a woman's identity when she stated there was no difference between genuine womanliness and the masquerade. In other words, the play really is the thing; a woman's subjectivity can be performed through what she wears.

But, what about a woman who draws her sense of self from her mother/female analyst, rather than from the father/masculine identity? Benjamin (1988) states that what a woman covets in the construction of her self-with-other is a recognition that her own desires exist: "[W]hat is wanted is recognition that one is a subject, an agent who can will things and make them happen" (p. 102). This desire does not have to be embodied by the phallus, as in the case where the woman's sense of self is as object of the phallus; rather, two women can be two subjects who each take pleasure with the other and who also take pleasure in each other through mutual recognition (1988)—woman as subject with her own desires, rather than woman as object of desire. And if a woman's desire for recognition includes sexual desire, and it does, then a woman's sexual subjectivity could also be portrayed through her body and her clothes.

Jackie began wearing stylized clothing that showed off her figure and I remember recognizing and feeling pleased at the idealization, introjection, and self differentiation that it seemed we were achieving in her treatment. I did not see Jackie's clothing as defensive; rather, my recognition was that what Jackie presented on the outside corresponded with her internal experience. During this same period she began dating men, and developed a relationship with a man who was twenty years her senior, around my age. They had an off again, on again relationship that I will discuss in more depth later. Jackie also developed a friendship with a woman she worked with who was lesbian. She began having sexual fantasies about her and would lament her inability to approach her friend sexually. She wanted a sexual experience with her, but felt too fearful of being rejected. These frequent sessions about her erotic feelings toward her friend led to discussions about sexual feelings for her mother, as well as to many flirtatious dialogues with me about being a sexual, seductive person. But Jackie said she didn't have erotic feelings toward me. In part, these feelings may have been dissociated. In addition, her response may have been defensive, since there was so much sexuality being discussed and her denial could have stemmed from a fear of being rejected.

An additional argument that supports my assessment of her reaction as a defensive one stemmed from my experience of her stories, since they were highly erotically charged and quite sexually stimulating. This is an example of our system of relating: I experienced passionate feelings that she denied having or communicating. She often thought I distorted the emotional content of her stories, or that my experience of our interactions originated solely with me—meaning the emotions we discussed didn't have a mutual creation. And I thought she was defensive, or dissociated, or maybe this was projective identification, or maybe she was right, it was just unanalyzed countertransference. Still, my feelings often felt sexual and erotic, and usually they seemed connected to her stories of sexual relations with her boyfriend, in particular the one who was my age.

While there were phases when Jackie looked attractive by dressing more stylishly, I often thought her clothing was more a narcissistic mirroring of my illusion—but then again, maybe I was defending feeling physically attracted to her. But I did not experience Jackie's appearance as sexually stimulating, or as lovable, or as warm and intimately inviting, and therefore she did not fit my definition of erotic, and maybe this was her experience of me. Where my erotic countertransference lived was in her narratives of sexual behaviors with her boyfriend and while this was certainly a part of her, it was also part of the masquerade.

Jackie met Andrew one evening when she was dining alone at a restaurant. For many years, I heard a great deal about their relationship because she was always ready to walk out, and other than this being a repetition of her earlier relationship with her father, she seemed to have little "real" reason to abandon Andrew. Sessions were focused on her paranoid fears of loss, fears of and wishes for merger with a dominant male, fear of and desire for intimacy, her longing to be known, and her inability to feel anger, all of which seemed to motivate her wish to leave Andrew. She often felt he ignored her because he was too busy, or that he intruded on her when he wasn't.

At the time, it seemed that when their relationship was in a good phase, so was ours, and she dressed in a stylish manner and we seemed mirrored in recognition. When Jackie's relationship with Andrew was in trouble, or perhaps when her feelings toward him mirrored her relationship with me, and this happened rarely, then she dressed in her mother's old clothes. Actually, my only knowledge of her mother was of her clothing. Jackie never spoke about her and if she did it was to pronounce her passive and withdrawn. My reaction to her mother's clothing was to feel rejected by Jackie, angry that she looked regressed or decompensated, and frustrated that she was messing up a perfectly good relationship with her boyfriend. At the time, I could not budge myself from feeling angry with her. It seemed as thought I carried the weight of her entire closet around my body, and even though I told her we seemed immobilized when she wore her mother's clothing, she could not add anything else to the mix. Very quickly, she would return to her new clothes, as though she had recovered from whatever emotion had infected her.

It was soon after Jackie and I began discussing her transference wish to be a more sexual woman that my erotic countertransference became increasingly more difficult to manage. During the next few months, Jackie spoke in detail about sex with Andrew. She began by setting the stage for the performance by discussing the bedroom, its darkness, the use of candles, fragrance, music. She elaborated on the warmth of the room, which impressed her because of the coldness of her own apartment, an acknowledged metaphor. She described Andrew's body, how he used it as well as how he used his powerful, seductive voice. He would whisper to her during their sex, both instructing her and asking what she desired and making her wonder whether or not he would grant her wish. At times he engaged her in playful acts of submission and domination, and while she repeatedly surrendered to his desires she secretly masked a frequent revulsion at her sexually submissive position.

When she first expressed this, I remember thinking that many women would give their eyeteeth for a sexual experience with this guy. My erotic countertransference was sparked by these stories. Usually, I felt submissive to my desire to hear more, and yet masochistic for wanting to hear more. Jackie seemed to dominate the treatment. I felt she wanted my surrender to her erotic desire. Ghent (1990) suggests that sometimes in analysis the roles of analyst and patient feel reversed in that the analyst surrenders *with* the patient. The patient's wish to be found, to be recognized by the other, the desire to be a subject, can often be expressed through the patient's masochistic narratives of being seduced into lovemaking, or being overpowered by the other (p. 122). Did Jackie's narratives disguise her desire to be recognized by the other? Or was her desire for recognition masked by her wish to not recognize me as a person?

For Jackie to experience her wish for recognition meant I was in power, and that she was dependent on my part of our relationship. Yet she seemed unable to tolerate dependence on another whom she could not control. Her only option was to dominate the other. Theoretically, the subject attempts to make the other give recognition without mutual recognition in return. "The primary consequence of the inability to reconcile dependence with independence, then, is the transformation of need for the other into domination of . . . [her]" (Benjamin 1988, p. 54). In a paper on masochism, Loewenstein (1957) had referred to this type of relation as the "seduction of the aggressor," which he understood as the repetition of losing love and finding love in the reenactment of the infantile trauma of castration and restitution—an enactment of the woman's forbidden masculine striving.

In Kaplan's (1991a) essay "Women Masquerading as Women," she states that "One of the features that distinguishes a perversion from other psychological symptoms is the fact that the strategy is expressed in a performance, an enactment, rather than in the more covert mental compromises seen in the analysis of a neurotic symptom or character disorder. In a perversion there is always an extensive enactment and always a fantasized or real audience . . . the perverse strategy is to focus attention on sexual performance" (p. 131). While Kaplan focuses her analysis primarily on the single subject, a number of object relations theorists emphasize the relational dimensions of the perverse strategy. To my mind, perversion is not simply a question of discharge of conflict, as Kaplan might say, but rather the use of a perversion is a communication with the other, it has a psychological function, and it establishes a system of relating.

Ogden's (1989) writings on projective identification describe this type of communication as that of one individual unconsciously projecting feelings onto another, evoking or inducing emotions that are comparable to the individual's ejected feelings. This serves a defensive purpose as well as functioning as a form of communication and object related-ness. The experience the recipient of projective identification feels is that she is "playing a role in someone else's internal drama and . . . feels unable to stop doing so" (p. 25). The pervert unconsciously imagines an audi-ence, and the audience is transformed into the audience she needs. Consequently, I am a part of the system, and Jackie's particular kind of relating and her particular kind of disguise have ramifications in the ways she deals with others and the way others feel.

What followed was a parade of sexual stories and behaviors mas-queraded by clothing, and again I was privy to two different styles or fashion statements by Jackie. The narratives and mannerisms that accompanied her seductive clothing detailed her sexual relationship with Andrew and were expressed with a slight smile. One issue she spoke of frequently was her knowledge of an earlier, long-distance, relationship that Andrew maintained with a former lover. He kept in contact by writing letters to this old girlfriend, who had lived in Europe for the last decade. His communications with her were advice-giving and occasion-ally involved helping her out financially. When Andrew ran errands and Jackie was left behind in his apartment, she would search his belong-ings to find old and new letters from the girlfriend. Jackie would then confront Andrew, who was repeatedly astounded that she was upset by his past relationship, and he would then attempt to comfort and reassure her that nothing romantic existed between the girlfriend and him any longer. He and Jackie would then have passionate sex during which he would profess his love, perhaps in submission to her anger and/or from a fear she would abandon him.

These sessions began with Jackie calmly narrating the climax first as she began the hour relating her sexual experiences to which I occa-sionally interpreted her hopes of my sensual surrender to the story. During these sessions, she would then back up and tell the events that had led to sex with Andrew, and identify with my feelings of surrender to sex. While I made many comments about these narratives, the set-tings, the performers involved, my subjective experience of the story, of her, and of her involvement, the interpretation that she dispassion-ately reacted to was of her infantile longing of wanting her domineering father to surrender to her oedipal wish and eliminate her passive mother.

Was this just a wish to use the male to beat back the mother in issues of dependence/independence? Maybe Andrew was being enlisted to beat me back? Or was I supposed to keep her submissive to Andrew? And why, during these sessions, was she dressed in an enticing manner, skin-tight dresses, high heels, makeup, why did she distract me by twirling her hair, slightly smiling all the while?

I remember once digging my fingernails into the leather armrest of my chair and stifling a desire to accuse her of creating blaring dissonance between affect and narrative, clothing and manner, performance and withholding, and so on. It was at this point in the treatment that I realized the mask was one of intersubjectivity, and what was reflected in the transference mask or masked transference was *my* countertransference. As she told these erotic stories, I began to experience her anger and frustration as my own, a projective identification. She, however, could not verbally communicate what she felt. But I knew from our history that any comment on my experience of her calm control, or what it covered, led to a fashion show of her reserve clothes, her masochistic surrender to my domination. The question was, which set of clothing disguised what? When I asked her it created a narcissistic injury that resulted in our both being punished. Jackie would retaliate by performing in her mother's old clothes. Her hair would seem to lose its style, there wouldn't be a trace of makeup or jewelry as she would be "forced" into a different masquerade, one that on the surface appeared as submission and merger, but felt like domination and hostility. Still, in this session I asked if she was experiencing anything in particular, any confusion, anger, or fear, as she told her story. I felt confused regarding my countertransference— whose feelings lived where? She responded that she was angry with her father, or maybe angry with Andrew, but she never seemed to feel much of anything toward me. I told her I was feeling uncomfortable, on edge, was I experiencing something "for" her? She wondered if I was becoming more aware of her anger toward men. I asked if there was any anger between us. She thought that was a strange question and wouldn't pursue it further. Still, I was now asking more and more questions much more frequently in an effort to clarify my emotions from hers.

Jackie was the only daughter of a very paranoid father and a depressed, passive, and submissive mother. Her father worked in a county job in the midwest and her mother was a housewife; both parents were about my age. It appeared that Jackie was her father's favorite and that he would often choose her for social events over her mother. There was also a younger brother of whom she was envious because he escaped the father's attentions. Jackie told stories about how she felt intruded on by her father in that he would anticipate and interpret her emotional responses and tease or berate her before she could defend herself. He rarely left her alone, entering her bedroom when she studied and sitting on her bed at night to watch her fall asleep. He was always attempting to stroke her physically, but she insisted his attentions were not overtly sexual. It is not surprising that she suffered from violent nightmares and weeklong bouts of insomnia as a child and adult.

It was, however, during college that Jackie experienced a traumatic emotional and physical assault—she was raped. In principle when a patient tells me she was raped, I believe her, and in this case too, I believe Jackie was raped. What made it difficult for me to feel the full impact of this incident was her dissociation, and again she narrated the event with a smile on her face. She was working on a tutorial with another student when one evening he began kissing her. She remembered saying "no" twice to him and when she dramatized her behavior, she did so in her soft voice and with her small smile. He didn't listen, placed her on the desk, and raped her. She stopped saying "no." When it was all over and she was getting dressed, he raped her again and she said "no" again. Jackie took both the student and the school to court, but she settled for a few thousand dollars before proceedings started. The student was not expelled. Jackie had a difficult time convincing people she had not encouraged the student's attentions or elicited sexual relations. Her friends abandoned her and she appears to have been very isolated for the last few years of her education. After this event, Jackie began treatment with a female therapist associated with the college—perhaps in an unconscious collusion in further victimization, since the therapist was paid by the same college that did not expel the student who raped Jackie.

Davies and Frawley (1994) propose that survivors of sexual abuse often regulate the severity of their victimizations as they concurrently experience empowerment over the events. In a sense, the abused person thus assumes control over her abuse and the perpetrator. However, this supposes a continued bondage to the original abuser and identification with the abuser's domination. In addition to providing an illusion of control, memories of the original abuse are kept masked, and this may be especially important for the patient who has no memories of the original abuse (p. 130). In her identification as both victim and abuser, the individual can often enact either role with her self or in relation to an other.

Because what is at stake here is the divided identity of the woman, let me return to Riviere (1929) and "Womanliness as a Masquerade." Who is the woman behind the mask? If the mask represents the woman, then the woman must also represent the mask. Identity is delicate and women often show the strain of their difficulty in attaining or maintaining it. For instance, in infancy and as a toddler, the little girl identifies with the holding mother. However, during rapprochement, when the girl is ready to separate from the mother she turns to the father. The female child wants what the male child wants regarding father, which is to identify with the father in separation from the mother and infant dependence. But the girl's identificatory love for the father is usually refused, as fathers typically recognize themselves in male children. When the father withdraws from the girl, she turns her identificatory love back onto her mother and usually experiences the father's detachment as a frustration of her aspirations for independence. She is left angry at her father's inability to recognize her desire, and often there is a degree of depression in reaction to the loss. However, the girl's return to the mother means that her wishes for independence and recognition of self are still intact. But if these wishes are also frustrated and the girl does not feel recognized by the mother, whom she may see as too powerless and passive, the girl is left with a residual desire for power. In later relationships, this often manifests in masochistic or submissive enactments. Yet if the girl can develop a sense of self from the mother, or if the female patient is able to develop a sense of self with the female analyst, then an identification with the female other could offer an integration and differentiation, as opposed to a defensiveness against individuation (Benjamin 1988).

This is the conflict Jackie and I faced in our striving for mutual recognition. Each of her masks successively rescued its predecessor and the process of differentiation was consistently thwarted. Who was I recognizing? In any treatment, the self must experience an effect on the other since this affinity affirms an existence of the self in an acknowledgment of sameness with and difference from the other. However, if the other is destroyed because the self feels controlled, then the self-experience is that of destruction. As a result, the self must control the other in order to master the fears and wishes of the self. If we depend on an other for recognition, then we are in that person's power and we must either surrender our desire for independence or else control the other—simply put, there is a demand for recognition without mutuality. If we cannot negotiate a balance for our need for dependence with our need for independence, then the need is transformed into a domination of the other (Benjamin 1988).

Jackie needed to control her therapy and did so by dominating me in a variety of ways, the most visible of which was through her masquerade of clothing. Flugel (1930), in his book *The Psychology of Clothes*, explains that clothes are an expression of the female self. "Whenever we bring a foreign body into relationship with the surface of the body . . . the consciousness of our personal existence is prolonged into the extremities and surfaces of this foreign body, and the consequence is— feelings, now of an expansion of our proper self, now of the acquisition of a kind and amount of motion foreign to our natural organs, now of an unusual degree of vigor, power of resistance, or steadiness in our bearing" (p. 34).

If a woman's subjectivity can exist or be expressed in terms of clothing, then, Jackie communicated at least two parts of her self through her two different masquerades. On the one hand, she existed as a sexual being, a woman who had power over others in usurping their attention through a sensual performance, and on the other, her alternate mask hid her desires for control through submission and surrender to a more powerful other. Or was there more? Did Jackie's submission and surrender only present a more impenetrable performance to those in relation with her? Were her mother's old clothes in fact more potent than her clothes that looked like mine? Was she wanting to repel or was she expressing a desire to receive, and which set of clothing masked what?

One day Jackie arrived for her session and I dreaded opening the door. I did not want to sit through her laments again and I somehow knew she'd be in her mother's clothes. She was dressed in a dark skirt that seemed two sizes too large, with a boxy blazer that nearly hung off her shoulders and made her neck look tiny in comparison. She wore no makeup and she had one strand of hair caught in the corner of her mouth. I was aware that in our previous session she must have felt too vulnerable—somehow it was either too sexualized or too emotional or too dissociated, and now I would have to sit through her moaning about how abused she was by everyone around her. One week I would be sexually stimulated by her stories, and the next I wanted to kick her out—and anger was the unconscious co-created communication that day.

I felt sick of these stories. In the past when I thought we were stuck in her compulsive retelling of abuses, I had either expressed empathy to her misery, or shared my experience of her need, or interpreted the genetic relationship, or discussed the anxious or defensive aspects of her situation, but more and more I felt as if I was faking it with her, masking what I felt. With hindsight, I was angry that I was disguising my feelings and that I felt manipulated into performing empathy when I felt enraged with her. I kept telling myself that I was just in a bad mood, she was who she always was, it must be me.

I was having difficulty claiming what I felt to myself. It was as though I should mask my own feelings from myself as I was finally realizing the full extent to which she did. And so, this time I brought my emotion into the room and asked, "Why am I the only one who seems to have emotions that exist between us? Why do we have to go over this again? Why doesn't anything ever change in here? It's either a session on abuse and victimization and you dress for the occasion in your mother's clothes, or it's a session on your achievements and your other set of clothing performs your accomplishments. Why is it always the same thing?" I said. She sat quietly staring at me and I could tell she was controlling herself because she was shaking a bit. She snapped back, "Who the hell do you think you are that you can talk like that to me? I pay you to listen to me, not to criticize me. After all this time that I've been coming here, you decide to tell me I'm not doing this according to your standards." "Well, what's different," I said, "one set of clothes over another? What's going on in here? What's happening between us?" "Go to hell!" she yelled as she stood up, shot me a venomous look and stormed out. I sat there seething at first and then I felt like crying because I'd lost control and hurt her. I wanted to hold on to someone and I thought she must be feeling the same thing. She'll come back and I'll work through this with her, I thought. The next morning I received her e-mail.

Was there no other possible outcome to this treatment but the one we performed? Had we only masked our caring and hateful feelings toward each other for those five years under different sets of clothing? Unfortunately, this may be so, since my being emotional with her ended the relationship. Why was our system of relating so full of distorted communications? Did she ever become a subject, differentiate a little, feel less merged with her father or mother, or not? Did someone else exist under the mask whom I never met and whom she didn't know either?

In this treatment, I was never sure what the masquerade meant, even though multiple interpretations were made by the many parts of both of us. Riviere (1929) thought that a woman's sexualization of her clothing symbolized unconscious masculinity, and that is one explanation, but I think the question is more complex. Was Jackie's choosing to use the division between her styles of dressing as her condition of subjectivity, or was it a negotiated differentiation that she made in identification with a sexual woman (me) and with a passive, depressed woman (her mother)? Or was her masquerade sadomasochism, and is that what terminated the treatment, or was it mine? Perhaps sadomasochism played a part in this woman's identity, and instead of its being destructive, maybe it eliminated a sense of loss or an inner division of self in such a way that the sadomasochism, or her mask of sadomasochism, *was* her subjectivity.

Throughout the writing of this chapter, I have experienced a multitude of emotions, but most unusual was the frustration I had in getting the words down on paper. I spent weeks looking for Jackie's chart and I kept missing her file as I searched the cabinets. Then, after each page was written, I counted the number of pages I'd finished, feeling I was almost "there."

About two weeks before I began writing this study of impasse, I realized I didn't have a copy of Riviere's (1929) essay "Womanliness as a Masquerade," which I wanted to use, and began what eventually became a frantic search of bookstores and Internet book sources, along with calling libraries listed as having the book. Nothing—it was long out of print. It was also missing from all the libraries in New York City. There's a copy in the Lincoln Center Library for the Performing Arts, but someone had stolen it from the reference shelves. An interesting irony. Finally, I located a copy at New York Psychoanalytic. I ran over and the librarian had pulled the book off the shelves for me and his assistant didn't know where he or the book was, so I had to run back the next day when the librarian was there and I finally had the damn thing. Later that same day, I went to teach a class at an analytic institute and happened to enter the classroom while the candidates were on break after their previous class. There, facing up on each of the twelve chairs, were twelve copies of Riviere's paper, which had just been handed out by the previous instructor. And then I thought, I really should get some sort of religion in my life.

But, as I wrote and thought about Jackie and our work and all my frustrations in preparing this chapter, I knew I was again experiencing very passionate feelings about her and that these emotions were out of her awareness—a re-creation of my feelings about her in therapy. Certainly, the treatment is over, it doesn't exist anymore, but I can't mask the erotic image of Jackie sitting in my chair with her garterbelt hooks showing below her short skirt telling me X-rated tales of sex with her boyfriend.

EPILOGUE

Perhaps the biggest difficulty in writing about impasse is how vulnerable it makes the therapist feel. Clinical papers, such as this one, are usually designed to demonstrate a theoretical point of view, but here I wanted to write in order to obtain closure on something that has felt left open for me.

The most famous paper I know on impasse is Freud's (1905b) Dora case, and over the years this case has been used to demonstrate every shortcoming that one might possibly attribute to an analyst: Freud as chauvinist, Freud as conveyer of sexuality, Freud as blind to misalliance, Freud as homophobic, Freud as part of an enactment, Freud as the voice of moral alarm.

It's hard to know just how much Freud realized about Dora since at the time he was so involved in the politics of the K. family. He says in his "Postscript" to "Fragment of an Analysis of a Case of Hysteria" (1905b) that he had the advantage of Dora coming back to him because she needed closure on their work as much as he did. Dora's struggle was that she was in fact in love with Frau K. meaning that she was able to make strong attachments; it was Freud who didn't offer a mutually powerful attachment in return. Because my patient was more withdrawn and not able to have made such a powerful attachment, I am left wondering what she wanted from me.

What did she want? I suppose what was most obvious was her desire to find a subject whom she wanted to be like. We were to mirror one another in sense of self, style, and ambition. In her identificatory love, I believe there was an unconscious wish to identify with the female subject who would provide an opportunity for integration and differentiation. Perhaps on some level a little of this happened, in that when Jackie felt her own needs were not being met she had a good-enough sense of self to leave when she felt abused.

But, was I also supposed to be a veiled or masked woman in the way Jackie was—in order to be a reflection of her? She wanted me to wait for her, with a fixed expression, until she was ready to feel more intimate or more trusting. I remember when I was a child in my hometown, there was a woman who stood in front of the local candy store wearing a bride's dress. The story went that her fiancé had arranged to meet her there and he never showed up. I recall seeing her stand in front of the candy store for most of the time I was growing up; no matter what the weather, she waited for him. Should I have waited longer for Jackie? Could I have tolerated not knowing what was going on in a better way? Unfortunately, because so much felt so unavailable and eventually so little felt tolerable, this was not possible at the time.

It wasn't that I didn't know the different layers of dynamics existing in the treatment. I was aware of most of them, although I could only question them at the time and she denied them each time. Uncertainty was the only certainty. My questions were always met with her small smile, a fixed look, and a denial. She did not consider my experience of our work as grist for the mill. She only experienced interpretations intellectually; they did not elicit emotional responses or insight. So why didn't I tell her earlier on that we were at an impasse? Because her outside life was continually changing, and while this was superficial it felt real at times. I kept hoping that I could hang on and wait her out, that she would eventually tell me what was hidden. But perhaps what was masked was too grotesque—I now wonder if her mask hid a psychosis, or at least a fear of one.

The answers to the questions in this paper are still unknown; and that is also the essence of Jackie and of this treatment. As analysts we can blame each other for poor technique, for mismatches, for collusions, and for enactments. We can identify with patients and feel empathy for the problems they feel in working with the more powerful therapist. But if we don't talk about our own failed treatments it means we may be keeping silent about the need to find better ways to work with such people, and that feels even more incomplete to me.

5

Gender Performance: Possibility or Regret?

When people begin psychotherapy or psychoanalysis, they often ask personal questions about the analyst in an attempt to establish sameness and differences. For instance, questions like "Are you married?" or "Do you have children?" are frequently asked, often in initial consultations. As treatment progresses and the therapeutic relationship becomes more intimate, questions become more personal. "Is your hair really that color?" is a question I would like to avoid answering since the response has to straddle both reality and fantasy, that is, it was that color naturally but it isn't anymore. What is interesting is that straight patients never ask if I'm straight, but many gay patients ask, "Are you lesbian?" June, a lesbian patient who has been in psychoanalysis with me for many years, was once teasing me for dressing in such a feminine way, lamenting that she never even needed to ask if I was straight because I was beyond the pale of lipstick lesbian and was obviously "a girlie girl." In jest, I asked how was she so certain I was a girl, maybe I was transgendered. She fell silent saying she needed to consider this and left the session in a deeply pensive mood. That evening when I checked my e-mail, I found she had left a message entitled "Sermon on the mons." I think it's important to quote her e-mail at length:

> My god, my narrow mindedness and fear astonish me. I feel like Joe McCarthy when it comes to the subject of transsexuals. Are you now or have you ever been a member of the opposite sex? I panicked. The floor moved and I, for a terrible moment, didn't know what the fuck you were.
>
> One's sex is bloody goddamned important. It is. What is your definition of a woman? We aren't only who we think we are . . . we're also who others think we are. I feel like a woman. I am perceived and treated like a woman and that, in turn, contributes to my sense of being a woman. Simply feeling like a woman doesn't make you a woman. And yes, parts do count for something. It's not for nothing that we are sometimes referred to by our genitals. The part signifies the whole. What's so wrong with that? We call Einstein a "brain." Remember the famous Jayne Mansfield intro on the Jack Paar Show? "And here *they* are. . . ."
>
> What instrument do you play? The wet organ or the skin flute? I'm not over my freaked out reaction to your question. Always be you. I know you as You. My mother once cut her hair short while I was away at summer camp. Who the hell is that lady, I thought.
>
> Your womanhood, or should I say, my experience of your womanhood looms large in my small mind. I'm in love with your way of being, but your body holds an enormous place in my mind also. Your femaleness touches me. I feel it. Your experiences as a female child are similar to mine. People responded to both of us as girls. We're the same in that way.
>
> Don't you know the difference that can never be the same? Cats are girls and dogs are boys . . . you can't make a cat into a dog.

What I like about this patient is how she organizes her thoughts and often makes me reorganize my own. Of course she was right, we had both been socialized as girls throughout our development and our female gender had created others' responses to us. But then I began to wonder, did my male transgendered patients have traditionally male experiences growing up? Even if they were responded to as male, wouldn't their experience be different than a male who was not transgendered? In my own development, I remember one particular experience of being handed a high school gym uniform complete with bloomers under the shorts. At that time when I was growing up and in that culture, I understood to hide my sexuality. My femininity, though, was promoted at school in that the girls were given more primping time after gym than the boys, who barely had time to shower before returning to class. But perhaps some of the boys wanted bloomers under their shorts, and I'm sure some girls felt very envious of the boys' experiences. Then, wouldn't a transgendered individual have felt compromised by this traditional gender-related experience, in a way that was different than, let's say, my own gender compromise? Would transgendered people just reject their experiences due to discomfort, or to the disharmony with their inner feeling of gender? And wouldn't such a rejection mean that a transgendered individual might not have accepted traditional gender-related experiences in growing up? Or is it instead that biological males who are transgendered only felt related to those gender experiences that were feminine, and vice versa?

In Fast's (1990) essays on gender development, she points out that children have an overinclusive sense of gender in that they identify with both parents. Preoedipal children believe they are or have the potential to be everything. They see no reason why anything they want to be should be impossible. Benjamin (1995a) also argues against the notion of "disidentification" (Greenson 1968), in which the male child turns away from the mother in the separation-individuation phase and identifies only with the father. In the late '60s, Greenson's research on transsexuals agreed with Stoller's (1968) in that "the male child's ability to disidentify with mother will determine the success or failure of his later identification with his father. These two phenomena, disidentifying with mother and counteridentifying with father, are interdependent and form a complementary series" (Greenson 1978, p. 306). However, according to both Greenson (1978) and Stoller (1968), in transsexualism the male child disidentifies with father and remains symbiotically tied to mother— the child develops against a sense of complementarity. Stoller considered this childhood symbiosis to be a wonderful closeness the adult transsexual just couldn't give up. To my way of thinking, this suggests the male child's gender identification has a rather tenuous pinball-like effect as it bounces from mother to father.

I prefer what Fast (1990) and particularly Benjamin (1995) says about the preoedipal child, whether it's a boy or a girl, in that children identify with both parents. For a child who has only begun to differentiate his own sense of self, it makes sense that the parents' gender wouldn't really matter regarding the child's identity. We need only think about children who grow up in households with same-sexed parents to know that these children differentiate their sense of self through identification with either parent. Identifying with the parent's gender is not a primary developmental issue; identifying with masculine and feminine behavior, however, is. Person and Ovesey (1983) term this "gender role identity," meaning that the child identifies with either a masculine or feminine self-image.

Initially, however, it was Stoller (1968, 1975) who modified Freud's (1905a) notion of masculinity and femininity in his concept of "core gender identity," meaning the child's belief in being either male or female. Stoller's notion of the male child's inability to differentiate from mother in infancy and early childhood laid the foundation for his ideas on transsexualism. Stoller thought the male child and the mother created a pathologically merged relationship that inhibited separation-individuation and that this skewed core gender identity. This merger, according to Stoller, had a penetrating impact on the boy's core gender identity, as it provided the bedrock for the infant's sense of femininity, a protofemininity for both sexes. Stoller (1975) stated that the boy's separation and struggle toward masculinity had its roots in a stage of oneness with mother and femaleness. It was the mother's inability to allow her son to separate, as well as father's unavailability, that produced degrees of pathological intrusive injuries to the boy's developing masculinity.

Coates and colleagues (1991) and Benjamin (1995) take issue with Stoller and state that it is neither merger nor symbiosis that creates transsexuals, but rather that "maternal withdrawal" can create an intense melancholic identification that has the effect of developing an excessive femininity in boys as well as girls (Benjamin 1995, p. 129), a conclusion I agree with. To my mind, this melancholic identification and excessive femininity in boys may lay the foundation for a profound sense of regret regarding an ill-suited gender later in adulthood, regret for both the gender he has and the gender he doesn't have. In choosing the word regret, I mean feelings of grief or pain tinged with disappointment, longing, or remorse, as in the dictionary definition of regret as an expression of distressing sorrow or disappointment.

Benjamin (1988, 1991, 1995) has proposed that in addition to object love, children develop identificatory love, which appears in the rapprochement phase and is directed toward the father. Traditionally, father represents the exciting outside world to the child, the potential for a separate subjectivity, and mother, a sense of nurturing and attachment. But, identification with father as a subject is important for both boys and girls in their efforts to experience themselves as a subject of desire, of autonomy, of a move into the world—and therefore an identification with an other who is experienced as powerful. But what if the child can't identify with father, if it feels too threatening to identify with him because it further promotes mother's withdrawal, or if father is abusive, rejecting, or humiliating? For the boy (and for the purpose of this chapter I am focusing on the biological boy), identificatory love with his father supports separation from the mother and also confirms the achievement of masculinity.

Coates and Wolfe (1995) argue that when a male child is unable to identify with the father, a "self-fusion fantasy with mother" (p. 9) develops in defense against separation anxiety. "In essence, the child substitutes an identification for a relationship and comes to confuse being mommy with being with mommy, this during a period when he lacks stable internal representations of self and other and when his cognitive understanding of the permanence of gender classification is still immature" (p. 9). Coates and Wolfe add a crucial element here, with regard to the solidification of cross-gender behavior, when they say the child not only *attempts* to stabilize the self by emotionally repairing the mother, but also the child *feels* or *believes* that he *has* revitalized the depressed mother and in so doing has solidified the relationship.

Butler's (1990) notion of identification differs from Benjamin's, and Coates and Wolfe's, when she says people identify not with a person, but with a fantasy. Butler seems to mean that we identify with the mother we wish we had or the father we wish we had, and we take up identifications in defense or in facilitation of our own desires. Our fantasies are constructed to experience our own desires. So, if we interweave Benjamin's (1995) idea on identificatory love—that gender is made up of the preoedipal child's identification with mother and father—and Coates and Wolfe's (1995)—identification as a substitute for a relationship—with Butler's view of identification as a fantasy within a fantasy—mother as we want her and father as we want him—then gender identity could be understood as an enacted fantasy relationship that reveals an identification.

The question then becomes, in what ways do we reveal or express our internal identifications, our fantasy within fantasy? It is my experience that we perform our sense of identity on our external canvas, our bodies, therefore creating an illusion of our self. By that I mean an image or symbolization that is a self-representation of our interior identity. So, in a sense, an individual's use of clothing performs the mimicked experience of gender itself in the early childhood identification with parents. "If the inner truth of gender is a fabrication and if a true gender is a fantasy instituted and inscribed on the surface of bodies, then it seems that genders can be neither true nor false but are only produced as the truth effects of a discourse of primary and stable identity" (Butler 1990, p. 337). To my mind, gender performs who we are and the performance presents different parts of what we experience at different times. Some people feel that performance is not genuine, that it's false and inauthentic. I disagree with that view because I question whether, if we were to take performance away, it would mean that what is left is more genuine.

All behavior is performance and gender as behavior is therefore performance. Butler (1995) suggests that gender is not expressed by specific masculine or feminine actions or verbal mannerisms—instead the performance of gender is that which originally produced "the illusion that there was an inner gender core" (p. 175). So, what is the illusion of an inner gender core? Is a drag queen's illusion of gender more or less real than my illusion of gender? Or is it just intensity in gender performance that makes it unreal or real? If so, what degree of intensity makes it unreal, or makes it real? Or is it the way we understand our own core gender identity that makes our gender performance real or unreal? Simone de Beauvoir (1952) said, "One is not born, but rather becomes, a woman" (p. 267).

To focus on gender performance is to stray from the historical method of psychoanalytic theorizing, which centers on mind experience rather than body phenomena. Winnicott (1949) was one of the early exceptions in his contention that in the developing child the psyche and soma are not distinguished from one another. He defined the psyche as ". . . the *imaginative elaboration of somatic parts, feeling, and functions, that is, of physical aliveness*" (p. 243, italics original). The psyche and soma form ". . . a process of mutual interrelation. . . . *felt by the individual* to form the core for the imaginative self" (p. 244). In an unpublished paper on narrative and uncertainty, Kaftal (1995) stated ". . . it is fallacy to think of the self as an indwelling essence, a true self, which is either uncovered or . . . has empathic life breathed into it during the course of treatment. The self is not something one is. . . . the self is something one does, something one does with others" (p. 13). Meaning, it is both the mind and body that perform the self.

In a (1998) paper on self and body Meissner laments the fact that self-perception and self-experience are understood as deriving from "self-valuing, self-satisfaction, self-ideals, and self-coherence," rather than the self-including-body-sensations. "Self has been viewed more in terms of central cognitive processes and attitudes . . . at the cost of undercutting the basis for all experiencing. . . . [leaving] unaddressed the experience of having feelings and acting [on them] as a center for interacting sensory events" (p. 141). Schilder (1935) wrote about the sociology of the body image, saying that the way we feel about our bodies and our selves is constantly communicated in social interactions. Our clothing, mannerisms, our posture and stance all make up this communicative function.

In Riviere's (1929) essay on female sexuality, she stated that "Womanliness . . . could be assumed and worn as a mask, both to hide the possession of masculinity and to avert the reprisals expected if [the woman] was found to possess it" (p. 38). Riviere, as a disciple of Freud, remained in Freud's fold as she wrote about a woman's penis envy and castration as the woman wanting to hide, mask, or veil her possession of power. In other words, the mask of womanliness veiled a castrated woman who had taken on a masculine identity, meaning a powerful identity. When a woman presents herself as sexual in her appearance, she can be experienced by others as either a powerful object, or as displaying sexual submission to the dominant masculine notion of beauty or seduction.

Still, if the woman feels she is achieving her own desires, and expressing her own subjectivity and identity through her physical ornamentation, then isn't she expressing her own sense of power through her chosen presentation or performance? Even Riviere complicated her notion of a woman's identity when she stated that there was no difference between genuine womanliness and the masquerade. In other words, the play really is the thing; a woman's identity can be performed through what she wears. So, if we assume that gender is a performance of childhood identifications; and that an individual can express her own desires through her physical ornamentation, her masquerade, her illusion; that female sexuality expresses a woman's defense against castration (or, in contemporary terms, that female sexuality expresses a woman's sense of power), then I have laid some foundation for the rest of this chapter on the transgendered, in which I suggest there is no such thing as genuineness in gender identity. There is no such thing as a natural gender; rather, gender is a performance of masculinity and femininity, and gender is a performance of illusion and masquerade. We are our presentation of gender and we perform our acceptance and our understanding or displeasure of gender.

I recently read a book about the life of Billy Tipton, a jazz musician who had grown up as Dorothy Tipton but who lived as a man from age 19 to 74. Billy had been "married" to five women and reared several adopted children. It wasn't until the autopsy that his family and friends, including his wives, realized Billy Tipton lived two lives, one of each gender. It was in reading this account (Middlebrook 1998) that I began to wonder which gender Billy had actually performed; it seemed he had performed both.

What I have presented so far is a glimpse of relevant gender theory, with some classical and some contemporary psychoanalytic perspectives. But, from this point on, what I found developing in writing this paper was my own internal dialogue of questions with no definitive answers. How do I discuss the way my transgendered patients and I understand each other? How do I inform the reader about our discussions on gender performance, multiple selves, masquerade, the different veils of the self?

How do I convey the idea of Scheherazade showing a different veil for a different story for a thousand and one Arabian nights and not Salome, whose veils covered a deathly secret? How do I talk about masquerade as a presentation of the self and not as a mask of things hidden? The genuine is not evident for all of us, and I wonder if it is for any of us. I tried on many different ideas as I thought about writing this essay, but they felt confining, ill-fitted. Every thread of thought seemed to have a flaw, and still other ideas felt so multilayered with sequined details I could barely begin to explain them. For me, the emotional struggle in writing on transgenderism became a metaphor for transgenderism itself. Consequently, although I have not been definitive here, I also feel that in treating the transgendered all definitions become redefined. What I will perform in this writing is my own internal dialogue of working with transgendered male-to-female patients (MTFs), since it is the best way I have of opening the boundaries of my mind and of my self, a crucial requirement in working with the transgendered.

When I first decided to write about transgenderism, I was going to discuss aggression, admiration, and satire as different roles the transgendered express in gender performance, and I thought I would illustrate these roles using clinical examples of two of my MTF patients. One patient is heterosexual and is anticipating hormone therapy and a sex change. He identifies as a demure, feminine lesbian and eventually wants to live permanently as a woman. The other patient is gay and has performed drag professionally for many years, winning awards and drag titles through his performances around the country. I felt I could write about the first patient's aggressive role in dressing, meaning his self-aggression or masochism, his use of a sexual dominatrix, his relationship with a rejecting lesbian, and I would tie all this in with his childhood, which had been riddled with physical aggression by his father and emotional neglect from his mother. In the second clinical example, I would discuss the gay patient's use of sex clubs, substance abuse, and his subservient, masochistic role with his wealthy lover. I would talk about his mother's depression, his father's absenteeism, his brother's sadism, and his sister's total rejection. I was going to address the role of admiration because both patients desired to be accepted as women at times, and admired and studied women in order to perform their gender desires. Last, I would talk about satire as a role both patients performed as well as elicited through humor, illusion, masquerade, and admiration of feminine gender. In other words, that paper would have focused on these two patients' subjectivities as they were expressed and masqueraded in gender performance of aggression, admiration, and satire.

So, in reviewing the early analytic literature on transsexualism, one of the articles was written by Greenson in 1968, in which he stated that in his work with transsexuals he found that men harbor an intense envy of the female, particularly the mother (p. 307). At that time this was a new perspective, as psychoanalytic literature was still fairly steeped in the classical notion that it was only women who envied men. Unfortunately, Greenson positioned this idea within the framework of Freud's theory that women suffered from penis envy and men from castration anxiety. Men had little to envy women for in a phallocentric world, so Greenson's new perspective severely pathologized transsexualism. Now, many analytic theoreticians later, the contemporary notion is that each gender envies the other for many reasons, and that aggressive envy is not so much a function of gender as it is a function of all humans.

Usually, when I begin writing a new essay, I review the psychoanalytic literature, starting with classical papers and moving through the ages until I've read sufficiently about the topic. But here, I felt so frustrated with the historical psychoanalytic literature on transsexualism that I thought it might be better to review the most recent publications on gender roles. I noted a paper titled, "Aggression, Envy, and Ambition: Circulating Tensions in Women's Psychic Life," by Adrienne Harris (1997). I felt it might address aggression and envy in relation to the feminine role. Instead, it focused on how aggression is inhibited or compromised for women because of their specific gender development, involving "maternal identification and the long legacy of repression and dissociation of hatred and anger in women's lives, particularly maternal hatred" (p. 303). I felt frustrated that Harris's idea of inhibited aggression in women's lives didn't speak to the aggressive role I wanted to illustrate in this chapter. It seemed to me that aggression, specifically self-aggression or masochism, might be even more repressed and inhibited—or maybe blatantly obvious—in the transgendered owing to their specific issues in development. In other words, I believe aggression would be experienced in an extreme way and consequently performed in an extreme way—meaning Harris's paper unfortunately wouldn't apply in my literature search.

So, as I read the literature and mulled over the tentative title for this chapter, I rested for a moment on gender performance as satire. I went back to read Stoller's (1978) early work on transsexuals, in which he suggested that drag was a satirical performance of femininity involving hostility, in that "humor is hostility subdued and graced by tolerance" (p. 32). Humor as it is used in drag, comes about because there is a reversal from trauma to triumph. Satire, therefore, is an expression of a wish for aggression according to Stoller—the drag queen mocks femininity and the female gender. To my mind, drag—or even cross-dressing if it is conceptualized as satire—can also be an achievement of admiration from an audience in its expression and attainment of otherness. Masquerade, illusion, drag, or gender performance is the climax of a mounting struggle to express the embodiment of the other. Maybe the transgendered have accomplished and display a sense of otherness that eludes the rest of us and manifests only as desire for the nontransgendered.

At this point, I felt limited by the literature, as well as by the first title I had chosen ("Gender Performance: Aggression, Admiration, or Satire?") as though nothing was helping me explore or further express what I wanted to say about my work with the transgendered. In a sense, I was experiencing what I frequently hear from my transgendered patients—a feeling of being limited and restrained—in this case by what I thought I was supposed to write, by what I originally thought I would present, and by feeling that there was much more I wanted to show and perform.

At first I wondered if I was searching for something larger than life, dramatic, something fit for the big screen, some huge performance of womanhood. I began to think about all the ways that the masquerade of womanliness has been captured by writers, directors, and artists on film—how they capture the genuineness of illusion. They seem to repeatedly express the idea that gender does not need to be controlled and that illusion can represent many aspects of the self, including aggression, admiration, and satire. Remember the killer in the movie *Dressed to Kill* (1930)—a man who cross-dressed to gain access to wealthy female victims. The killer's aggression toward women led him to masquerade as a woman in order to allow him the ultimate deceit of taking the actual life of women in addition to his performance of being a woman.

Also, in the 1997 movie of Henry James's novel, *The Wings of the Dove* in which Kate Croy entices her own boyfriend to seduce and marry her terminally ill wealthy friend, Millie Theale, in order to inherit Millie's wealth. In one particularly deceitful scene, Kate enables her boyfriend's seduction of Millie. Kate begins the scene herself as she masquerades in cross-dress costume to lure Millie into an erotic web while waiting for the boyfriend's entrance. It's a story that presents a masquerade that veils deceit as well as womanliness. In a sense, it was as though a destabilizing of Kate's gender became a signature of erotism.

Do the creative artists of filmmaking, those who capture life in narratives and stories, know, or are they somehow more aware of all the functions femininity can perform? Certainly, artists are astute students of performance, illusion, and facade—and they are creators of inauthenticity and masquerade; they promote genuineness through fabrication. Do they in fact possess greater mastery in the presentation of inner worlds on external canvases than the rest of us? Have artists found careers that enable them to maintain their childhood notion of gender differentiation—that "anything is possible"? I'm reminded of the movie, *Ed Wood* (1994). Ed Wood made grade Z monster movies nearly fifty years ago that showed outrageous scenes of invasions and carnage, and as it turns out, was a rather infamous cross-dresser in the socially sedate '50s—perhaps he was publicly struggling with this notion of "anything is possible."

In *Orlando* (1992), the filmmakers capture Virginia Woolf's idea of gender ambiguity. Here, Lord Orlando struggles to attain the woman he admires and whom he wants to keep as his own. In his desire to have his feminine love object he lives for centuries, eventually evolving into Lady Orlando, the woman he originally admired. His newly found womanhood encapsulates his sense of self as both male and female. Is this the ultimate humanity, that "anything is possible," no matter how many centuries it takes? Are the nontransgendered at a disadvantage since we do not have the experience of femaleness and maleness to the extent or intensity the transgendered do? Are the movies just an unreal presentation of what is unreal in life, or are they perhaps reflections of what is real for a larger portion of society than we know about?

In the film *Ma Vie en Rose* (1997), the director creates a narrative of a young boy who feels he is a girl. It's a story about the desire for admiration, and a satire of a family and community that won't let the child be who *she* wants to be, a twist on the way I wanted to use satire. The director seems to have captured the emotional struggle I wanted to convey about the transgendered. And so, the more I thought about it, the more I realized that while aggression, admiration, and satire were aspects of what I wanted to discuss, my tentative title did not reach the deeper emotions I experienced with my transgendered patients and did not touch what these patients narrated. The more I listen to their underlying feelings regarding aggression, admiration, and satire, the more I realize these were also masquerades, veils that covered the deeper experience they spoke of, an experience that sounds like regret for living in a world that does not accept that "anything is possible."

PERFORMANCE, MASOCHISM, AND REGRET

Angelo, a transgendered MTF who identifies as lesbian, related an incident he experienced with his lesbian lover. Angelo had dressed to go out for the evening; he was wearing a little black dress, pumps, and had spent hours perfecting his makeup in preparation for his date with Tanya, a biologically female lesbian. I will use the masculine pronoun in reference to Angelo since in treatment he wears masculine clothing and refers to himself as a man, even when he's dressed in his feminine clothing. Angelo and his girlfriend went to the Clit Club, a lesbian bar, and he said it was one of those evenings when he struggled to feel comfortable with his appearance, fearful he wouldn't be accepted by the women in the club. At one point, another woman tried to pick up Tanya as Angelo watched. He felt unable to stop the event fearing Tanya would reject him entirely and storm off, which she frequently did. In their relationship, she seems to exploit his already existing masochism. Later in the evening, Tanya informed Angelo that the three of them would go to Angelo's house for sex.

During sex, however, Tanya was only interested in the other woman, leaving Angelo excluded. He felt his body was not enough, wrongly shaped. He regretted being there as he was and wished he was post-op. Angelo complained about how he continually needed to wear his truss, shave his body, spend hours making himself up, and how Tanya still preferred other lesbians to him. I remembered that old saying, "You have to tolerate pain, if you want to be beautiful" and wondered to what degree masochism motivated his gender performance.

Angelo has only recently begun interviewing doctors about surgery and hormones. It has been a stressful time, as it seems clear to both of us that in having the operation Angelo will lose his family. In a sense, he is waiting for his mother to pass away before beginning hormones, feeling that she will reject him if his physical appearance changes. Is this also an unconscious desire to become the family matriarch, replacing his mother when she dies?

I have been treating Angelo for five years and he usually comes to sessions dressed as a man on the way home from his hospital job. Every so often he arrives in what he calls his androgynous look, which is really quite striking as he's over six feet tall and wears long tunics over tights, his dark hair comes to his shoulders, and he deepens his eyes with a little makeup.

For many years, Angelo said he and his mother were very close; they had similar ideas, values, and attitudes, and he has taken care of her since his father passed away ten years ago. She's had a serious physical illness for the last few years and Angelo feels his own needs can't be met as long as his mother is ill. This is not unusual in their relationship. Soon after Angelo was born his maternal grandmother died of cancer, and Angelo's mother was devastated for many years. Angelo remembers times when he was very young, stroking his mother to comfort her as she sobbed about the loss of her own mother. My sense is that his mother was quite depressed, and not emotionally available to him, particularly during his early years. On the surface, Angelo's relationship with his mother could seem symbiotic and merged in the way Stoller, Greenson, and other early theorists on transsexualism suggest, but when Angelo describes his mother, she appears preoccupied, aloof, and actually disoriented. My sense is that she was not emotionally available for any of the children, and particularly not for Angelo, who was the oldest of four and who was born just a few months before the maternal grandmother died.

Angelo's father was quite paranoid and physically and emotionally abusive. I feel that it was in his relationship with his father that Angelo perfected "performance." His father would frequently become instantly angry at what Angelo felt were minor infractions. He would insist that Angelo and occasionally his brother strip naked and lie on the bed while he beat them. Angelo's mother would cry and leave the room during these events. He has no memory of her interfering with the actual beatings, although she would try to talk her husband out of them before they began—and in so doing may well have talked him into some of them. Moments after the beating took place, sometimes even before Angelo was dressed, his father would return to the room and plead for forgiveness. He would say he hadn't meant to hurt him, and demand that Angelo kiss him and tell him how much he loved him and how great a father he was. In a sense, Angelo's father taught him that there's no naturalness in the world. His father forced him to think differently from the way Angelo actually thought or felt. "Trust me and not your own eyes" was the message. I am sure that in this masochistic position Angelo perfected the art of illusion and masquerade, which eventually rerouted his identification away from his father and may have given impetus to his particular development of gender performance. Angelo remembers having to deny his father's brutality only moments after suffering under it. He had to soften his face and caress his father in order to make him feel better. If he didn't, his father would not stop the harangue, which could escalate into another beating. Affection was a major performance and "anything was possible" in this household.

In one disturbing session, Angelo brought in a tape recording made when he was 3 years old, of Christmastime with his father. One the tape, Angelo's father tells him to sing a holiday song, which he proceeds to do. I listened to a child's small voice on the tape struggling to sing while his father constantly interrupted, bellowing out, "That's not the right word, Angelo," "What's the matter with you, sing it right," "Don't you know anything, Angelo!" "Sing it this way, Angelo." After turning off the tape, Angelo and I sat in stunned silence as he covered his eyes and started to cry and I wished I had the luxury. With hindsight, what I found interesting about that tape recording is that Angelo did sing for his father, and incorporated all his corrections—he performed as demanded as a 3-year-old.

Angelo's narratives are filled with sadness and regret about not being able to repair his depressed mother, regret about not being the son his father wanted, and not being accepted for who he is. Are extreme experiences of domination and masochism crucial ingredients in cooking the transgendered soup? It is my assumption that they are not, otherwise many more of us would be transgendered—and not all of my transgendered patients have experienced abuse.

I remember strolling in the theater district one evening and seeing something I haven't been able to get out of my mind. A couple was walking down the street toward me. The woman was transgendered and was walking a few steps behind her male companion. She looked as though she was feeling dominated and emotionally beaten. Was her performance a trap to enlist a third party, or was it an attempt at failed freedom—a regretted internal negotiation? The sadness it stirred in me was quite powerful, and similar to the feelings I have when working with Angelo.

Angelo tells stories about his use of a female dominatrix in a particularly masochistic striving for womanhood. He travels to her house late at night and on arriving changes into a sex-slave outfit. He then spends hours cleaning his dominatrix's house as she berates him. Is this a constructed reflection of his relationship with his father?

In the transference, Angelo seems to never get enough from me, he constantly questions my opinion about his behavior, perhaps eliciting, expecting, and/or fearing verbal sadism or my rejection. Do I think he's feminine? Is his face too masculine? Does he do what other women do? Aren't women supposed to be demure, and what do feminists think about this or that? He's always providing me with reading material on transgenderism, or asking whether I see hidden meaning about his femininity in his dreams, which he supplies in duplicate.

My subjective experience or countertransference is that I feel quite exhausted after our sessions. I feel that every part of me has been tugged or pulled, intellectually, emotionally, and physically. For instance, once when I had injured both my knees and had some stiffness walking, Angelo noticed, left his chair, sat at my feet and began stroking my shins. I remember saying to myself "Oh, please just go back to your seat and stop doing that." Perhaps in this moment I played one of my own performances, since I feared a reaction or an interpretation would humiliate him and repeat his father's sins. I had it in my mind that he used to stroke his mother to make her feel better when she was depressed and also stroked his father after he beat him, and so told him I didn't think I shaved as frequently as he did. He laughed and returned to his chair. This interaction prompted a discussion about how he is often surprised that people experience him differently than he intends. He said he was often perceived as intrusive or controlling or dominating in a way that was similar to his father. He asked if I had minded his touch and then wondered why I never wanted a hug after sessions. The thought of being entitled to one's own reaction to another's touch was novel to him. Should I perform the affect he expected, I asked? Is there a difference between a performed affect and a gender performance? Angelo's performances felt natural whether they were performances of emotion or gender. Does the level of emotional intensity or the form of a performance mean that the affect or the behavior was unreal?

DRAG, ADMIRATION, AND REGRET

About a year ago, I began working with Brad, a gay man who performed drag. I'd like to digress for a moment, because I think Butler (1995) makes an interesting point about drag when she talks about gender performativity as related to the phenomenon of gender melancholia. She suggests that, inherent in mimicry or in the satirization of gender expressed through drag, there is a performance of dissatisfied longing. In other words, drag is an enactment or acting out of unacknowledged early childhood loss that was never grieved. She believes that in drag performance ungrieved loss reiterates a gendered idealization and an uninhabitability of a particular gender. She continues by stating that drag performance allegorizes a loss it cannot grieve. Drag explains, by portrayal, the incorporative phantasy of melancholia whereby an object, either maternal or paternal, is taken in through fantasy in an attempt to hold on to the object or as a way of refusing to let it go. "Gender itself might be understood in part as the 'acting out' of unresolved grief" (p. 176).

While I agree that an inability to grieve is an enormous factor in Brad's life, I feel that regret is an element of grief that may be even more elusive. Regret implies a critical self-judgment about our own chosen involvement in life. Regret suggests sorrow and disappointment in our mistakes and the resulting losses.

In the past, Brad had worked around the country in various shows performing as a lip-synch artist, and apparently had done quite well, since he won many contests. He now lived with a lover he had met in a sex club a few years ago and has been unemployed since then. I didn't learn how they met until a year into the treatment because Brad regretted the circumstance. He had been visiting friends and after getting high felt compelled to go to a sex club. He regretted what he considered the necessity and compulsive desire to frequent sex clubs, saying he didn't feel he had control over his sexual appetite when he was high. He did, however, enjoy sexually stimulating other men by the way he looked, the way he could strike a pose, or the way he could lure men to him by seeming disinterested. He would pretend self-involvement, as though he were entirely preoccupied in gratifying his own needs—narcissism and disdain as attraction. His disinterest intrigued men. He was sexually thrilled that they always approached him, but the route he took to attain his desires felt sadistic to him. Ignore men and they will seek you out, he said sarcastically, certain his sexuality was like that of Odysseus's sirens, a luring domination.

To mention a related situation, one of my heterosexual male patients, Peter, discussed in Chapter 2, also has compulsive sex. Recently he told me about entering a sex chat room on the Internet. He placed an ad listing himself as a 20-year-old woman with intense sexual cravings for religious men. He said that within minutes he had a few hundred male respondents and decided to play in the chat room with one married man who seemed more articulate and willing than the others. Peter verbally baited the married man and provoked him into a defensive position. When the married man, thinking Peter was a woman, called him a bitch, Peter enticed the man further, saying his domination was sexually stimulating. As Peter was narrating this to me, he began laughing, saying men are incredibly easy to manipulate, and insisted it is women who have the ultimate power in relationships. Does each gender view the other as dominant?

In returning to Brad, it was he who suggested I see *Ma Vie en Rose*, as he identified with the main character. Brad remembered how envious he was when his sister received confirmation in church. He was a year younger and had a similar body type. He began sneaking into her closet and trying on her confirmation dress and veil. He couldn't believe how lucky she was. A few years later his sister got a dress that was very '60s, with a pink plastic handbag and shoes to match. Brad said he would race home after school to put on the outfit, use his sister's makeup, and lip-synch to recordings of female singers. Eventually his mother found out, and beat him repeatedly for nearly a week. She insisted he was trying to humiliate her, that he was aggressively trying to ruin her life by satirizing it. His dressing up in women's clothing reflected her failure as a mother. Was her humiliation also fueled by the recognition that he performed being a woman better than she did? Was his performance of entering young womanhood any less real than his sister's?

Brad described his mother as distant and uncommunicative. He never really said much about her, saying he couldn't remember his childhood because it was so painful. He thought the members of his family never spoke to each other and he hadn't been in touch with them for years. I never had a sense of Brad's father except that he was always working and never around. Brad's older brother, however, was quite sadistic and physically aggressive, and Brad remembers suffering many beatings from his brother and feeling unable to report this to either parent. In hindsight, I now realize I had very little data on Brad's history, and no real sense of any of the family members—and herein lies the loss, which I assume was ungrieved and regretted.

Brad left home immediately after high school and began hanging out at sex clubs every night. It is amazing to me that he didn't contract the HIV virus; it surprised him, too. Perhaps it was in these early years that Brad realized "young meat" like himself was desired by others and that this provided him with a way to have a sense of power and domination over men. Eventually, he learned he could truly serve up a wonder-ful dish if he expanded the performance to include drag. I saw quite a few pictures of Brad in drag. He was exquisite and more dressed-up, more made-up, more elaborate and ornamental than I have ever been. I remember once going to a Russian nightclub in Brighton Beach. I was told to dress up, and made it there in a black dress with boa feathers around a low neck. In comparison to the pictures I saw of Brad, I was underdressed. Still, was my dressing up any more or less real than Brad's? His was more intense, but then maybe he was just better at presenting an external description of a feminine internality.

Brad stopped performing drag about five years ago. He said he had won all the trophies he needed and just wanted to keep house for his lover now. I felt upset that Brad, and for that matter Angelo, were not feminists. I wanted them to become successful, powerful women striving for social and economic equality. Instead, Brad—in identification and perhaps mimicry—had duplicated his mother's position in their family as he isolated himself and waited for his male lover to come home from work. It took awhile for me to realize that Brad drank excessively. He successfully masked this secret from me for most of his treatment, and it was only my sense that he seemed so unproductive that made me think something had to be incapacitating him every evening. Eventually, he admitted it was substance abuse. After a period of time and much effort in treatment, Brad stopped drinking and began attending daily AA meet-ings. Still, I think there was another secret I never learned about, one that eventually made him leave treatment and New York to live in the country with his lover.

When I last saw Brad, he said he had to help a friend move to another city and would miss some upcoming sessions. During this period, he left a message saying he was now looking for a country house for his lover and would return after that. Then I received a letter saying he had permanently moved into the country house, and left New York and me. Before leaving treatment, he had been discussing feeling torn between his lover and me. He felt our sessions brought on arguments between them, and his lover was threatening to stop paying for his treatment. Brad must have realized that "anything *was not* possible," and he made a choice.

CONCLUSION

Lately, I have begun working with another transgendered patient, also MTF. Since she dresses as a woman when I see her, I will use female pronouns. In a recent session, she spoke to me about pity, saying that getting people to pity transgenderism is an unfortunate first step to entering mainstream culture. I recently read a review of a new film, *Boys Don't Cry* (1999) about Brandon Teena. Teena was a female-to-male (FTM) adolescent killed for dressing as a man. It does seem that more recent films, including, *Ma Vie en Rose* (1997), seem to portray transgenderism in a sympathetic manner, and I wonder if I have written this chapter in the same emotional vein, hoping for empathy from the reader regarding both transgenderism and for the experience of capturing treatment with transgendered individuals on paper. Regretfully, I have no answers to any of the questions I have presented, and when I think them over they only produce more questions—so, for me "anything is not possible."

With hindsight, this chapter has been a clinical exploration of "not knowing" and of tolerating the state of not knowing, both with my patients and with myself, in order to see where our mutual meanderings take us. For Angelo, our explorations have led to his looking for a doctor to begin hormone treatment; for Brad, I believe he felt caught between his lover and his therapy, and had to make a choice that made sense for him. For myself, I remain curious about what I believe, questioning my ideas, my values, and my inner experiences as I hope to wonder and wander even more.

In *Unformulated Experience: From Dissociation to Imagination in Psychoanalysis*, Donnel Stern (1997) suggests the analyst needs "to be curious as possible, open to all the alternate formulations one finds unfinished in oneself, including one's reactions to the other. The uncertainty of the unformulated [in one's self and in otherness] is preserved, even nurtured. Alternatives are allowed to percolate and glimmer, emerging as indeterminate shapers. . . . the other person is seen from all sides" (p. 196). His words conclude my performance.

6

The Sacrificed Sister

Late one evening a few years ago I received a phone call from a private detective. He began a brief conversation by asking a few questions. These felt unnerving because only I knew the answers: "Are you the Florence Rosiello who lived for the first two years of life in St. Paul, Minnesota before your parents divorced in the early 1950s?" "Was your mother's maiden name Jones, and was your father's surname Veteri?" "Did your mother remarry when you were 5 and did she and your stepfather have a daughter when you were 9?" He continued, "Did you know that your biological father remarried in the early 1960s and that he and his second wife had a daughter, Sara, who is eleven years younger than you?" Finally, "Sara hired me to look for you," he said. "Her mother is ill and she recently told Sara about your existence to ease her conscience. Sara has been kept from all your father's family so that no one ever told her about you. She has her own family now, but no extended family, no siblings. She doesn't trust her mother to help find you and hired me instead. Can I call and tell her your phone number? Will you talk with her?"

I did know about Sara. In my twenties, I had found my biological father through my own searchings and asked to meet him. At the time,

I had wanted to know why he had never answered my letters or my phone calls as a child, and why had he abandoned me so entirely. He asked me never to call him at home again, told me I had a half sister, and that he and his wife didn't want her to know about me, and that was that.

Now, Sara wanted to know me, but who was she? I told the private detective I would talk to her—"Have her call me." A few minutes later she did. Sara told me my father had died eight years earlier. She gave his medical history, and after the clinical data we began talking about ourselves. She informed me that she was five feet, five inches tall, had brown hair she dyed red, weighed 110 pounds, and looked like Joseph, her/my/our father. I said, "Oh, how interesting, me too." She asked to visit with her husband and we set up a date a few weeks later. Sara was very excited about our meeting. I was not; instead I was anxious. Who was she? What would she be like? What if she was like him? What did she want from me? Why did I think she wanted anything in particular other than friendship or companionship or sisterhood?

This now meant I had two half sisters. One from my father's second marriage and one from my mother's second marriage. I knew the one from my mother's marriage—Annie. She was the one I grew up with, the one I nearly raised, the one who lived with me in New York City when she was an adolescent studying ballet. The one to whose three children I am godmother, from her two marriages that I've helped her through. The one I still provide for financially, the one I talk to every week—the one I thought was a toy my mother brought home from the hospital just for me when I was 9. The one I know and the one I unconsciously sacrificed to my mother's desire for merger, to my mother's excessive availability and intrusiveness. And Annie was the sibling who unconsciously surrendered to the sacrifice.

I was not the daughter my mother desired. As early as I can remember we always locked horns, as she put it. Maybe it was that I spent my early years being raised by my mother's mother. She didn't like my mother either, which solidified our mutual disdain and gave me a sense of empowerment. My mother wanted a beautiful daughter, a talented one, a trophy daughter, in a sense. She complained that I was none of those and lamented my academic problems as well. My half-sister Annie, on the other hand, was perfect for her. Tall, dark, a classic beauty, a talented ballet dancer with scholarships to the New York City ballet schools, an "A" student in school, a freelance model. She was just what my mother had wanted. But when my sister was very young she was often left in my care while my mother pursued her own career as a fashion coordinator and model. In a sense she left me alone, and from that I learned to take care of myself and my sister. Still, my mother would often compete with me for the kudos I did receive. For instance, I was a better amateur actress than she was, I had more friends than she did, I was often able to get my sister to do things she couldn't get her to do, and I was my grandmother's best friend. I found that when we did compete for different parts in the same play or for who had better friends, she would angrily admit defeat and envy and leave me alone, and my stepfather followed her lead.

What is interesting is that I often characterize my sister's personality as featherlike, willowy, dependent, and desiring merger with demanding men who want to control her in the way our mother did. My mother saw my sister as a more perfect version of 'her' and defined Annie's experiences as though they were her own or as if my sister's experiences affected only her and not Annie. She fought my sister's battles as though they were hers and while Annie struggled with her as much as she psychically was able to, and while I frequently protected my sister from my mother's intrusions, Annie often passively gave in to gratify my mother's desires. It was as though the three of us in our particular triangulation had made an unconscious agreement: my mother wanted a merged, symbiotic relationship with one of us and my sister was chosen as victim; and as victim she surrendered and submitted to my mother's desires. For my sister there is only otherness, only the needs and desires of the more powerful other—and in this she is a masochistic reflection of an other's powerful needs. She still makes no demands of her own. Even professionally, Annie has little power or financial stability, although she now teaches ballet and raises her children and is focused on making a third marriage before the age of 40.

Sara's character, as my biological father's daughter, also appears merged and excessively responsive to her mother's emotional demands— a masochistic position. Yet, what seems more evident is her level of hysteria and dependent personality dynamics. Sara doesn't work outside the home and instead raises her two children, supported by her lawyer husband. Both of my sisters lead lives similar to those of their respective mothers, an identification with the same-sex parent. In addition, I believe both mothers desired merger from these daughters, in their excessive availability to perceived needs, as well as to exploit mother–daughter sameness and denial of difference. Both mothers attempted an undoing or cessation of their daughters' self-differentiation and autonomy. As adults, neither daughter moved more than a few blocks away from the family, nor did either daughter strain the relationship with mother by threatening it with a career or any powerful interference. Neither Annie nor Sara seems to have developed a sense of self as subject.

Sara was ill-prepared for our first meeting. While she was correct—she did look like our father—the similarity was only in coloring. I, however, am a dead ringer, a female version of him, down to the same mole in the same place on my face. Sara was quite surprised by my appearance, and as we traced my life historically, looking though old pictures—well, actually fragments of pictures where my mother had cut or ripped my father out of the picture—Sara began to cry. She developed a migraine, had to lie down, had to take a short solitary walk, kept apologizing for the education he'd paid for, for the privileges he had given her, for her parents' behavior, for his never sending child support, and on and on. She looked miserable when she left, unable to stop sobbing. Then, within a month of my first hearing from her, she placed a frantic call to my office, tearfully saying she wanted to leave her husband, she needed my help, and would I call her immediately. Other similar phone calls came flooding in—could I help her with this, what was my advice on that, could she visit again, would I visit her, would I meet her children—and then a request to meet her mother. Did I want this? Did I want Sara? Wouldn't I take time and focus away from Annie if I "saved" Sara? Annie asked, "Where will you spend holidays if you have another sister? Do I have to meet her? What are her children to my children? Are you their aunt, too?" What triangulation was this? I appeared to be in power regarding both sisters, yet I felt manipulated and pulled at by these two dependent women.

It seemed that if I were to spend time with Sara, or let her demand time from me, then Annie could again feel she was making another sacrifice—and I would be letting her make another sacrifice to another demanding woman. I was already frightened by Sara's needs and her desire for immediate gratification and told myself that I might wind up on the *Sally Jesse Raphael* show in a segment called "Triangulated Half-Sisters Who Scare Each Other." I decided to let Sara go and asked her not to call for a while. Perhaps in the end I performed my father's sin and abandoned her. Or maybe I saved myself or Annie from another demanding woman. Did I just act selfishly, narcissistically? To my mind, it felt like I gave something to Annie by not asking her to make another sacrifice for me. And so, I sacrificed Sara in the doing of it.

How emotionally difficult or psychically easy was it to perform with Sara what my father had performed with me—a perverse triangulation. If I assume, as I do, that both half-sisters identified with and internalized their respective, excessively available mothers, then with whom did I identify? Who did I internalize? I would like to say that I internalized my grandmother, as she was quite nurturing and emotionally giving, but I am little like her. Actually, I remember that during my analytic training one of my instructors commented that I was an excellent clinician, but that I really wasn't very maternal, and I took that as a compliment.

My own identification—or the identification I consciously like—was with my absent father. In fantasy, I did not feel threatened by Sara's association with him. He was an outsider in her merged relationship with her mother, I imagined. When I truly let my fantasies fly, I pretended that when he looked at her, he had thoughts of me that racked him with guilt for his misguided life. In my imagined relationship to my father, he knew I was his reflection—I was who he was, we were both outsiders, survivors of women who desired merger. He and I were powerful in the outside world in our exciting, creative professional lives.

In psychoanalytic theory, identification can be used either as a substitution for or as a defense against abandonment. I believe I developed an identification with a fantasy father, with the father my mother detested, the one she insisted I was like whenever I struggled to meet my own needs, which was whenever I needed emotional and psychic distance from her. I often found her looking at me as I grew up, lamenting the way all my physical features, as well as my personality, were exactly like his. "You're just like your father. You're stubborn, miserly, you think only about doing what you want and not about helping me," she would insist during arguments. She frequently taunted, "I gave up the possibility of having my own life and married your stepfather so you could have a family. You're an ingrate." "Go live with you father, you're so much like him." I have often wondered about and accused her of intercepting my letters to him, thinking that had he gotten them he might have wanted me, recognized my needs and given me the life I fantasized. He would take me away to the Italian side of the family, a big group of people who looked like me. They would absorb me into a way of life that suited me, a life in which my father thought I was important, where he would recognize my abilities, my self as different and the same as his, a place where he would muse "I was just like him."

Benjamin (1995) suggests that in the rapprochement phase the father plays an important part in representing separation and autonomy, as well as desire, and this is for boys as well as girls. In rapprochement, the child begins to differentiate *from* both parents through identification with the sameness and difference *of* both parents. Mother is experienced and identified with as the source of nurturance, warmth, and protection. Father typically represents the outside world, creating a sense of freedom for the young child. Still, identification with father means an identification with a like subject who represents the desire for the outside world and independence. In the child's identificatory love of the father not only is there an association with particular aspects of the boy's or girl's idealization of him, but also with the father's representation of the outside world's excitement and stimulation. Benjamin (1995) writes, "This identification with the ideal [other/father] has a defensive function, protecting the child from experiencing the loss of control over mother that is generally experienced in this phase. But it is not only defensive, insofar as the ideal father represents longings that the child may partially realize in her effort to define herself as a subject of desire, [it is also] . . . identificatory love of the father, [and] an identification with difference in otherness is crucial" (p. 130). For the young girl, it is important that she be able to use her fantasy of father, who represents a sense of power, to aid her in her efforts toward freedom in the outside world. Such a fantasy of father can compensate for the girl's loss of control

in relation to mother. A disidentification with mother, if mother is emotionally withdrawn, can undo the mother's unavailability (Benjamin 1995).

If the girl's identificatory love has been recognized by the father she
will not have to envy his masculinity or power. In fantasy and because
of my mother's pronouncements, I felt recognized by my fantasy father.
This fantasized recognition helped structure a self identification and
helped me to have a sense of being a subject of desire.

Ogden (1989) discusses the psychological reorganization experienced by the female child before the Oedipus complex begins. He presents
the notion of there being a triangulated set of whole-object relationships
within which the father is experienced as a love object and the mother
as an ambivalently loved rival. Ogden theorizes that "the little girl falls
in love with the mother-as-father and with the father-as-mother [in other
words]. . . . The little girl falls in love with the mother who is engaged
in an unconscious identification with her own father" (p. 119)—that is,
the mother's father. Ogden provides an engaging example of this in
describing a mother and daughter clothes-shopping expedition. As the
daughter tries on clothes, mother (in an unconscious identification with
her own father) emotionally presents a third party, a father. The little
girl experiences her mother's involvement, either admiration, recognition, or criticism, as her own father found in her mother's gaze. What
Ogden is talking about is not the actual involvement of the little girl's
father, but rather the mother as a "conduit to a relationship with 'the
other'" (p. 120). In keeping with Winnicott's (1960) notion that "there
is no such thing as an infant," (p. 39) Ogden (1989) is saying that there
is no such thing as an oedipal dyad, only a triangulation of object relations found in a two-person relationship—father is always present, either
in reality or not.

To put this another way, Ogden (1989) suggests that the mother,
in unconscious identification with her own father, emotionally presents
this third party to the daughter. I will extend this idea to include other
important males in the mother's life, some of whom may overshadow
the mother's father, and in so doing I again hope to address the importance of siblings in development of self. My mother and her younger
brother were inseparable when growing up, and considered themselves
twins. They believed they parented each other under the watch of their

longtime housekeeper. Between them there was a mutual identification, recognition, and mirroring of the other's sameness and differences. In particular, my mother idealized her brother's physical aggressiveness, often telling stories of how he protected her, how he could beat up any kid around—no one was stronger than her brother. He considered my mother to be a beauty who attracted his male friends and who crowded the family home with her exquisite girlfriends. They provided each other with a sense of empowerment and accomplishment in their own differentiation of self. In a sense, they were subject and object of each other's desire in their fantasy twinship.

For me, my mother's relationship with her brother provided a triangulated set of whole-object relationships that supported my developing belief that I had the potential to accomplish my desires. In one story, my mother told of her brother fighting off an intruder who was attempting to harm her. In her narrative, brother and sister triumph over the intruder after an extensive battle and drive him away. This is perhaps the only story from my mother's life that ever impressed me, perhaps because her physical aggressiveness seemed so out of character. When I first heard her tell it, her youthful strength seemed split off from who she was in adulthood. Her need to control and merge was much more evident, and while this had a superficial appearance of powerfulness, even as a child I experienced her as weak and vulnerable. But I admired her strength in this story and the way she and her brother had joined together to provide a powerful union. I remember thinking that I "inherited" my uncle's strength and aggressiveness—in other words, my mother emotionally presented her unconscious identification with her brother, and in triangulation I identified with her brother/my uncle. I remember wishing to be his daughter eliminating her entirely and claiming his strength and power as my own. In my perceived difference, I experienced a separation from my mother that was really a transformation of self—myself as subject and inheritor of my mother's past power, given by her brother.

But what about my own father as a powerful male figure? All I had was a fantasy father who would have attended to all my needs and childhood wishes and recognized me as being like him. Did the fantasy of my father's recognition enable the development of an identificatory love that was not available to my sisters due to their mother's excessive availability? Was recognition by their respective fathers diluted by their mothers' wish for merger as these women attempted to exclude psychological triangulation with the father? If so, doesn't a lack of recognition from father leave such women looking to repeat this early trauma, so that as an adult the daughter attempts to meet her desires through a man rather than through her self?

Benjamin (1995) suggests that "a lack of recognition and the denial of the identificatory bond [between father and daughter] damage[s] the sense of being a sexual subject and leads the woman to look for her desire through a man—and frequently develops into masochistic fantasies of surrendering to the ideal man's power" (p. 130).

Of these three sisters, have any escaped sacrifice? How does the surviving sister live with the awareness that she has sacrificed her sibling to the merging parent, or does the notion of self as survivor just imply faulty agency and privilege? While I eclipsed my mother's domination, I also eclipsed a real relationship with her, and this stands out in the light of not having an actual relationship with my father. What I sacrificed was an attachment to an emotionally present parental figure—a longing I still maintain in sorrow, anger, and particularly in regret. In my relationship with my half-sister, with whom I grew up, we are forever plagued with fears and wishes of the other's excessive availability. While we are intimate and we nurture each other in many ways, neither of us would claim to have a maternal role with the other, only one that is sisterly. Our mother's domination has left us only passively related to each other. I doubt that my half-sisters feel we mattered or were seen as subjects in our own right, to our respective mothers—I certainly don't. As an adult, I am left with a fear of abandonment that looms large in all relationships, sometimes eliminating them when they might have added importance in my life. All three of us were sacrificed in our intimate lives—and as adults, being involved in intimate relatedness remains a struggle.

Personally or professionally, none of these sisters escaped masochism. My half-sisters' lack of professional success has left my successes tinged with culpability. Are these masochistic dynamics specific to same-sex siblings or are they even more evident in opposite-sex siblings? Is it always the female child who is sacrificed to the excessively available parent? And is this parent always the mother?

MASOCHISM

In "The Economic Problem of Masochism" (1924), Freud described three types of masochism. The first is a sexual masochism that relates sexual excitement with psychic tension, meaning pleasure is derived from pain in fusion, defusion, and refusion of sexual and death instincts. The second is feminine masochism, which dovetailed the Oedipus complex with the beating fantasy, meaning that for those individuals sexual arousal and release were inhibited due to a defensive regression of Oedipal desires. Such individuals unconsciously wished for the father through the fantasy of being a naughty, female child. Therefore, identification with the female and the wish to have father created sexual satisfaction. The third type is moral masochism, which loosened the relation of pain/pleasure to sexuality. Freud explained that it is now the superego that becomes an object of the ego's regressive, sexualized wish to be beaten by the father. An ultramorality sets in as the moral masochist attempts to satisfy his oedipal wishes through the desire for pain, humiliation, and submission at the hands of all authorities (Glick and Meyers 1988).

Many post-Freudian analysts who wrote on masochism stayed within the Freudian fold in holding that pain is a condition for pleasure—although they shifted their focus from oedipal to preoedipal conflicts (Berliner 1958, Bernstein 1957, Brenner 1959, Bychowski 1959, Eidelberg 1959, Eisenbud 1967, Menaker 1953, Nydes 1963, Socarides 1958). Analytic writers of this period typically stressed that masochism originated as an ego or narcissistic defense against a punitive environment (Bergler 1949, Keiser 1949, Loewenstein 1945, 1957, Nacht 1938). In addition, self-aggression or the idea of "victory through defeat" (Reik 1941) became an important focus (Brenman 1952, Horney 1935).

More importantly, contemporary analysts (such as Bach 1991, 1994, Cooper 1983, 1988, Ghent 1990, Stolorow 1975, Stolorow et al. 1994, Stolorow and Lachmann 1980) discuss masochism as a defensive attempt at self-restoration. The notion of masochism as reparative makes it a primary, rather than secondary function, often originating in relation "to merger with the idealized image of the parent, or in feelings of illusory control over a narcissistic infantile vulnerability" (Rosiello 1993, p. 31).

THE THERAPIST AS SUBJECT

When I began writing this chapter, I thought about the way we as analysts report what we do—and who we are in what we do—to our colleagues. How do we tell each other about our work? Whenever we write about theory, or about transference–countertransference feelings, or about subjectivity, analysts reveal parts of themselves. Sometimes the analyst as subject is a primary focus of the essay. For instance, Freud openly discussed his self-analysis, using himself both as subject and object (Bollas 1989) in "The Interpretation of Dreams." He was also the first to write about sibling transference in his Dora case (1905b). Many have speculated that Kohut presented his own self-analysis in "The Two Analyses of Mr. Z," in that he was Mr. Z in the two analyzes and the second analysis was a self-analysis (T. Kohut 1994). Of course, we reveal ourselves secondarily when we write about our countertransference, and some think that our particular topics belie our private interests. Either primarily or secondarily, the author presents something about herself in conveying how she does psychoanalysis. To my way of thinking, the analyst's self-analysis as a source of introspection is a way to have a prepared mind in understanding the patient and treatment. In our profession we share how we work and what created the origins of how we work with one another. Practitioners of other sciences or arts have it a little easier when sharing what they do to their colleagues. For instance, biologists have a more structured task because in their profession more standards are in place regarding writing and presenting the self in it. But what are the standards for psychoanalytic writers who present themselves as subjects? Should we say more or less about ourselves in our papers to maintain a professional transference?

My thoughts about this essay originated in a personal experience and created a playground within which to consider the sibling transference–countertransference matrix. I was in the mix from the beginning—maybe I was the first ingredient—an already existing component in understanding patients who developed sibling transference. But what risks does the analyst run in so openly setting out food for thought?

Bollas (1989) writes about colleagues who promote a "'confessional voice' to bare disclosure of mind, affect, and self in their work" (p. 52) to the professional community. He comments on the way colleagues must sit through the clinician's discussion of his own honesty, which the audience frequently doesn't believe or is annoyed with, anyway. Of course, there are other analysts who have been able to present themselves as a subject in their writings, either as object of a self-analysis, or in conscious musing on unconscious context expressed to an audience. These analysts appeal to their internal dialogue in an authentic way that provides a basis for interpretive work with patients, and this was my goal in working with the patients I will discuss later. However, writing about the analyst as subject remains an atypical psychoanalytic phenomenon.

During the era of traditional psychoanalysis, for instance, the concepts of abstinence and of the analyst as a blank screen seemed pervasive both in the consulting room and in psychoanalytic writings. Perhaps this was reinforced by Freud's negative reaction to Ferenczi's notions of mutuality and use of the active technique, with the analyst analyzing the patient and the patient analyzing the analyst. Still, Ferenczi was considered one of the foremost clinicians of his day. Did his belief that it is crucial to reveal ourselves when conducting an analysis enhance his clinical skills? Many colleagues accused Ferenczi of madness in the last years of his life (Aron 1996), a response perhaps stemming from Freud's rejection of Ferenczi's ideas on mutuality in treatment, some of which included Ferenczi's loving his patients in a literal, albeit parental way.

The analyst as subject seems to have gone underground, at least in the literature, until the late 1950s when Searles (1959) quite openly wrote about his oedipal love in the countertransference. He told his readers "I have experienced romantic and erotic desires to marry, and fantasies of being married to, the patient" (p. 284). He likened this struggle to his experience in the resolution of his Oedipus complex late in his personal analysis. At the time Searles wrote this paper, it was extremely unusual for the analyst to present himself as a subject in psychoanalytic writings, and many of his colleagues thought he had lost control of his countertransference.

In 1969, in her book *The Hands of the Living God*, Milner used herself as subject through describing her struggles to understand her thoughts as well as those of the schizophrenic patient she was writing about. Her writing has a poetic quality and absorbs the reader into her way of thinking about her patient and about herself. What is also interesting in much of Milner's work (1988) is how frequently she uses the personal pronoun "I" in the first line of many of her essays. Typically this style is considered too narcissistic for psychoanalytic writings even in contemporary psychoanalytic literature.

Contemporary psychoanalytic literature has taken an interesting twist with regard to the analyst as subject, in that self-disclosure of the analyst's feelings to or about the patient is currently creating a professional controversy. But self-disclosure is different from viewing the analyst as subject, in that we get data when we think about the analyst as subject because it means *two* people are interacting. In self-disclosure, what the analyst chooses to do with the data is derived from two subjectivities, and this can either be disclosed to the patient by the analyst or not. In other words, what we do with self-disclosure is different than what we do with narrated or written self-analysis. I will address self-disclosure more fully later in this chapter.

CLINICAL ILLUSTRATIONS

For the last few years, since that phone call from the private detective and the ensuing events, I have wanted to write about siblings, specifically the development and outcome of sacrificing a sister. As I thought about the dynamics I experienced and considered my sisters' emotions, I was aware that I had been hearing similar narratives from my patients. Interestingly enough, I heard them from women who were talking about their relationships with their sisters, typically triangulated with a merged parent. Certainly, as therapists, we all have patients who create or have originated such dynamics in their personal lives, and we work with this material as a matter of course. But how does this manifest in the transference–countertransference matrix and what are the patients' and our subjective experiences? What do we mutually create?

Cassie

Cassie came to treatment a few years ago frustrated with her inability to leave her dead-end job, her difficulty developing a committed relationship with a man, and her relations with her family. She had grown up in the midwest and was the younger of two daughters. Cassie describes her older sister, Julie, as being entirely different. Julie was petite, pretty, very popular, dated throughout high school and college, and married a man who came into an enormous inheritance a year after the marriage. They settled into a post-academic life of independent wealth in New York.

Cassie, however, was immensely unpopular in school and in college and, having followed her sister to New York, maintained a rather empty social life well into her treatment. While she credits her social and emotional discomfort to her family history, she is certain that much of her psychic pain derives from her physical presentation. She is over six feet tall with rather masculine, yet handsome features, large-boned, and describes herself as unfeminine. Her clothes are mannish, but stylish in a hip-hop sort of way. She is, however, quite brilliant and gifted, is particularly fluent in other languages, and had spent a year abroad, in Saint Petersburg, studying. She now works for a very corporate company where she feels out of place, and, I believe, she must look it, too. She felt particularly displaced when she went to Russia a few years ago and developed her first relationship with a man.

Within a few weeks, she and Darius became inseparable. He moved in, expected her to pay for his housing, his food, all his entertainment, and every bit of his cocaine. He wanted her to partake and she did, having little experience with cocaine and none with men prior to entering Russia. Very quickly, Darius became demanding of her time and paranoid about her movements without him. He became instantly jealous, imagining her short trips to the market as long journeys looking for men. From her description, I assume he was in a cocaine psychosis but maybe it was just his own. She went from being his erotic foreigner to his submissive slave, literally. In one particular instance, he pounced on her from behind the door when she returned home from a walk with friends. He then attempted to strangle her as her friends protested, although they did not intervene. It wasn't until she nearly lost consciousness that one of the men talked Darius out of continuing his attack. Then he asked for her forgiveness, which she easily gave.

A short time later, Darius attacked Cassie with a knife and cut her. This time she realized each attack was getting more violent. She also knew she had somehow ended up in a dependent stupor, a mixture of drugs and violence, masochism and sadism.

Cassie believed that her experience with Darius's sadism and her own masochism were similar to her experience growing up with her mother and sister. Apparently, her mother and Julie were constantly at odds, always quarreling, engaged in obsessive debates about everything and nothing. Cassie's father appears to have retreated passively to his study and left parenting to the mother. Her mother was described as extremely obsessive, intrusive, excessively available, desiring merger with Cassie and rejecting Julie as selfish, headstrong, and obstinate. The mother, however, did admire Julie's ability to be social, popular, and pretty, but saw those qualities as superficial and unworthy of her attentions. The mother found solace in Cassie, who she called her best friend, someone who always agreed with her, someone who she could always get to agree with her, if badgered enough.

Cassie frequently speaks of the way her mother greets her as an example of her mother's wish for merger. She will put her arms around Cassie's neck, stand on her toes, pull Cassie's head toward her own as she struggles to kiss her entire face, cooing and using baby talk as enticement. These are not quick exchanges, but instead last for long minutes as her mother attempts to touch Cassie's shoulders, her back, and eventually holds onto her hands until Cassie wrestles herself free. This is followed by protestations that only Cassie can comfort her, only Cassie understands her, she is the good, wonderful, giving child. Cassie tells about these interactions with disgust and a sense of having been slimed by her mother's desires.

She also frequently laments the fact that her mother is incapable of allowing change. When Cassie was an adolescent and made plans with the few friends she had, she was unable to tell her mother if their plans changed. Her mother would launch into battering mode: "Why did your plans change? Who changed them? Why did your friends think they could just change your plans? You told me you were going to the movies and now you want to go to the dance? What's wrong with the movies? Who is going to the dance?" This would go on for hours. Consequently, Darius' intrusiveness, desire for merger, and physical abuses felt like her mother's intrusiveness, symbiotic demands, and emotional abuses—a continuation of a familiar sacrificial dynamic.

In contrast, Julie seems to have escaped a merged relationship with her mother. Julie was very active in high school, she dated, had lots of friends, and spent as much time away from home as possible. Cassie found herself frequently at home, always intruded on, always seen as her mother's confidant, always expected to be the perfect child. Julie encountered no resistance about leaving home for college, while Cassie struggled with her mother to attend the same school. Actually, there was a period of many years where Julie and her mother did not speak to each other, and this seemed fine with them both. Cassie, meanwhile, agonized over her mother's undiluted attention. Cassie feels her sister was more mutually related than her mother, although she felt her sister was sadistic as an adolescent. Still, Julie often tried to protect her, and to help her defend herself against their mother, and tried to mother her herself. Cassie believes that without Julie her childhood would have been much worse and that her mother would have had no limitations on intrusions. It would seem that Julie's need to be different from her mother, her many outside interests, and an identification with her absent father enabled her to escape the mother's desire for merger.

In her family, Cassie was the sacrificed sister, a position straddling the poles of merger/differentiation and masochism/sadism within a triadic relationship. Cassie was sacrificed in an intersubjective triangulated agreement. For example, Julie's rejection of her mother's excessive intrusiveness created dramatic arguments between them. This terrified Cassie, who feared her mother would turn her rage against her. Surrendering to her mother's domination felt less violent than not surrendering, even though surrendering still meant emotional pain. When the mother did become angry with her, Cassie became mute and dissolved into apologies laced with masochistic recitals of her unworthiness and wrongdoing. After a period of stony silence, broken by Cassie's pleas for forgiveness, the mother would eventually concede, and then accuse Julie of misguiding Cassie. In this family, Julie was Cassie's good-enough mother in that Julie was kinder and more accepting of Cassie's differences and sameness, more aware that Cassie had her own needs and desires. In Julie's attempts for otherness and development of self, she encouraged Cassie's meager attempts at separation from the mother's wishes to merge. She would often push Cassie to confront her mother and I believe there were rare moments when she did, but generally Cassie was too fearful of her mother's wrath.

In a sense, Cassie secretly identified with her sister; this would have been a dangerous identification if openly expressed. Julie epitomized potential and success in the outside world, as well as escape from a despotic parent, and she also recognized Cassie as a separate subject. Julie's vicious arguments with her mother modified the mother's omnipotence in Cassie's attempt at differentiation from mother. In other words, Julie's triumphs over the mother counterbalanced Cassie's sense of her mother's omnipotence. In a reversal of power relations Julie turned the tables on the mother's despotism, and this created a fantasy of shared feeling and perceptions between the sisters. Their union constructed the capacity to recognize the mother as another subject, and the fantasy of maternal omnipotence was aligned with the duality of shared perceptions and feelings between siblings—an intersubjective reality.

Yet, in this case, there was also an identification with the mother as subject, resulting in a double identification—one with Julie and one with the mother—as well as a recognition that mother was different from both sisters. In Cassie's identification with her sister, she attained a degree of differentiation from the mother. Julie escaped the mother's intrusiveness by sacrificing Cassie to her mother's needs; Cassie's sacrifice was experienced as a masochistic one that eventually became a tribute to her mother's sadism. The mother's verbal cruelty toward both her children, her insensitivity to their needs, her constant degradations and viciousness, her obsessive wish for total power and control over her children, and her rejection and disapproval of her husband's attempts at parenting left Cassie overwhelmed with masochistic feelings. If we fear retaliation by the controlling, powerful other, sadomasochistic fantasies are created from the breakdown of mutuality. Surrender to the more powerful other becomes the condition of survival (Benjamin 1995b).

In treatment, Cassie appears to have developed a sibling transference, and I say this because when the transference does venture into the maternal, Cassie becomes emotionally deadened, flat, and exceedingly obsessional, a defense in reaction to and in identification with her mother. This is not to say there is no maternal transference; there is at times, but Cassie and I are more comfortable in the somewhat differently configured maternal sibling transference. The desire for and fear of merger are more kept at bay in our sibling transference–countertransference dynamics.

The sibling transference is usually characterized in psychoanalytic literature as being one filled with competitiveness, envy, fondness, hostility, and manipulative or aggressive behaviors, as well as nurturance and attachment (Agger 1988, Des Rosiers 1993, Graham 1988, Kernberg and Richards 1988, Parens 1988, Rosner 1985, Volkan and Ast 1997). It is also typically seen as a triadic relationship, in two-child homes, where the transference corresponds to the sibling rivalry for the mother. While this is an aspect of the sibling transference, Cassie seems to feel that I am a more experienced sibling, from whom she elicits comments on dating, making friends, questions about where to go to find this or that, cool places to hang out (as if I'd know), and on and on. These questions continue to pop up in her treatment, which is quite intimate and in depth as she searches to understand herself, her mother and sister, and most recently her new, very pleasant boyfriend. My subjective experience or countertransference is perhaps the best indicator of the type and depth of her transference, which I characterize as akin to two girls in a dorm room talking about life and the development of one's self. This is not to say that Cassie doesn't express a full range of feelings, although it did take quite a while before she acknowledged anger toward me, and when she did, it was in hindsight although she was still emotional. What I find most interesting about Cassie's treatment (she's always been on the couch), is that she spends the entire session with her eyes closed. Is this an attempt to keep me out visually, or to keep me in? I've often wondered if, behind her eyelids, she imagines me to be younger than I am, closer in age as two sisters might be.

THE SACRIFICED SISTER   127

She has often spoken about how different I am from her mother, who is actually a few years younger than I am. In her mind, her mother seems to have missed the cultural and feminist struggles of the 1960s, but Cassie has determined and actually proved to herself that I did not. She enters my office on her own, coming in as I speed past to grab a bite in the kitchen. Early on in her treatment, I once returned to the office to find her looking through all my CDs. She was elated when she saw *Santana, The Best of The Cream,Van Morrison, Canned Heat, Eric Clapton,* and the newer ones, *R.E.M., The Gypsy Kings, Squirrel Nut Zippers, Buena Vista Social Club,* popular music that spans decades, as well as blues and jazz. That section of my office is behind my desk, so in a sense she was being intrusive, as if identified with her mother's self-entitlement to the privacy of others, and we discussed this. On the other hand, she was thrilled and presented a fantasy about my adolescent experiences, how she hoped I had marched on Washington, D.C. during the Vietnam War era, burned my bra in support of feminist ideas, and had worn bellbottoms and moccasins to college. Her mother had done none of this and I've often wondered how she managed to escape the influence of this era so completely.

In my experience of Cassie I sense something of what my sister must have understood of our relationship, as though I'm an exciting object, a subject of my own desires, a person who holds the potential and novelty of adventures of a different generation. Surely there is envy in that, but maybe not jealousy. Jealousy is not always an aspect of envy, particularly when idealization and identification are more dominant factors. In my countertransference, I feel very intimately related to Cassie, and frequently wish I could go to clubs with her, or out to movies, or hang out in our mutually imagined dorm room, giggling about boys and sharing theories of our personal universe. It is interesting, in my countertransference, that I feel that she will never leave treatment, a wishful lament that I know is unreal and not therapeutic. My countertransference wish is tinged with my own personal desire for people to remain with me. I become, in fantasy, the good-enough sister who never abandons anyone. This is a restorative dream that in life is not true—it is only a counter-maternal desire.

Bianca

Bianca is an exquisitely exotic, beautiful woman in her late thirties. Her perfect body is slender and she keeps it tightly bound through her dancing. She works in the creative arts and only within the last few years of treatment has she become moderately successful. Watching her move about in the treatment chair is an experience in itself as she snakes over the armrests, seductively manipulates her long hair (each time changing her look), dramatically emotes every word she utters, and engages me completely. She is humorous, articulate, erotic, paranoid, and entirely narcissistic and histrionic.

Bianca grew up in a bohemian New York City household. Her parents are well educated, have done well financially, and are both attractive. She has a sister who is a few years younger than I am and Bianca is the same age as my sister, Annie. Bianca is also the sacrificed sister. Is it always the youngest child who is sacrificed to the parent desiring merger in a two-sibling household?

Bianca describes her mother as a beautiful but emotionally scattered woman who appears to flit from room to room, never realizing she is orchestrating too many projects at once. Interestingly, she is reported to shut down emotionally when not engaged or distracted by some crisis that she typically has designed. Bianca's father is a CFO in a large corporation; he is usually preoccupied with work, although later in life he has become more involved with his two daughters whom he regularly instructs with criticisms.

When Bianca was 5, an incident occurred that characterizes her developmental years and her interactions with her family. Her mother was away for a few days, perhaps taking a respite from her chaotic marriage. Bianca's father took the two girls for a walk and asked them to wait while he visited a female friend. Bianca remembers being left when it was still light and not seeing her father again until it was dark. She felt petrified waiting and soon became hysterical, crying and screaming and running up and down the sidewalk searching for her father. Some people came by and tried to calm her, and maybe her sister, Melanie, who is a few years older, explained their predicament so that they all left without helping. But Bianca was frightened they would never be retrieved, afraid her parents had deserted her, and that she was left to Melanie's care.

Bianca's parents divorced soon thereafter and her mother moved away to another city. The father also moved but took an apartment with a girlfriend in the same neighborhood. At this time Melanie was an adolescent and Bianca was around 10 or so. Incredibly, both parents abandoned the girls, and Melanie raised Bianca during her preadolescent and adolescent years. While there were housekeepers and maids, no adult lived with the sisters. I don't know that much about the mother, but early on in treatment Bianca related an incident that happened when she went to stay with her mother while her own apartment was being renovated. Bianca and her boyfriend had ordered a take-out dinner and were sharing it, unaware of her mother's plans for the evening. Her mother came home, opened all the food containers, and asked why they were having this type of food. They said they had ordered some for her, too. The mother turned away and started crying, moving from room to room, rejected by their meal choice and some magical miscommunication. Her pitch increased as she became more emotional about not being considered, consulted, waited for, and how she was used, exploited, ignored, and abused. Bianca and her boyfriend sat stunned, not really understanding what they saw. When this event was related in treatment, Bianca feared she had been selfish, uncaring, and neglectful of her mother. Was this a masochistic identification with her mother's masochism and desire for symbiotic communication? This interaction is a typical one for her mother.

When I first began treating Bianca, she spoke about having been in treatment with a well-known male therapist for five years. A colleague of Bianca's had referred her to me because she now wanted a female analyst. Bianca's sister, Melanie, was doubtful of my credentials, however, and told her she should be seeing a therapist at Melanie's own therapist's institute. In an incredibly competitive moment, I sat erect and damn near rattled off my CV, needing to triumph over Melanie's therapist and Melanie, and "my institute was better than their institute." Next session, Bianca asked why I had felt so threatened. I didn't understand the full dynamic at the time, although I felt mortified at my response, but my sibling rivalry became clearer as we went on.

Melanie appears to be the sister who escaped the mother's chaotic intrusiveness, developing a powerful identificatory love with her absent father. Melanie is in the same profession, in the same position, and in a similar corporation as her father, and so is her husband. Bianca's father seems quite proud of Melanie; they appear to have little conflict and share similar values and attitudes. They live in the same neighborhood and speak nearly every day, often about Bianca and her inability to manage her own life. Bianca and her father have only recently found a way to relate to each other. Within the last few years, Bianca realized that her father likes to give advice and that if she takes it and reports back he is pleased with her. Now both the father and Melanie phone Bianca and instruct her on how to live her life. Bianca welcomes her father's attentions, having felt denied them all her life, yet also feels he is intrusive and demanding.

The sisters seemed tangled in separation and attachment during childhood. Bianca remembers having difficulty ever being away from Melanie, who scorned Bianca's dependence. At school, Bianca's separation from Melanie frequently resulted in vomiting and sobbing episodes that would not stop until Bianca was taken from her class and placed next to her sister in her sister's classroom. She would hold on to Melanie, who struggled physically to escape. At home, unsupervised after both parents moved out, Melanie and Bianca wound up in many violent and physical fights. They would bite each other, pull hair, and wrestle, perhaps as a metaphor of failed attempts at merger and autonomy. Bianca remembers being black and blue during most of her adolescence in literally fighting for Melanie's attentions. In adolescence, Bianca became anorexic and then abused drugs and alcohol into her late twenties. During this time, she developed masochistic relationships with men who either abused her emotionally, or abused substances with her. Melanie's sacrifice and sadism toward Bianca led to Bianca's intense masochistic struggles as an adult.

It was a few years into the treatment before I really understood what was happening with Bianca. She would begin a session by relating an event, and follow with pronouncements about how she should have handled a situation. At first it just seemed masochistic—everything was a problem, all events were painful, or the aftermath, when she realized

how she should have conducted herself, was painful. She felt humiliation, intense shame, and her behavior was always criticized. As time went
on, I realized that the way she criticized herself had a dissociated quality: the event was emotional, but the criticism was not. Then, I noticed
that the idioms she used in her criticisms were different than those she
used in telling the event. Someone else was creating her narratives. I
began asking her how she had come to her critical conclusions and she
provided intense explanations, with histrionics substituted for related
emotions. As this became more evident, I asked if Melanie had helped
her understand her actions. She said no, later perhaps fearing I would
develop another sibling rivalry and eliminate her sister; later she agreed
to this when I asked again. It took many years to realize just how crowded
her sessions were with criticisms from her sister.

Recently, Bianca developed a relationship with a man who is not
abusive. This is the first relationship in which she has ever been monogamous. For a year, she pretended to be what he wanted and he fell deeply
in love with her. Eventually, he wanted more emotional intimacy, and
she felt frightened that she could not produce an authentic self within
an intimate relationship. She feared he would leave and began contacting her previous, abusive boyfriend who was still obsessed with her.

This was a difficult period in treatment. I made every interpretation possible, every communication about her masochism, her desire to
repeat earlier trauma, and her wish to keep her self merged with abusive
and sadistic others. I interpreted the transference, how I must feel abusive
to her now, as well as my countertransference, how I felt the need to
save her as she had wanted her sister to save her when growing up. I
spoke about my experience of feeling controlled by her, useless, abused
by her rejection of all my comments. She said she felt fearful of me,
whatever I wanted she didn't own.

During one session, I realized I was nearly in tears from frustration
and found myself pleading with her to let me in, to let us have an intimate
moment. Perhaps this was a similar dynamic she felt with her sister
(perhaps one I had wished to have with my own mother). Bianca started
crying, in response or in resonance, and then I watched her regress to a
level I've never seen with any other patient. Sessions became chaotic and
she became frantic in her emotional demands; she was unable to stop

crying for the next few weeks. Phone calls began coming in, dramatic calls about paranoid experiences. Everyone was leaving her, and she feared I would as well. It was like watching her at 5 years old, out on the street, looking for her father after he'd left her for hours with her sister. She could barely get through a workday without sobbing, she was creating bizarre situations with her new boyfriend, accusing him of womanizing, and there were scenes with her previous boyfriend on street corners. Her sister was furious with her, and her father was criticizing her. She loudly protested I was making sure she was dependent on me, "You want me to trust you and you'll leave me. You're all I have. I can't even maintain a relationship with my boyfriend unless you help me. What do you want from me?" "Just you," I answered, "I just want a part of who you really are." Within the next few months, I saw her every day, at least once a day. Gradually I could see her regression subside as she began to trust I would not leave her, and I felt more frequently allowed to see her more private self.

Who had we become to each other? Was I the older maternal sister who would finally save her? Was she the younger sister who wanted to be saved, different than my own sister who never entered treatment and who seems stuck in dependent, masochistic relationships with men? What were we enacting? I asked her if she had a sense of what was developing between us. She knew we were relating differently, or maybe she just knew we were related, like siblings. She felt authentic in our work and was having similar experiences with her boyfriend. Now she thought I kept her in the relationship with her boyfriend, helped her get through her workdays with colleagues, and her business was doing quite well. She wanted a more distant relationship with her father and sister and felt able to recuperate more quickly after discussions with them. She was intimate with me, and thought I would not abuse her, and I guess that meant that I wouldn't merge with her, no matter how intimate our work.

What were my feelings about her? Over time I began to understand that she was the sister I wanted, one I might actually fix, one I could help survive earlier merged relationships. Could I finally defeat the rejecting, all-powerful mother? Whose mother was I imagining, hers or mine? Was I lost in some transference–countertransference collusion, or not?

COUNTERTRANSFERENCE LOVE

I have become very aware of what I feel toward Bianca and, clinically, it would be called the worst four-letter word in psychoanalysis—love. I fantasize that she's my sister and that I can be of use to her, always, and that she will continue to become successful in life because of our work. Yet, I don't believe Bianca's feelings for me are as powerful as mine for her. While she cares about me, I think I am the one who experiences loving feelings toward her.

But what do I mean by love? For me, love includes the potential for loss. It is only a momentary feeling, yet in this moment, love is sustained by a hope of development, and laced with longing that compels it to go forward. Searles (1965) thought that the establishment of a mutually loving relationship was the heart of treatment, "[a] feeling of boundless love is the only soil from which the patient's healthy ego-differentiation and maturation can subsequently grow" (p. 24). Hirsch (1986) thought that countertransference love is probably inevitable in, and maybe essential for, a successful analysis.

Coen (1996) takes this a step further saying that "without access to their own strong loving and hating feelings, therapists cannot carry intensive treatments to conclusion" (p. 14). Gabbard (1994) stated that often therapists are uncomfortable with loving feelings and instead focus on sexual feelings toward their patients. It feels safer for patient and analyst to focus on erotic feelings rather than on wishes to be loved and to love.

Awhile back I saw the Craig Lukas play *The Dying Gaul* (1998), and found it an intriguing story about love and betrayal, truth and confession. In one particular scene the therapist in the play narrates how he has fallen in love with his male patient. He determines he must confess to the patient and end treatment. The patient, for the first time, confronts the therapist. The patient explains that love is a part of every relationship and that the therapist must integrate it for himself. The therapist must maintain the treatment and love, as the patient could not tolerate the loss of the therapist or risk losing his love. The point this character makes is, Why should he be denied the therapist's love? Why shouldn't it exist? How can anyone, either patient or analyst be free of desire?

In order to write this chapter, I took off a week from seeing patients. It happened that I had continued treating Bianca five to six times a week. When we resumed our work together after my break, she was furious that I had been unavailable, and I was stunned by her anger. I wondered aloud how she could be so angry when I had spent the week thinking about her. Had she forgotten I asked permission to discuss our work?

Usually, patients feel pleased when they think they're referred to in a clinical paper. They ask about the topic, discuss their fantasies and fears, and bask in narcissistic pleasure at being special. Bianca, however, wanted details: How was I using her relationship with her sister, what was my hypothesis, my purpose in writing the paper? Finally, she demanded to know the origins of my thoughts on the sacrificed sister. Should I tell her about my experience with Sara and Annie? If I did, would my answer take the issue of the analyst's use of self-disclosure to an extreme?

SELF-DISCLOSURE

In contemporary psychoanalytic literature, self-disclosure typically refers to the disclosure of the analyst's emotional reaction to the patient, not a disclosure of facts about the analyst's life. Hirsch (1996) states that there is no indication that *purposeful* self-disclosure of factual data is at all integral to treatment, rather it is the analyst's *unwitting participation* in an enactment or a self-disclosure that reconfigures analytic develop-ments. Those analysts more critical of self-disclosure state that purpose-ful self-revelations may disrupt the necessary asymmetry in the thera-peutic relationship (Greenberg 1991, Hamilton 1990, Hoffman 1992).

In a paper titled "The Role of the Analyst's Inadvertent Self-Revelations," Frank (1997) states that the use of self-disclosure can mean treatment has become too symmetrical and that the analytic discipline has broken down, creating a need to restore a more productive thera-peutic alignment, but he also says it is the analyst's own authenticity that is most important in guiding the therapeutic response. Frank does add that some analysts can disclose more about themselves than others in a productive manner. Kaftal (1997), in opposition, suggests that "the analyst's primary task is to provide a unique transitional space in treatment in which the 'reality' [authenticity] and 'not reality' [inauthenticity] of both participants are subsumed by the overriding ethic of interpersonal play" (p. 344), which must take place in a safe context. Kaftal goes on to say that to speak of self-disclosure versus authenticity presupposes an objective stance on the part of the analyst, as though the analyst could internally measure the reality of what is authentic, adding that "the issue [in self-disclosure] should be not the analyst's self-revelation but the range of relationships of which the analyst is capable, a range that might, in fact, be much broader and deeper than he is capable of in 'reality'" (p. 345). Orange and Stolorow (1998) question why self-disclosure continues to be debated in the literature, believing that "the psychoanalytic family requires of is members the suppression of spontaneity and self-expression" (p. 532).

In an attempt to deepen my relationship with Bianca, to better know her, and to widen the analytic playing field, I let Bianca know the sibling origins of the "other woman" in the room. As I told her the story, much in the manner I've written about it here, I realized she was receptive and interested. She listened intently, interjecting sameness and difference whenever she felt a kinship with my narrative. On finishing, we both sat in silence until she said there was something else she wanted. Could she bring in her camera to take a series of pinhole pictures of me? "What would you do with my picture," I asked. "Paint it, eventually," she answered. "Why, what'll you do with it after it's painted?" I had the horrible thought that her friends would visit her house, she'd show them a picture of her analyst, and that would set off the tone for a party. Still, after my initial reaction, I understood she wanted more than my illusion. She wanted to keep me, to make an internalization of the analyst in a very real, artistic way. I interpreted this to her and she made an interpretation in response, "You're very eccentric," she said, and related a fantasy she had about my life that was quite accurate, and I realized she'd been taking mental pictures of me for quite some time. In the next session, for the first time since she began treatment, she brought in her photography portfolio, and I saw her ability to capture beauty and sadness and knowing another on film. Bianca had received many artistic awards, particularly when she was in her twenties and working on her masters. However, after receiving a grant to paint and photograph in Europe she felt undeserving, rejected the award and her art, and then decompensated, aided by drug and alcohol use.

For now, I am to be Bianca's subject and she mine. We will take an image of each other, create an illusion either on paper or through photography. We will use our own particular artistic mediums to capture the other, the self, and our relationship—our family photo album. To my mind, we have found a way to live in each other's home in fantasy and reality.

7

The Tango, Female Fetish, and Phobia

Danced in an embrace, the male Tango dancer indicates through silent gestures that he wants his partner to dance a different step than the one he himself is dancing. He presses her back or signals her right hand with his left. His limbs, as well as hers, seem to move independently, as if detached from the dancers' bodies. The torsos stay still while the legs perform perhaps unrelated movements, sometimes as if to escape one's own body, sometimes the other's, sometimes to exaggerate sameness or difference from the other, more frequently to objectify—to limit intimacy. The dancers know that, from the outside, others experience them as together, mutual, entwined within coupled performance. The tango is danced to express mutual pain and in a way the dancers' experience of each other tears them apart. Still, they dance their emotions, feel the differences in each other's movement, include and exclude their audience as they communicate in unspoken, coded messages that others struggle to read and understand. Power and surrender are the dominant themes of the suggestive tango: one partner advances while the other never escapes the embrace.

My patient's message posted on-line at the web site read: "I am a non-disabled woman and have found that I have an affinity or particular attraction for women with disabilities, specifically amputees. I realize that my statement/admission may be construed as objectification and, in fact, some may think that I am offensive. I apologize in advance. It should, however, be understood that people do not choose how we feel or whom we have feelings for."

I can't say that I chose to become infatuated with tango dancing, rather it happened as I struggled with each step, and my feelings for it intensified as I learned to let the music pulsate within me. In dancing the tango, I find myself desiring my partner's silent instruction, his control, his manipulation of my body and mind. I perform different movements and think of little more than my torso twisting, the toe of my shoe scraping seductively along the wood floor, my hair flicking as I quickly move my head in another direction. I watch my silhouette in the mirror and am excited by the emotions expressed in my loss of control to another's instruction. I am seduced, seductress, and surrendered. For a few late nights a week, I enter a fantasy as well as a reality different from that my consulting room affords. My body releases not only the residue of my own daily emotions, but also the burden of my patients' narratives. I am free, momentarily—for an hour or two—to emote through my body. Here my passion for dance, with its inherent sexuality, is socially acceptable albeit a little eccentric. My patient's sexualized fetishistic passion for amputees is not. This got me to thinking, where does the union of relationship begin? What is the conviction of the body to the mind, of phobia to fetish, of dancing to fantasy?

The lyrics in tango music communicate self-absorbed distraction and the emotional isolation felt in abandonment and lost love. In watching tango dancers, the audience realizes they symbolize lovers or former lovers. We see that the dancers are establishing intimate links or are showing us that their intertwining indicates separation. In other words, each body divorces itself from its own limbs as well as from the embrace of the partner, and also, paradoxically, merges into the space of the other. Tango dancing personifies separation, isolation, and rupture, all the while performing for the audience the antithesis of tenderness and unity. Watching dancers perform this control of isolated and split-off limbs, the audience understands the dancers are only able to loosen the body by first making sure of—or questioning—the wholeness of it (Taylor 1998).

JUNE

June has been in analysis for five years yet it is only within the last year that I learned about her fetish toward amputees. For a long time, she simply didn't use the word amputee. I guessed the word after a long struggle to piece together the missing parts of her sexual behavior. When I finally said it, after I finally understood it, she released a moan of gratitude or relief that her secret was known by another.

A few times a week, late at night, June logs on to the Internet to view pictures of amputees. She finds herself unable to resist, motivated by some unknown, mysterious sexual desire. She sits for hours looking at different pictures of men or women. June masturbates while voyeuristically viewing the amputated stump, and considers her attraction to the stump as phallic in origin. She also fetishizes the wheelchair and crutches, with or without amputees. All three can evoke sexual arousal, masturbation, and orgasm. June identifies as lesbian, though her desire for amputees has no gender lines.

Although I had only become aware of June's fetish well into the treatment, I knew from the beginning that she had a pigeon phobia. Early on, she sufficiently described them so that I was able to guess the word "pigeon." She had been unable to say "pigeon" or "amputee" out loud. June is terrified that a pigeon might fly close to her, get caught in her long hair, or brush against her. She fears looking at their faces, believing they look evil, with intent to harm. Worse yet, she cannot look at them from behind, insisting they look too phallic and ugly—a description similar to what attracts her to the amputee. Her most powerful fear, however, is of getting pigeon feathers caught in her throat and choking to death. She can't watch a movie with pigeons in it, read a magazine if it has pictures of pigeons, or even look at a lone pigeon feather on the ground.

June's phobia reveals almost nothing about the object except that pigeons have the power to frighten her. Questions about pigeons and her associated fantasies and interpretations evoke very little except a report that she is familiar with pigeons—where they lurk, how they move, directions they fly. She is also replete with phallic interpretations of pigeons gathered from many years with previous therapists. While

June's constant vigilance against pigeons eliminates almost any repetition of confrontation with the terror-filled object, her fear creates a need for her to repeatedly reassure herself that she can avoid it.

A phobia, in a sense, shows the capacity of the body to be controlled by fantasy, a conviction of the body to the mind. It is as though the phobic object is directing the subject's body, and the body waits in anticipation of the terror. According to her, June is the victim of the terror-laden pigeon, not the one who terrorizes. Yet in all her avoidance of the object, she sustains a relationship to it that is fueled by her terror. Her phobia provides her with power and concurrently violates and disempowers her, an emotional dissonance I see as shared by those who dance tango. What is ordinary becomes an emotionally charged symptom, "like an unconscious estrangement technique . . . not so much an erotization of danger but [rather an erotization] of significance" (Phillips 1993, p. 109).

For some people, phobic terror feels comparable or even similar to sexual excitement, and maintaining a fear- or hate-object may be as important as creating a love-object; for them, the hate-object creates an opportunity to keep a love-object. In this case, June's pigeon phobia directs her hate away from her anxiety-riddled mother onto pigeons, allowing her to keep the opportunity to be lovingly related to her mother, who I will discuss later. This redirection of emotion is essential if the individual cannot tolerate her hate of the object, or recognize the hate as her own. Recognizing one's own hate (or another's hate) creates a sense of control in the outside world; not being able to do so means one exists in a more terrifying environment. "A phobia is a conviction that bad things are unspeakable and therefore that the unspeakable is always bad" (Phillips 1993, p. 112).

June's phobia developed when she was 8 years old. It seems to have coincided with her father's losing his position in a large corporation and the family's moving south for a job opportunity, and began after her mother allowed a pigeon to fly close to her. One other event that may have powerfully influenced her development was an operation on June's uterus when she was just a few years old. This would have included a hospital stay and separation from family members—perhaps June's first experience with separation or isolation from a body part.

June's mother is a very anxious woman, quite sarcastic, an intellectual, and a person who bemoans her life whenever her needs are denied. She is also extremely intrusive, demanding merger with all family members, particularly June. Actually, June's parents, believing themselves infertile, adopted a son six years before June was born. This adopted older brother has not spoken to June's mother for years; he refers to her as deranged, demanding, and crazy, and relates only to June and the father.

When I first began working with June she would often talk about being forced to visit her family. Her mother would first search for her by leaving multiple phone messages, then she would call June's friends looking for her and talk about June to these friends. When she finally found June, her mother would wail about missing her and worry about soon being dead and gone. On arriving at her parents' home, June would swallow a few of her mother's tranquilizers (her mother gave them to her) and wash the pills down with glasses of whiskey (which her mother handed her). She felt she could tolerate her mother's intrusiveness after anesthetizing herself, cutting off self from body. This frightened me no end, as I envisioned June brain-dead from the combination of drugs and alcohol, by her mother's hand.

June's father seems to be a passive figure who she refers to as "my mother's husband." He is perhaps the only person June admits to hating. Interestingly, she says she can have satisfying sex with men. To my mind, she has sex with men because she dissociates, she splits off emotionally in order to leave her body alone with its own experience.

As I mentioned earlier, when June was a few years old she had an operation on her uterus. She remembers liking the nurses at the hospital and receiving special privileges from her family. I have often wondered what aspects of her phobia and fetish were fueled by this experience. June became particularly close to her brother during her recovery and to this day still considers her adopted brother to be more paternal than her father. For example, in one particular incident that occurred in her adolescence she credits her brother for saving her life. In this story, June tells about becoming anorexic and letting her weight drop to less than ninety pounds. After one more aborted evening meal, June's brother pulled her away from the dinner table and her uneaten food and beat her quite violently. Her parents were unaware of this and June has maintained this sadomasochistic secret. I wonder about the erotization of this event, of its similarity to the erotic stimulation around her phobia and its relation to her developing her sexual fetish of amputees, wheelchairs, and crutches.

FETISHISM

In Freud's (1905a) paper, "Three Essays on the Theory of Sexuality," he wrote that the choice of fetish was determined by sexual experiences of childhood, and that it was related to the constitutional predisposition of the individual. A fetish was a substitute for the mother's phallus where the child (Freud specifically referred to the boy), was unwilling to believe mother did not have a phallus. A fetish, therefore, protects the child from the threat of castration, and from the threat of homosexuality—meaning that sex with a woman involved him with a phallic woman.

According to Freud, fetishism came about when the child's development was interrupted by the trauma of seeing the female genitals; in other words, it was an obsessional objectification of a particular trauma concerning the oedipal constellation. Freud thought a fetish was only pathological if it was substituted for an actual sexual object. Consequently, a fetish was defensive, as it allowed individuals to disavow a frightening situation or object "by excising those features of reality that triggered for them the original fantasy of danger" (Reed 1996, p. 1153). Certainly, June's fetish toward amputees could easily be understood in traditional terms—that is, her hospitalization and surgery created a defensive reaction to a childhood perception of a lost female body part. Her hospital stay included excessive nurturance and attention of caretakers, and it could be assumed that she sexualized these events as they took place during the oedipal phase in her development.

What I find interesting is that Freud's notion about fetish is not antithetical to his ideas on phobias: "Freud's view invited an illicit reenactment from the past, a place where, quite unwittingly, a memory could be cast. . . . What the phobic [individual] fears, unconsciously, is not only the replication of this truant past, but its modification in ways that cannot be anticipated. If one loses the replica one might lose the original" (Phillips 1993, p. 107). It almost seems as though the fetish trauma might lead to either a fetish or phobia symptom—and in June's case, it led to both.

Rank (1922) and Sachs (1923) specifically related fetish to phobia saying that perversions represent the child's defensive attempt to protect against anxieties by a process of excessive libidinization. This libidinization is then obsessively directed toward particular parts of the body (or particular objects) that feel threatened in fantasy. In addition, this fantasy can disguise a particular libidinized object or subject through its displacement in the fetish or phobic choice. It can also be the mode of gratification itself that is libidinized, and not the objects or subjects the individual believes to be in danger in the fantasy. From this perspective, in her phobia June libidinized the lost object or subject or the lost limb in the fetish as the loss of the pigeon that suddenly flies away without warning.

Glover (1932b) in his paper, "Perversion-Formation and Reality-Sense," related fetishism to certain obsessional phobic states that he considered negative fetishistic phenomena in the oedipal phase of the child's development. He thought phobias could alternate with an erotic fetishistic interest in the same parts of the body. Both phobias and fetishes represent the contracted range of an expanding reassurance system in response to excessive anxiety. In other words, both phobic and fetishistic obsessions defend against the fear of castration or loss.

In Gillespie's 1940 essay on fetishism, he emphasized that sadism originated in a mixture of pregenital disturbances from oral and anal trends. He thought both the use and the type of inanimate object were determined by a defense against sadism that could destroy the object. The contribution of sadism to fetishism, as well as to phobia, is an important concept in the literature. To my mind, sadism is integral in the development of both fetish and phobia. The desire to hurt, punish, humiliate, and degrade are essential aspects of the individual's fantasy of controlling her own body as well as the object/objectified body. Certainly, June is quite sadistic in her sexual relations with women, whom she swears she "fucks like a man" and whom she leaves before her lovers realize they are alone in the bed.

In Bak's (1968) paper "The Phallic Woman: The Ubiquitous Fantasy in Perversions" he stated that in perversions a substitution of sexual, perverse solutions was developed via regression in order to safeguard the object from the child's aggression. The fetish was a defensive result of separation anxiety and identification when the child erotized the phallic mother. While this makes sense to me, I disagree with an earlier companion paper written by Bak (1956) in which he differentiated perversions from sadomasochistic perversions; the latter, he believed, were when the object was immobilized and actually tied down with ropes. He thought this was due to the individual's clinging to the fear that the object would move away.

To my mind, sadomasochism isn't just tied to the use of ropes. Some form of sadomasochism is evident in all fetishes and all phobias. Perversions of fetish and phobia inherently exist as the arch between sadism and masochism. They are what hold sadism and masochism together, and this is what makes them frequently indistinguishable, inseparable as fuel from fire and indeterminable as to which begets the other. June contends that the fetishist feels like victim/victimizer, and that as a phobic individual, she constantly struggles with love–hate and masochistic-sadistic punishment, either of the self through her own behavior, or through the other's mutual or seduced involvement.

In Greenacre's (1979) paper entitled "Fetishism," she stated that the fetish is a makeshift defense against an usually strong castration complex—one so strong that an illusion of actual castration is easily aroused and experienced as a body sensation. I agree with Greenacre's reference to body sensation, but I disagree with her differentiation between fetishes that are sexual and those that are not. For instance, in an earlier paper Greenacre (1960) said that those fetishes that are not sexual are related to separation anxiety.

> It has been especially clear that in women neurotic fetishistic practices might retain still active elements of the intense masculinity complex which continues to interfere with adequate sexual responsiveness. It is probable that in both sexes, the fetishistic use of [and here Greenacre is referring to her clinical example of the patient who fetishizes pills, she says] . . . contains, and defends against, strong

infantile dependence on the mother and wish for the breast, and similarly may interfere with adequate mature sexual functioning. [p. 196]

But, separation anxiety need not exclude sexual issues, and as sensual beings, it seems difficult to decide where and when sexuality factors into another person. Sexuality is present in all issues, just as some level of sadomasochism is evident in all of us.

In a more recent paper, Richards (1990) wrote in reference to an essay by Hermine Hug-Hellmuth titled "A Case of Female Foot or More Properly Boot Fetishism." Richards specifically addresses the problem of psychoanalysts not recognizing fetish and perversions in women since this prohibits any opportunity to analyze them. She wonders if this lack of psychoanalytic recognition protects women from the social condemnation of having perversions.

Richards (1990) also laments that because analysts don't look for fetish in the women they treat, this would result in treatment failures in the analysis of such symptoms in women. These are Richards's most salient points: Why don't we look for fetishistic behaviors in women, and why aren't our female patients more forthcoming? Why didn't I know about June's fetish until four years into the treatment? There is still a powerful prejudice against women as sexual subjects and even less acceptance for women having sexual perversions.

Kaplan (1991), in her book *Female Perversions*, states that the fetish is emotionally designed to represent absences and losses of every kind, meaning it is not just phallic castration. Kaplan includes vagina mutilation anxiety as a basis for fetish and this specifically speaks to June's early hospital experience. Kaplan also includes "castrations, deprivations, separations, illnesses, abandonments, annihilations, and deaths—as well as representing the powers that can diagnose, protect, ameliorate, heal, remedy, fix, and resurrect. The sexual fetish is . . . a versatile memorial" (p. 122). She suggests that phobias are "a fearful avoidance of situations and places that symbolize situations and places where a [woman's] vengeful feelings might be acted out" (p. 174). Unfortunately, Kaplan separates the object of obsessional attraction (the fetish) and the object of obsessional fear (the phobia), as though they have little to do with each other. As I indicated earlier, for me, these are only opposite ends of the same perverse obsessional pole, different symptoms of what is in some cases the same trauma.

A more postmodern feminist view of fetish is proposed by Apter (1991), who defines fetish using a gynotextual language. She suggests that the sexual fetish can stand in for "lover, parent, child, or female double, the female fetish belongs to an erotic economy of severance and disappropriation, itself less fixed on a fiction of castration anxiety" (p. 122). Apter cites Mary Kelly's work in *Post-Partum Document* (1985), in which Kelly maintains that with the female fetish castration anxiety is displaced by the gynocentric notion of "loss, fluids, and ghostly stains . . ." (p. 122). For Apter, as for Kelly, "the transgressively eroticized mourning of missing love objects becomes substantial in its own right [as the origin of fetish], weaned from supraphallic explanation" (p. 122).

Apter (1991) also refers to Freud's 1938 paper "Splitting of the Ego" and here I think she ties together fetish and phobia, although it's interesting that she does so by citing Freud's remarks:

> when faced with a conflict between the instinct's demand and reality, the child may select not to chose between them, opting instead for a means of satisfying both sides. . . . [E]verything has to be paid for in one way or another, and this success is achieved at the price of a rift in the ego which never heals but which increases as time goes on. The two contrary reactions to the conflict persist as the centerpoint of a split in the ego. [pp. 130–131]

An idealized fetish symbol may rise up on one side and a devaluation of the real [the phobic object], occur on the other.

In coming to understand the origins of phobia and fetish, it is interesting to observe the way that even contemporary psychoanalytic literature routes back and through traditional explanations of them. Is there something inherently different about fetish and phobia that lends traditional interpretations to them? My understanding of fetish and phobia has been developed within a more relational, contemporary approach (see Richards 1996) within clinical treatment. It's not the patient's mind that takes precedence in such treatments, but the patient's body that explains theory and clinical application, and in these instances it takes the therapist's use of her own body to interpret personal experience to her own mind.

BODY EXPERIENCE AS THERAPEUTIC ACTION

"The music starts," he says. "There is passion in the tremor of the violin and in the syncopation of the accordion and yet the dancers are not immediately caught up in a fury of orgasmic flicks and twists." The words of my dance instructor reverberate in my mind as I feel the sensations in my body, "Tango dancers begin slowly" he says, "feeling, familiarizing, testing, yielding. Slowly entranced, the dancer's defenses to the tango are lowered. There is exchange of power and control, submission, yielding, exchanges—these all have their technical merit. Over time the dancers are taken in, taken over, controlled by their passions, aggressions, and defenses, which are now contained in the tango." My dance instructor continues, "It is the *nature of the dance* that makes tango an inner communication between partners and allows the relationship of the dancers within the tango to be studied from without" (Poucher 1999, personal communication).

June e-mailed me, writing: "Well, the hell with keeping it all inside. I'll tell you something about pigeons and amputees. Pigeons, I have rarely seen straight on. Amputees, in pictures, I have seen straight on. My focus is extraordinary when it comes to amputees. The image feels quiet; the quiet after the storm. Pigeons are the terror before the terrible. Pigeons are the before and amputees are the after."

She writes, "Amputees and pigeons have so much energy and power attached to them. The amputee energy is reined in, yet utterly powerful and knowable. The pigeon's energy is chaotic, confused, and unknowable. I want to be close to and fuck the amputee. I want to throw up upon seeing the pigeon. The amp and I are equal because we are both in a state of vulnerability. Arousal is vulnerability. Mutual need. The mutual dependence is out in the open, so neither one of us will betray the other. I will talk about this all with you. It's true that I am sometimes difficult. Well, you've certainly put a lot of time and thought into me. What more do I need? I mean . . . am I waiting for? It's now or later; might the hell as well be now. Remember that show, *This Is Your Life*? Okay, you be Ralph Edwards and I'll be the celebrity guest. Anyway, being phobic is like living a painting or a poem. Symbolism abounds. Stuck inside a dream."

I wondered, what is the experience of living a painting or a poem? Is it like a fantasy experience? Is it a relational balance between environmental and endogenous forces, a mind–body involvement? I remember going to my initial dance class. A mirrored ball hung in the center of the ceiling, lights flickered around the edge of the room, dancers glided across the floor, each mysteriously knowing the other's intentions. My instructor whispered that I was a quick study and that this would be my problem, because I could be taught and dance on before I completely understood the movement or instruction. He asked what I wanted from learning to dance. My dissociated response surprised me, and so I kept it to myself: I wanted to be controlled by the dance, by another who would provide me with an experience of a different communication of affect. In hindsight, what I was desiring was a connection to or understanding of body sensations that, as a new dancer, I could not as yet contain in my mind.

During one tango lesson, I realized that I had become attuned to my instructor's touch and was dancing through body response rather than by cognitively anticipating a combination of dance steps. While I was aware of what I saw around me, my surroundings were felt as an inner experience, an outer world internalized. Each step moved the feelings further inside, as opposed to emotionally stepping outside myself. I did not feel dissociated. Rather, the experience felt all-encompassing, engaging a certain wholeness, an enclosure or containment of separateness and difference into merger with another.

After I had written a few pages of this chapter, I went on my winter vacation, which is my usual group bicycling tour of another country. This particular trip was different for me, in that it was on a mountain bike on dirt roads in a jungle in a Third World country, and I am used to biking on paved roads in New Jersey. At the end of the trip, my back bicycle wheel hit a rock and I flew into the air only to crash down onto the bike seat. I fractured my pelvic bone and was left to return home on crutches to finish writing about my patient who, among other things, has a crutch fetish. My tango life was temporarily interrupted as I moved about my office on wooden crutches, wounded physically and narcissistically in my temporary handicap. I found myself entirely caught up in my body, watching my muscles disappear, feeling weakened, exhausted, and totally unable to tolerate my physical state.

One day I wondered aloud about June's experience of my being on crutches. "How much body needs to be there?" she responded. "A head? That's all." She then told me one of her favorite movies is *Boxing Helena* (1993), a film about a man who captures a woman who obsesses him, and, in order to keep her prisoner, cuts off her limbs, slowly mutilating her until she is little more than necessary organs. She said, "Amputeeism is forever, just like death. I'm aroused by the physical limitations of the amputee." June continued, "I found myself masturbating to *Boxing Helena* repeatedly. I don't remember how many times I saw it. Did you see the movie *Crash* (1996)? There was an amputee in it and characters in the movie would fuck bleeding body parts after car crashes. This desire of mine is a mystery to me. It's a thing I don't know. It's like living with a stranger inside of me."

What is the experience of living with a stranger inside? I have no reference point, no sameness with this mind–body state. All of my otherness contains elements of my self. As June spoke about her fetish, I felt disgusted, ill, repulsed. I found myself fantasizing—dancing off into my mind as she narrated her sexual desires toward amputees. I could not tolerate listening to her sexual involvement with this fetish. Her discussion about dismemberment in the movies made me sick. I remembered, as she spoke, that I had once tried to watch *Boxing Helena* and found I could not sit still after I realized the main character was about to be mutilated by amputation. I hadn't thought about this scene for years, but I still felt shaken and disturbed by the image and now I couldn't seem to get the scene—or the anxiety related to it—out of my mind. Yet I knew I had to find a way of listening, of tolerating my feelings of being nauseated by her story. June was not being aggressive in telling her story, she was anguished and shamed as she spoke. She was desperately attempting to talk about her involvement with fetish and her own self-disgust in doing so.

It was during one of these agonizing and nauseating analytic hours on June's fetish that I realized I had been fantasizing about my dancing lessons, at first in an unconscious and then conscious attempt to remain in the room with her. I wondered how my fantasies were intermingling with hers—information somatically retrieved by the other in affective communication of subjective experience. I found myself tangoing on, in an altered mind–body state, as I listened to June describe her sexual experience as she watched a man mutilate a woman's body in *Boxing Helena*, and watched a man have sex with an amputated, bloody limb in the movie *Crash*. The more she spoke, the more I fantasized dancing to the tango, surrendering my psyche-soma to particular movements of isolation of body parts from torso and embraced merger with another in different directions. Were we in a sense co-creating an inner-world experience, or movement through outer-world sameness/difference, masochism/sadism, and desire/disgust?

My experience of her narrative felt as if I had a conscious desire for a projective identification experience, which, I believe, would turn the unconscious defense of projective identification into something else. More accurately, it was a co-created body experience of another's affect-laden communication that could not be tolerated by the listener. It seemed important to experience a body-to-body communication in the hopes of explaining to myself what June was experiencing and to allow the possibility of translating her emotional state into verbal representations that I could tolerate. In essence, I found a potential space (Winnicott 1971) where I could listen to June's desires of sex with amputees, contain her desperate desire for wholeness, and translate the hidden affect to her.

It is in potential space that imagination and fantasy develop in dialectic with reality. In the absence of reality there is only fantasy, and when the dialectic between reality and fantasy becomes limited in order to avoid meaning through denial or in dissociation, as when there is a "splitting of the ego" (Freud 1927), there is fetishism. It was June, along with my "twoness" (Winnicott 1958) that created the third—potential space. Within our intersubjective sphere of metaphor, symbols, and illusion, June and I filled in missing puzzle pieces denied through her mind-reality and perceived in my body-fantasy. Our unity, our created otherness in potential space, our "nature of the dance" in its thirdness all helped to germinate the seeds of June's development into a separate subject.

Stolorow and Atwood (1992) in a chapter entitled "The Mind and the Body," state that for some patients there are different groups of experience that may highlight a disunity of mind and body. Typically, the patient was characterized by a childhood identification with some external view of the self, experienced from a critical perspective. "This identification is so complete that the sense of the self as an embodied subjectivity is eclipsed by an externally situated view of self-as-object" (p. 48). This experience develops from the child's interactions with the caregiver who insists on the child's meeting expectations beyond the child's developmental ability. In attempts to maintain the needed bond to the caregiver, "the child abandons her own unmirrored experience and embraces an outside perspective in its place. This accommodation may result in a sense of being located outside one's body; the body then becomes the focus of critical scrutiny and evaluation and often of intense shame and self-consciousness" (p. 48). In June's case, her sense of self may be located outside her own body and that body could be experienced as the amputee's body—or perhaps her body is experienced as the missing parts or limbs of the amputee. In my fantasy or countertransference, perhaps June located her sense of self in my body to contain her narrative, along with her shame and her own disgust of her attraction to amputees. In other words, she used the capacity of my body to control her fantasy, as did I as we slowly began to dance in potential space.

The first steps in our *cabeceo* started a while ago, and began after a long silence. June spoke about being excessively sexually excited by paraplegics. "I watched the Barbara Walters interview with Christopher Reeve and got very aroused by it. What I found most sexual was that his wife helped him. Every time she helped him I could feel myself becoming aroused. There's this old *Penthouse* magazine that I've read and reread. In it there's a naked spread of female amputees. I kept wondering [she said], What is their sex like? How do disabled people have sex? I'm dying to know how it gets done. My fantasy is that both people, the amputee and the other person, are both aroused. I think it must feel very mutual . . . everybody is equal in bed. Sometimes I've had sex with people who have scars. I like to just masturbate myself on the scar. If I had sex with an amputee, I'd masturbate on the stump."

I cannot feel empathy toward her or with this statement. I feel repulsed and want the visual and the visceral away from me. I know I should want to hear more about her experience, but I cannot formulate a comment geared to further exploration, I only have a desire to silence her, to cut off her voice. I want to make her desire only nondisabled people.

I cannot tolerate my own thoughts, I am disgusted by them. I begin thinking about the homeless woman who begs on the corner, seated in a wheelchair, exposing her stump below the knee. June has told me she often talks to this woman, buys her coffee, makes her comfortable, chats with her. I have always avoided her. I feel disgust at my avoidance of this homeless woman. In a sense, I've created an emotional identification or resonance with my patient's disgusted experience of her own fetish. Yet, I followed her *marca*, her lead, as she spoke about isolated body parts, a splitting off of limbs, as she narrated her part in our developing dance. My *figura*, or following, my independent movements with this dance seemed signaled by her voice, a left hand of sorts speaking a ruptured communication of limbs separated from torsos danced in disgust.

I felt ill as I listened to June's narrative. Was I lost in my own disgust? Was my imagination taking her fantasy further than she might have? I began to hate her as I stared at her. My aggression peaked and I felt it racing through my body, realizing that it seemed to clear my view of her. I watched her stroke her chest bone. How small she looked on my couch, how pretty her hair, how soft her skin seemed. I wondered, why isn't she crying? I thought, I want her to cry right after I scream at her to stop.

I am full of conflicting emotions and find myself wondering how I would look if my hair were a long as hers. How would it look moving about my face as I dance? Would I pull it up, pile it on top of my head? Is my face as narrow as hers? How would I look dancing if I had some of her features? What is that dance combination? How do I move? I can feel my instructor's hand placed on my back, indicating my next danced opportunity. I'm dancing—moving, feeling my body. Whose feeling is this? I'm gliding along the floor, sliding from heel to toes and back. I feel light, excited, I fantasize seeing the floor swirl beneath me.

Have I defended against her narrative by fantasizing dancing away? Or have I experienced a somatic understanding of something that she experiences with her amputees? "Do you feel lightheaded as you talk about sex with amputees? Is the room swirling? Do you see body shapes dancing about in your mind? Are you aroused, excited, stimulated?" I use my body's experience to inform my response, although I am aware there is more involved than just affective attunement or projective identification; this is a different emotional mutuality of metaphor and illusion.

I wonder if my own fantasy isn't a refuge against disgusting imagery, a dissociation, a defense. Is this her aggressive pathology or mine, or are we both just merged in feelings of shame? While my disgust may be part of the problem, I also consider it could be part of the solution. Disgust creates victimization, but it may also empower the self against the stimulus that creates it (Miller 1993). Perhaps June was looking for my handicap, my limitations, maybe she amputated my experience of intimacy with her, but I was beginning to think and feel that she amplified it. With hindsight, I realize she had unconsciously asked me to dance something different than what she verbally indicated. Our independence of each other was to create a third, a nature of the dance, a potential space. Our unrelated bodies of different emotional narratives were to embrace and dance steps of exclusion and difference, fetish and phobia, and in so doing our agreement created an inclusion of the other, a sameness of shared emotion through different, yet mutually experienced illusion.

I told June of my metaphor, the illusion of dancing along with her narrative, my experience of being with her body in danced movement, of the control, domination, and alternating surrender that I experienced in following her lead. I also told her of my repulsion, and how it stood next to my desire to understand her subjectivity in connection to amputees. We shared our intimate experiences with each other as she, over many months, began to express concern for me as a whole, separate individual who was capable of feeling like her, but who did not have the exact feelings as her own. She began to experience herself as a separate subject in our "threeness" of symbol, symbolized, and interpreting subject.

In the last few months, June has developed a loving, sexual relationship with a woman who has a successful career. It is her first long-term relationship with a woman who has a richly developed social and professional life.

In Aron and Anderson's (1998) book *Relational Perspectives on the Body*, Aron writes in the chapter titled "The Clinical Body and the Reflexive Mind" about self-reflective functioning (based on Bach's [1985, 1994] understanding of reflective self-awareness of self-subjectification and self-objectification of self and other's thoughts and actions). Aron defines self-reflective functioning as "the dialectical process of experiencing oneself as a subject as well as of reflecting on oneself as an object" (p. 4). A related notion is that of "mentalization," a term used by Fonagy and Target (1985, 1996, 1998, Target and Fonagy 1996) that is described as an intersubjective theory of mind, developed in the infant–mother dyad where the infant learns to reflect on feelings and thoughts of self and others. Fonagy and Target theorize that self-reflective functioning is the core of self-structure. Self-reflective functioning or mentalization makes possible our understanding of another's state of mind, her intentions, or her experiences as either different or similar to our own in development of selfhood. Where this reflective process has failed, individuals may create representations of mental states through the body, as when emotional pain is expressed through self-mutilation.

I would like to take these ideas in a slightly different direction and add that some individuals may create representations of mental states that are intolerable for another to contain, but that the other-as-analyst creates her own mind–body state that allows containment or holding of the experience of the patient. This may be an intersubjective mind–body experience that communicates affect in an other's body as a different experience—a potential space in which one plays with the idea of being the other while knowing that one is not. In a sense, having my fantasy, dancing with it as a means of emotional interpretation—and then conveying this to the patient—created a sense of feeling like the other in different ways. And my expressed shared experience aided in the creation of June's feeling of concern for another as a whole and separate being who was similar to herself.

This is similar to projective identification, but not exactly. Projective identification is the analyst's emotional experience of the patient's dissociated, denied, or unformulated affect. "Projective identification is the negative of playing; it is a coercive enlistment of another person to perform a role in the projector's externalized unconscious fantasy" (Ogden 1990). Rather, I am referring to the patient's articulated, affect-laden data that cannot be contained or tolerated in the mind of the therapist. The therapist consciously or unconsciously then alters the patient's material through illusion, fantasy, and metaphor as interoperation of conveyed emotion from the patient.

This process can produce a different affective body-state created by the analyst's fantasy that then provides a capacity to tolerate the patient's affect. The patient's articulated affect and action are then experienced through the analyst's mind–body as fantasy that negotiates and translates the patient's data into informed affect. It is a dialectic of symbol, symbolized, and interpreting subject within the self and between therapist and patient. This work has led to a decrease in June's use of fetishism as the dialectic of continually playing in potential space forecloses "nonexperience" (Ogden 1990).

As I see it, June found an affective route in my body that created my understanding of her emotional experience of sexuality and desire, as well as a body experience of limbs disconnected from torso, a floating, swirling sensation merged with domination and control in relation to an other. Initially, my disgust aided in knowing the intensity of her desire, while my desire of something other than her narrative created a capacity within my body to contain my fantasy-experience of her narrative. This is June's experience of her own desires, her fetish, and her phobia, which I somatically felt as I danced the tango in my mind's fantasy.

My dance instructor (Poucher 1999, personal communication) said about the tango: "In adhering to the nature of the dance, the dancers create for each other a means of aggression and a possibility of violation that is more metaphorically than concretely attached to such human virtues as sexuality, love, fear, and abstraction. The dancers agree to make themselves vulnerable. They desire the vulnerability of the partner and fear their own. The dancer is controlled by the thing that creates an aggressive reaction to the partner's vulnerability, but at the same time makes fulfillment of such aggression impossible."

8

Supervision of the Erotic Transference

There is no predesigned template for treatment—neither eroticisms nor angst are scripted between patient and analyst. My own experience as a patient, and now as a therapist, illuminated for me the fact that erotic transference experience is less frequent for most people than other transference developments. I did not develop an erotic transference. My last analyst was a woman in her late seventies who reminded me of my grandmother; together, we struggled with feelings that were antithetical to an erotic transference, such as loss, abandonment, and the imminent death of my mother.

Similarly, for most of my patients, the erotic transference has never developed— for these patients sexuality is not central with regard to their sense of self, life situation, or in their interactions with others. I am not saying these individuals are nonsexual; they are sexual, but sex just isn't a meaningful factor or motivation in these treatments. For them, other issues are more important and these other issues, therefore, become the treatment focus.

There are other patients, perhaps a smaller population of patients, for whom sexuality and loving emotions are crucial in self-definition, in subjective experience, and in relationships. At this time in my own life, I find sexuality and loving emotions seem to matter to me, although not at the expense of other emotions. Still, I have a particular attunement to sexual or loving feeling in myself and with patients who have a similar response to comparable feelings. Writing these chapters on the topic of erotic transference–countertransference developments was an attempt to record these few experiences.

Over the years, a few therapists have sought me out for supervision after hearing or reading one of my papers on erotic transference–countertransference. Sometimes these supervisees have come to address a patient's treatment issues on sexuality. Most supervisees I have worked with, however, have just requested a generalized supervision for all types of patients with all types of problems.

Of those who have come for supervision on patients who have developed an erotic transference, one or two have fled after several meetings. One opted to leave after realizing supervision was actually going to include discussing developments related to sexual and/or loving feelings between therapist and patient. And the other left because she feared erotic feelings might develop between supervisor and supervisee, maybe fearing or wishful that one of us would surrender to the other's domination. Most, however, have stayed for years, and during our work they have discussed a variety of treatment issues, which sometimes include sex and love.

This chapter focuses on a supervision experience in which the supervisee, Dana, wanted to learn how to treat sexual and loving feelings between analyst and patient using a relational approach. One of Dana's male patients, Chad, had developed an erotic transference and she was experiencing an erotic countertransference reaction.

Dana's past two supervisors, both male, had been trained in contemporary, interpersonal analysis. She saw these supervisors in consecutive years, on a weekly basis. The interpersonal theory used by her supervisors focuses on relationships, both internal and external, and views the person as negotiating human interactions in search of satisfactions and securities while always trying to keep anxiety to a minimum.

According to Dana, both supervisors encouraged the interpretation of her patient's loving and sexual feelings as a defense against intimate feelings, and saw these feelings as originating in unresolved issues of the patient's earlier relationships. These supervisors encouraged Dana to work through her patient's erotic feelings and to move the patient into a more treatable neurotic transference. They felt the patient's eroticisms protected the patient, (as well as those individuals in relation to him) not only from his desire for intimacy, but also from his own aggressive feelings.

While there are similarities and differences between the relational theory and interpersonal theory, nonetheless the former is derived from the latter; to contrast and compare the two in greater depth is beyond the scope of this essay. I will focus instead on the Relational Approach, making occasional references to interpersonal theory only in an effort to explain the supervisory experience with Dana.

The Relational Approach differs from Interpersonal Theory in that it is an eclectic combination of contemporary psychoanalytic theories, and bridges other theories that focus on intrapsychic or interpersonal factors, internal or external object relations, and one- or two-person psychologies (Aron 1996). The primary focus in this theory is on relationships, which are regarded as central in human life and development. Relationships include those that are both past and present, internal and external, as well as imagined or real relationships that create the individual's character and pathology. Relational theorists are interested in intrapsychic and interpersonal motivations and meanings regarding the vicissitudes of human development.

What I find most appealing about the relational theory of the mind is that it negates neither the importance of the body nor the importance of sexuality in human development. Interpersonal theory, for example, did not accept drive theory and rejected infantile sexuality, theorizing instead that erogenous zones were not important in individual development. In addition, the interpersonal theorists denied the centrality of the oedipal complex over preoedipal longings, therefore reducing the clinical importance of sexual conflicts (Aron 1996).

The interpersonal theorists' move from sexuality as a motivator in human development was a reaction to the classical drive theory, which focused on intrapsychic aims (those aims usually being sexual) in the individual's desire to reduce internal tension. The Relational Approach, in a shift from interpersonal treatment and somewhat toward drive theory, refocused attention on "temperament, bodily events, physiological responsivity, distinctive patterns of regulation, and sensitivity" (Ghent 1992, p. xviii).

In relational theory, the person is considered an interactional being who struggles within his environment to make contact with others and self in an effort to negotiate his desire to be known and to know an other. "*Desire* is experienced always in *the context of relatedness* and it is that context which defines its meaning" (Mitchell 1988, p. 3). Desire, then refers to both psyche and soma both in knowing an other or knowing the self. Our mind and our body's response in relation, internally or externally, imagined or real are a part of the interactional mix.

Freud's (1915b) notion about the body is evoked in the Relational Approach, in that the sensations of our skin surfaces, touch and feelings, are crucial in forming our images of ourselves (Aron and Anderson 1998), and in knowing an other. This statement conjures up interesting thoughts. I remember a story told by a patient who related an experience of being intimate with her lover. She spoke about lying with him as he gently moved his hands over her body. At first, she thought he was merely stroking her rib cage, feeling the texture of her skin and the warmth of her body. But when she asked, he responded he was touching the contours of her body while thinking about her inner structure. He wanted to experience her external and internal composition; in a sense, it was an attempt to merge and differentiate her being. As they lay next to each other she found they were breathing in a syncronized pattern—his inhaled breath capturing and taking in her exhaled breath. Breathing in her breath was a way of holding her within him for a moment. Inhaling her breath meant maintaining and keeping her inner scent, her flavor, now "known" through his senses. My patient's lover wanted to know the multiplicities of her inner and outer being. He was penetrating through his touch, his gaze, and through breath, as well as holding his emotional illusion of her, in his desire to know her in convergence with her desire to be known and know him through various means of acumen, sagacity, and discernment of inner and outer essence.

Mitchell (1988) was one of the first relational theorists to posit sexuality as fundamental in relationships. He highlighted four points, the first occurring in association with infant and early childhood experiences that are felt by the infant externally and internally. The body organizes early relational experiences for, and to, later interpersonal and intrapsychic events of the person. The second point Mitchell makes is that sexuality means an interpenetration of one body with another, either real or imagined. This interpenetration creates emotional desires that "represent longings, conflicts, and negotiations in the relations between self and others. Sex is a powerful organizer of experience. Bodily sensations and sensual pleasures define one's skin . . . one's boundaries; and the dialectics of bodily and sexual intimacies position one in relation to the other" (p. 103). The third is that body sensations offer up a language or vocabulary for expression of intrapsychic and interpersonal dynamics that includes love/hate, conflict/resolution, pleasure/tension, and suffering/passion. Lastly, the child's experience of exclusion from or inclusion into the parents' sexuality makes metaphoric meaning and motivation in life's struggle to negotiate the interpersonal realms of emotional accessibility or isolation in relation to another.

In a way, relational theory places a pragmatic emphasis on using everything at hand in treatment, as for instance the use of self and other, both the patient's transference and the therapist's countertransference experiences. While all theories recognize transference–countertransference, the Relational Approach places a particular importance on countertransference and the analyst's experience of intersubjectivity in understanding treatment, transference, and the patient. The traditional psychoanalytic notion of abstinence and objectivity in creating insight and interpretation as crucial to cure has been replaced in relational theory by the therapist's reliance on the "real relationship" between self and patient (Philipson 1993).

In addition, the relational theory accentuates intersubjectivity and its focus on recognition of self and other. Benjamin's (1995) concept of intersubjectivity in relational theory highlights the use of transference–countertransference, the patient's as well as the analyst's subjectivity, "the unknowability or knowability of the patient's subjectivity" (p. 24) by the analyst, and the analyst's known or unknown subjectivity. In other words, treatment consists of "the intense scrutiny of the meeting of two minds, each with a multiplicity of its own" (p. 24).

The therapist's subjective experience or countertransference is seen as a therapeutic tool that aids in understanding what the patient is experiencing. When relevant, countertransference or emotional reactions are sometimes disclosed to the patient. The therapeutic "tide is shifting toward the analyst openly expressing emotion, thereby facilitating the patient's healthy pursuits of confirming reality and experiencing shared affect. Rather than frustrating our patients under the assumption that they intend to lead us astray, we now consider seriously that they may instead be leading us in the right direction" (Maroda 1999, pp. 55–56). It is this relational notion of two interacting subjectivities, of a "real relationship," and the importance of body experience and sexuality that factored into the supervision of Dana and into her desire to know her patient.

In beginning supervision, Dana feared her intense loving emotions would cloud her countertransference and prohibit an analysis of her patient's erotic feelings. She was struggling with exploration rather than exploitation, she wondered what was seduction and what was abstinence, she regretted any possible collusion with her patient's desires as well as feared the elimination of her own feelings in her work.

In Dana's previous supervisions, she frequently felt her male supervisors were attempting to protect her male patient from a seductress. Dana also mentioned early on in our work that she had experienced sexual feelings toward one of these supervisors, further complicating the erotic dynamics. She told her supervisor of these feelings, aware of her embarrassment around these desires. He acknowledged her emotions in one of their sessions and supervision moved on. Her supervisor continued to focus on the patient and not on Dana's erotic feelings toward himself.

Supervisors typically handle their supervisees' emotions or transference in this way, no matter what type of feeling is presented. This is done in an attempt to avoid interfering with the supervisee's personal analysis or turning supervision into analysis. As a general rule, the supervisee's transference to the supervisor is not usually interpreted or worked through outside the supervisee's own analysis. Dana was left frustrated at not having her supervisor's help in talking about her erotic emotions toward him. In addition, she continued to feel lost in her loving and sexual feelings toward her patient. As a result she began to withhold from her supervisor much of what transpired emotionally between herself and Chad. Desire, deception, and domination seemed to guide her supervisee experience.

In Dana's second supervision with a male supervisor, she reported that she and this supervisor struggled somewhat aggressively with each other. Their work developed into an impasse with neither having the desired impact on the other. Is this an example of aggression replacing sexuality or defending against it and was Dana sexually attracted to this supervisor as well?

In a didactic supervisory relationship, the supervisee is typically intellectually surrendered to the instructor who imparts knowledge. So why didn't Dana acquiesce to her male supervisors' clinical expertise and learn what they had to teach? One reason might be an oedipal dynamic, in that Dana was trying to protect her male patient from her male supervisors, and she needed to be in control of their influence on her and on her patient. Or was it a wish for merger and fear of separation in that Dana unconsciously wanted to duplicate with her supervisors the erotic feelings she experienced with this particular patient? Or did Dana want to know her patient, as well as have her supervisors know and recognize her subjectivity?

To my mind, what Dana desired was both a didactic and an experiential erotic transference–countertransference relationship with her patient, as well as with her supervisors. She wanted to know her male patient, her self, and also be known by her male supervisors. She still wanted to be known by an other when she chose supervision with me, although perhaps now a bit disillusioned with her desire. However, my being female posed a homoerotic conflict that Dana was not prepared to work through or with in supervision. Homoerotics between heterosexual women are rarely discussed in relation to treatment, and talked about even less in supervision.

In teaching Dana about relational theory and its forays into sexuality and desire, I realized I lean more heavily than most relational therapists do toward the intrapsychic notion of sexuality in relying on Freud's (1905a) first formulation of anaclisis or attachment in infancy. According to LaPlanche and Pontalis (1973), Freud hypothesized that an anaclitic relationship existed between libido and self-preservation. It is this link between "the subject's basing himself on the object of the self-preservative instincts in his choice of a love object" (p. 29) that, for me, highlights the importance of sexuality in intersubjectivity. Freud meant that as the infant attempts to nourish itself and grow, the infant is also gratifying primitive urges at the breast. Sucking at mother's breast is an oral activity and there is a pleasure derived from sucking. Freud (1905a) said, "the satisfaction of the erotogenic zone is associated in the first instance, with the satisfaction of the need for nourishment" (pp. 181–182). In other words, the first object for the infant is mother's breast, which is cathected as the first place for sexual discharge. Consequently, the self-preservative needs have a relationship to the object from the beginning, and sexuality functions in anaclisis or attachment with these needs. Therefore, sexuality exists in the very functioning of bodily activities as well as all sorts of other activities, such as emotional or intellectual activities between individuals. It is the warp and woof of human relatedness and human existence.

I adhere to this notion of sexuality and work with eroticisms and loving feelings between patient and analyst as a matter of course in intimate relations. While many patients I have treated refer to their erotic feelings about others, themselves, and sometimes me, a few patients have never mentioned sex. With this latter group, discussions on this topic are rarely, if ever, brought up. I encourage the patient's musings on having or not having sexual or loving feelings and analyze their response, but in general I am respectful of each individual's personal frame for inner world exploration. This holds true in my work with supervisees as well.

I was hired at a party, actually. It was a gala celebration given by one of the psychoanalytic institutes and all my colleagues were dressed in sequins or suits, making for a rather sexualized atmosphere. I was seated at a table with colleagues when I felt a hand on my shoulder and, turning around, was greeted by Dana, who then moved on. An hour later she repeated the act, but this time lingered longer and after some agitation asked for supervision on a male patient who had developed an erotic transference. I had known about Dana's work with this patient from a paper presentation she made to the candidates in training. She was about to begin her fourth and final year before graduating from the institute.

It was only after supervising her for a year, after which she abruptly terminated, that I later understood her delay and agitation.

In one of our early meetings, Dana related the erotic transference–countertransference developments with Chad. It seems that in their first session, near the end of it, he said he saw her underwear as she sat in her chair. Dana remembered being too embarrassed to respond and remained silent even after she regained her composure. What complicated her reaction was her certainty that he had not seen this. She remains steadfast in this commitment.

The "underwear sighting incident" created the treatment forum for the next few years of sessions together—wordlessness, shame, and being controlled by another were constant triangulations. These triangulations were relived in Dana's supervisions, and the supervisions themselves made up triangulated relationships. This is not to say that Dana and Chad didn't talk; they did, but when the undercurrent was erotic their interactions were stilted. For example, Dana related an incident where Chad had sat wordless for a time, intently staring away from her. Although Dana thought Chad was secreting lustful desires, she could rarely find the words to help him explore this. When she was able to ask, Chad denied his sexual feelings and responded that it was Dana who felt them. Neither of them believed that, she told him, and at times, seemingly shameful, he agreed. Dana's feelings for Chad left her in a similar shameful position; she had wanted to address her feelings in supervision but felt unable to do so. Unsure of how to work with the mutual desire between herself and Chad, she tried to keep treatment relatively still in an effort not to spill her containment of their feelings.

Dana's consulting room seemed sexually charged; both she and her patient appeared to be sexually excited during the sessions, and each was openly denying the libidinal tension between them to the other. Was Dana's experience a projective identification? According to Ogden (1982), projective identification takes place when the patient unconsciously projects feelings into the therapist. The therapist then experiences the patient's emotions as though they were her own inner creation. While this is the most common experience of projective identification, other experiences of it can be a sense of being taken over internally by the patient, or feeling that the patient's unconscious fantasy has actually pressured the therapist to respond with similar affect to the projection. Dana, however, felt her erotic feelings about Chad were her own creation, not his projected creation—she added that she had felt sexually attracted to him the moment she saw him in the waiting room. She thought Chad had had a similar erotic reaction to his first sight of her, too.

When we began working together, Dana was interpreting to Chad the sexual feelings between them as a defense against aggressive feelings toward women, his mother, his girlfriend, and toward her, and treatment appeared at an impasse. Chad was now spending even more of their sessions silent or maybe brooding that his feelings were hindered from expression, and Dana spent much of the session fantasizing being in love with this patient and angry at "nothing being discussed" regarding their erotic feelings.

It was this notion of impasse, of nothing-being-discussed, in a sense, that intrigued me. In my fantasy, Dana and Chad seemed like two high school kids going out on a date, both brimming with adolescent hormones, not knowing how to talk to each other, and feeling self-conscious and inexperienced in the sexualization of proximity. Then I had another fantasy of being trapped in an elevator with a good-looking man. What do you say? Who says what first? Do you say nothing and just look at each other, or look away? It's the very silence that makes it erotic. It's the lack of words—what's not being said—that carries sexual tension.

Before beginning supervision, I remember asking Dana if she felt there was any danger in her enacting her fantasies with Chad and she replied there wasn't. Some therapists might be advised not to enter into an erotic transference–countertransference mix, those specifically who are fearful of sexuality. Dana appeared to be a good candidate for working with erotic feelings because, on the one hand, while she was concerned about eroticisms in treatment, she wasn't afraid of working with them, only inexperienced. On the other hand, and more important in her being a good candidate, Dana's manner has a seductive edge in that there's a relaxed flirtatiousness in her interactions. In a sense, her style and character are sensuous and, as a matter of course, these wind up in the therapeutic mix.

Still, what initially seemed so striking about Dana's clinical presentation in supervision was her level of upset and her agitation. These also appeared to relate to her hesitancy the evening when she had asked for supervision. She seemed to fear being reprimanded or receiving criticisms that would duplicate her past supervisory experiences. She was relieved to know a little about my work and felt comforted that a few of my patients had sexualized feelings about me. I, however, was interested in learning what she had not told the other supervisors, which was what she felt about Chad and had not yet told anyone. I was intrigued with the dynamics created in the intersubjective space between Dana and Chad that had not been verbalized. I wanted to know more about her "nothing-being-discussed" comment, about words as defense or as evocative of potential space.

In starting, we began where she was and with my experience of sitting with her agitation, which felt like being with someone ashamed of sexuality—that is, Chad's and Dana's mutual state. While Dana told her patient's history of being afraid and shamed of having sexual feelings, she added her own shame and fear of professional criticism in having sexual feelings for a patient. She had presented the sexualized feelings between her and the patient to her classmates, to faculty, and to supervisors at her training institute and their response was empathy for a difficult dynamic. It was almost as though Dana had co-created a mental illness or a condition with her patient, and not that her treatment had developed into an intimate and erotic dynamic.

In 1990, Ghent's paper entitled "Masochism, Submission, Surrender," focused on the many complexities of the patient's use of surrender as being an essential element in being known by another. Ghent defines surrender as "conveying a quality of liberation and expansion of the self as a corollary to the letting down of defensive barriers" (p. 108). He goes on to say that the patient longs for surrender, which is "the wish to be found, recognized, penetrated to the core, so as to become real, or as Winnicott put it in another context 'to come into being'" (p. 122).

Ghent (1990) then states that there is an overextending, penetrative aspect of surrender in the desire to truly know and emotionally discover the other. In a sense, there is a desire to experience the other from within the other. Winnicott (1969) refers to this as a "use" of the other, as the individual strives to find the "true other" (p. 125).

Bollas (1986) suggests that surrendering to another is a process and, as such, surrender becomes a necessary element in being known by another. It is in the process of surrendering, according to Bollas, that the self is able to transform. Maroda (1999) takes this notion a step further, saying the process of surrender not only transforms the self, but that

> surrender is *the* self-altering process. In the moment that a person surrenders he or she is irrevocably changed. In [treatment] . . . the "object" is, of course, the analyst, and the "process" is psychoanalysis. The patient surrenders through the medium of the emotional merger with the analyst and their shared regression. But the surrender itself is not to the person of the analyst, but rather a giving over to the patient's own emotional experience—losing herself to herself—within the containing framework of the analytic setting. [p. 54]

Letting go or surrender in treatment links itself with regression in that the transformative experience of altering the self also entails facing losses and fears. For instance, fearing abandonment, isolation, regret, or disgrace within the controlled dissolution of self-boundaries of thera-peutic regression can create a sense of fragmentation, derailment, or distortion of a wish in the service of self-development. Consequently, regression and surrender, both tinged with negativity in common lan-guage, can be progressive forces in therapy. The negativity in both is their shared complement of shame in regard to an unknown presenta-tion of self to an other. There is a humiliating and anxiety-ridden po-tential in any treatment progression that is based on judgment and ex-posure of a private self (Wurmser 1999); new experiences are often accompanied by shame. Still, regression dovetailed with surrender di-rects the patient into his own shape and his own sense of self-as-subject in recognition of other-as-separate—and acts as a creative inner force toward psychic order.

Ghent (1990) states that "The successful use of the object, or being used by the object in the form of surrender, is one's bid at overcoming the fear of the other" (p. 126). This creates an interesting dynamic in treatment in that the therapist must not fear being used by the person surrendering, which means that both the therapist and the patient sur-render to the other's needs. Ghent goes on to say that it is "the success-ful use and surrender, in which both survive and use and have therefore transcended fear of the other, [that] are necessary precursors in the development of love. In fact, a deep sense of love is what is actually felt, in either of these experiences" (p. 126).

Therefore, within the process of surrendering to the other, loving feelings or (the next step) sexual excitement can be expected develop-ments. In desiring love or sexual interaction, each individual is involved in object usage and wishes to surrender to the other in the hopes of being known. This consequence of surrender is the basis of erotic transfer-ence–countertransference developments in treatment.

But what about regression and surrender in the limited situation of supervision? It is usual to think that the supervisee should keep "it" to herself—that is, regress and surrender in your own treatment, not in supervision. When a patient regresses and perhaps acts out in treatment, it is one thing, but when a supervisee regresses and maybe acts out in supervision, it is another, because supervisor and supervisee are col-leagues and often peers. The relationship is frequently quite symmetri-cal, different than the asymmetry between patient and therapist. There is a greater taboo on emotional expression in supervision, and the greater the taboo, the greater the shame. Sexuality or just plain sex is quite shameful since without mutuality, sexual desire that is recounted or ex-perienced in supervision can feel humiliating.

Some of us remember how it was in high school or college when our adolescent sexual desires for a chosen lover of the month were frequently rejected. I remember keeping many of those sexual wishes secret from peers, fearing humiliation if similar feelings were not returned from the chosen other. Shame and secrecy and surrender have much in common.

Morrison (1999) addresses what he considers to be "a *contagious* intensity of shame," or "an *intersubjective matrix* of shame," where "a particular shame experience [stemming from internal sources is evoked in an interpersonal context and is] elicited in *collaboration* with some-one else who is experiencing shame" (p. 322). Morrison thinks of this phenomenon as resonance on the therapist's part with the patient's shame, and sees it as an element of projective identification since it high-lights the patient's dual goal of getting rid of a bad feeling as well as of communicating the bad feeling to the therapist. While I agree with the notion of affective resonance, I disagree with Morrison's including it in projective identification, because that would mean resonance begins with one person and gets projected into another. Rather, in Dana and Chad's situation, theirs was an immediate, mutual, sexual desire and they had to go back to discuss it.

Dana remembers being told by her peers, by faculty she asked, and by supervisors that being able to tolerate Chad's silently communicated sexual stimulation was "brave." At the time, she wanted to announce, "Don't call me brave, it's just being." Dana thought her questions to others about working with erotic transference–countertransference left people stumped, no one had an answer. More frequently, she felt like a seductress, ashamed of her feelings toward Chad.

This got me thinking, what exactly *is* seduction? A common defi-nition is that seduction is the act of leading someone astray, sometimes with sexual intent. Then is it seduction when we physically attract some-one else, or when they attract us? If we see someone walking down the street and they look appealing or intriguing to us, are they being seduc-tive? Is seduction like a proposition, or is it availability?

To my mind, seduction is a way of being, a manner of relating, a sensual particularity, as well as an action that attracts or charms or has alluring qualities. I once watched my 2-year-old nephew cup my sister's face in his hands, look longingly into her eyes, and ask for a desired dessert . . . which he got. Is being seductive also . . . being resourceful?

Freud (1915b) thought the psychoanalytic situation itself created a seduction, in which the patient naturally had erotic feelings for the therapist. "Transference love," he said, "is provoked by the analytic situa-tion" (p. 168). There are two particulars that Freud raised in this tech-nique paper on transference love. One is in regard to honesty; here he said, "psycho-analytic treatment is founded on truthfulness" (p. 164). The other is mentioned in his critique on transference love as resistance: "Can we truly say that the state of being in love which becomes mani-fest in analytic treatment is not a real one?" In considering truthfulness and realness, if Chad experiences Dana as seductive and vice versa is this just defense or is it a truthful response? Isn't it a mistake to inter-pret or make such feelings unreal, that is, to consider transference as just infantile longing? Isn't hiding such feelings dishonest? And, can patient and therapist really hide such feelings from the other or do we just not verbalize them?

I think what makes people seductive is our feeling that they're being real with us. When we're real or honest with others, they feel emotion-ally engaged by the experience, and we have, therefore, been success-fully seductive in that interaction.

Still, successfully seducing someone feels shameful to those thera-pists who work with the erotic transference–countertransference. Is any therapist exempt from these emotions, except through defense? I remem-ber the time I first experienced sexual feelings toward a patient. He was an attractive young man who put himself through a masters program in business by hustling or prostituting himself to men. I began treating him during the time when the first wave of AIDS hit the gay population in the mid-1980s, when I was in my own psychoanalytic training. This patient was on the couch for six sessions a week, with two sessions on Fridays, one in the morning and one in the evening, for many years. He would lie with his arms stretched out toward my chair behind him.

The supervisor I had at that time, ironically a male who used Inter-personal Theory, thought I was being seductive because I let this patient talk about his sexual exploits without interpreting this as aggression. I explained to the supervisor that when I interpreted aggressive origins, the treatment became explosive and threatened the patient's emotional stability.

Interpreting aggression didn't feel like an honest response to me or to my patient. Something else seemed more real between us and I believe it was the intensity of our feelings for each other. In a sense, I surren-dered to the seductive stories Joe told as he stroked his outstretched arms, and in that way I was seduced as well as seductive as I let his words stimu-late me. Is this collusion? Sure, but not entirely.

Collusion is another negatively weighted word in psychoanalytic language; sometimes it means a merged or symbiotic level of not know-ing or denial with an other. But, collusion can also be progressive and stimulate therapeutic action. Collusion is a necessary ingredient in intersubjectivity in the development of intimacy—people infer collusion when they feel like-minded and emotionally related to another. Sometimes collusion creates the meeting point of similarity or twinship where self-in-relation begins.

Collusion in association with seduction can create a playground for affective communication. It can be a milieu for developing potential space. For example, had I interpreted Joe's desire to control me through his sexualized narratives, he most likely would have responded aggressively, taking us into something that did not feel real. What was real was the intensity of his emotions as he related interactions with others—and his narrative and the affect surrounding these stories was sexual. This was real. The words didn't matter; actually, they were sexual, but they could have been any words. Words were secondary to the primary communication of mutual affect that we experienced. Joe said he felt known and accepted by me. He didn't change his narrative because he hadn't entered treatment in order to amend *my* psychoanalytic language. And in a sense, I mastered the situation because I entered *his* dynamic. This was a more real interaction. I didn't know how to explain this at the time to my supervisor or even to myself. My supervisor said my treatment of Joe was a collusion to stay emotionally distant, and that I protected Joe and myself from his aggression—and that may be, or not. Perhaps it was more that my patient and I unknowingly understood something about our intersubjective experience that we could not articulate, but our emotions for each other communicated realness. Words might have made us even more inarticulate and less real to self and other.

How else do we communicate to another who we really are? One nonverbal factor that influences our intersubjective experience is our manner of dressing. One day Dana entered my office wearing a long, clingy black dress. She apologized for wearing it and said she would change before going to see patients. It seemed fine to me and I suggested she leave it on and work with whatever arose in treatment. She laughed and said she thought that I could get away with it, but that it might be too sexually stimulating for her. So to Dana's mind, loose-fitting outfits were less erotic. Since her treatment of Chad was so sexually charged, I couldn't understand her logic. What did her clothes matter? The eroticism between herself and Chad was so heightened, what harm would a clingy dress do to an already existing bonfire?

I have been told that my clothing is frequently seen as too seductive. A few colleagues have criticized my dress as a factor in why some of my patients have developed an erotic transference. This means I evoke the erotic transference, but if so then wouldn't that mean all my patients should have sexual feelings about me?

For many years, I attempted to wear conservative clothing, especially during my analytic training and for a few years afterward. I felt sexually neutered, restricted, and hidden. My clothing now represents an aspect of what I think about myself and an awareness of my desire to be recognized as a sexual subject—an expression of power as well as sexual vulnerability are both conveyed. My clothing also links me with my mother, an admittedly rare identification for me as I seldom find anything similar between us. My mother was very sexualized in her way of dressing, as had been my grandmother, her mother—a maternal line of viewed female sexuality. My dress, except during my analytic training, expressed the familial desire to compete for attention, recognition, and praise. I remember once standing on a stool to be fitted for a new short skirt my grandmother was sewing for me, both parents watching as I modeled. "It should be shorter," my father said. My mother agreed as my grandmother pinned up the hem. Objectification or sexualized self as subject? Both, I assume.

My patients say I dress like they do, and that is true. These patients also say that through my manner of dress, I present myself as sexual and they interpret this to mean I seem sexually uninhibited enough not to be offended listening to patients' sexual issues. So for some patients the way I dress may evoke an erotic transference, while for others it may create a milieu where they feel safe to discuss sexual function and dysfunction.

Still, how we dress as therapists brings up another interesting point: Why did my patient, Joe and one or two others whom I treated during my analytic training, when I dressed much more conservatively, develop an erotic transference? And why did Chad develop sexual feelings for Dana who dressed in longer skirts? The meaning I take from this dichotomy is that sexualized clothing does not necessarily skew the transference to eroticisms, although it may send a message, correctly or incorrectly, that the therapist can listen to sexual issues with fewer judgmental overtones.

An aside: I changed my style of dressing in the early 1990s during the time I was leading an AIDS group of eight gay men (Rosiello 1995). More accurately, I should say I surrendered to my own desire to dress as I liked and this decision to dress more honestly (or dressing as disclosure of my own character) was influenced by my work with these group members. Maroda (1999) states that "Mutual surrender is a relational achievement [in treatment], not a given. It is the culmination of the working through of the transference–countertransference, and often follows a storm or conflict between analyst and patient. It does not come easily to either person, and can only occur with experience and mutual trust" (p. 56). Maroda lists several reasons therapists resist surrender: first, because analytic training teaches us to resist in an effort not to collude with the patient's intentions; second, because regression and surrender are emotionally exhausting to experience; third, because we must face our own primitive defenses when patients break through to us; fourth, because we fear a loss of the patient, an abandonment when we are emotionally vulnerable; and fifth, because we fear losing control of treatment boundaries or having to reestablish them. Nevertheless, how can we ask our patients to surrender if we are not open to such surrender ourselves?

At the time I was leading the AIDS group, I was theoretically opposed to any mode of surrender and particularly opposed to surrender of self-disclosure by the therapist. My treatment style was more traditional and heavily informed by self psychology, a classical Kohutian one-person psychology perspective. The group, however, demanded that I become as emotionally available or as real as they all wanted to be, or else they would emotionally eliminate me from the group.

Truth was crucial to these group members in their last months. There was no time for working through group resistance or transference—that was for later, if there was a later. I surrendered to facilitate group surrender to treatment process. The group members needed to brave emotional honesty and work through the real threat of AIDS, and this particular group forum provided an opportunity for mutual surrender. This is not to say that I blurted out my thoughts without concern for therapeutic impact; it didn't mean wild countertransference either. It meant constructing emotional responses that were real and intimate, not emotionally distant, intellectual interpretations. Intrapsychic and interpersonal motivations and meanings cannot be ignored. Rather, they are presented in the emotional moment, with more personal cost to the therapist's involvement. Over time, I fell in love with this group and I felt they reciprocated during our mutual surrender.

In the group's third year, they all died. I heard many personal last rites. One man in particular, a famous film critic and lecturer whom everyone was very fond of, said he wished there had been one person in his life who could have known him for himself and not for his fame. It was tempting to say, ". . . but, we know and love you," but it wouldn't have been real to him. He was right. None of us knew or loved him the way he needed to feel it. The group's silence at that time was one of the most honest experiences I have ever had and one of the saddest. In a few months, I lost six group members: only two group members were left, John being one of them. Then my mother died from cancer and I realized I could no longer emotionally manage losing the remaining two group members. A week after I left the group, John died. I guess we timed it. John had been my antagonist and eventually my ultimate supporter. This bout with surrender, sexuality, life, and death remains an influence on who I feel I have become. My manner of dress changed at that time and now states my commitment to my past experiences, most of which were influenced by sexuality. One last thing: a few people have asked why I only wear black, an occurrence that coincides with the end of the AIDS group and my mother's death. I'm not sure, actually; perhaps I'm still mourning, or maybe the absence of color creates a sense of freedom in simplification.

Early in my work with Dana, she expressed her feeling of freedom in being able to discuss erotic transference–countertransference in supervision. In treating Chad, she was now responding to his staring at her, saying, "The way you're looking at me feels very loving and deeply emotional. Tell me your experience of what we're sharing, or is our closeness more available to you in silence?" Chad now seemed quite emotionally involved in treatment and for a time, Dana and Chad appeared to Honeymoon, as did Dana and I.

It was around this time that Dana wore her clingy black dress to our session, and our relationship took on a different hue and became sexualized—or rather, wearing the dress indicated a sexualization had already begun. Until this point, Dana seemed relieved to find a supervisor who did not criticize her erotic countertransference accounts and our work was somewhat influenced by her growing idealization of me. Now her idealization became sexualized.

Shortly thereafter, Chad began talking more about his girlfriend and sheepishly announced their intended marriage. Dana felt countertransference feelings of envy, as well as relief that Chad was considering marriage to a long-term lover. She understood that his relationship with his girlfriend signified, in part, his transference desire to love an available woman and build a life with her. Another aspect of Dana, however, felt more desirous of continuous loving feelings, and experienced Chad's wish to get married as rejection.

In association, Dana's feeling about me seemed to alter concurrently with her feelings about Chad. On the one hand, she was becoming more flirtatious in supervision. On the other hand, she seemed to be unabashedly competing with me. For instance, one day I was using an example from my own work to support the idea that sexual feelings seemed more available to me than loving feelings toward patients. I thought this was probably defensive on my part, as being loving often feels maternal and I have a difficult time accepting that I actually have maternal feelings. I then asked if I could use some of Dana's clinical treatment of Chad for clinical illustration in a paper I was writing about loving feelings in treatment.

Dana almost immediately responded that she wanted to write about it herself. She added that she really didn't have trouble feeling maternal or nurturing or loving either; she had little conflict with these desires. Thinking back on this experience, in discussing loving feelings in relation to sexual feelings, I had showed a vulnerable hand and she came up with a royal flush. Perhaps this dynamic is expectable when a supervisee is about to depend on her own therapeutic abilities as she prepares to terminate supervision. Is the difference between supervision and treatment that the supervisee surrenders to her own mind and not to the supervisor's?

Still, I felt fairly shamed in my confession about love verses sex, somewhat aggressed against, and wondering how far I was to fall in her eyes. Was I to keep Chad single so that the two of them could enjoy their eroticisms without the intrusions of Chad's girlfriend or the intrusions of Dana's past supervisors, so Dana and Chad could have an extended transference–countertransference tryst? Was she angry that I had failed to keep Chad monogamous, with her? She didn't think so, but I got the sense she was glad she could work in the erotic transference better than I could, or that her relationship with Chad was more loving than my relationships were with my patients, and maybe that was and is true.

I began to hear less about Chad in supervision and more about theory and psychoanalytic literature and questions about building a private practice as Dana neared ending her analytic training. Then I remember listening to Dana tell me she had contracted with another female analyst for supervision in the upcoming year. I was surprised. What was wrong with the female supervisor she already had? The closer Chad got to marriage, the closer Dana and I got to "divorce," and when we were looking at the few remaining months I again began hearing of her previous supervisory experiences.

Dana now seemed focused on one past male supervisor. In their supervision, she had once told him of having erotic feelings toward him. She was still trying to organize the dynamics that created her feelings and was struggling with the conflict about their existence. I asked if her erotic feelings toward me had now become more conflicted, perhaps negative. It seemed so blatantly obvious and transferential that Dana was talking about our relationship. She agreed and continued talking about her feelings for Chad and his betrayal of her—a further confirmation of what I thought she was feeling in our relationship.

In writing this essay and in suggesting to Dana that she write up her own experience of our supervisory work together, it was interesting to note we both had different memories of this incident in which I confronted her on her sexual feelings. An early draft of her paper seemed to show she had no memory of my having asked her about her sexual feelings toward me. She had originally thought I neglected to address the sexuality between us. This was not my recollection, however, as I remember bringing up these feelings and of her response being affirmative and then dropped, with her saying it was parallel process. Dana's suggestion of parallel process angered me, because her intellectualization of this intersubjective experience left me without a partner in the struggle for meaning. I told Dana her leaving supervision meant we would not understand the sexual dynamics between us. She agreed, saying she was not ready to have such a discussion and added she would return in the future to address the erotic feelings in our supervision.

Some people would say there really isn't a notion of surrender in supervision. Surrender is not expected or evoked in supervision. While I agree in theory, in the practical moment of supervision, surrender does exist. Initially, Dana surrendered to an idealization of me in that she experienced a sense of freedom, affirmation, and recognition of her feelings regarding her patient—a type of surrender in "becoming real" (Ghent 1990) or "coming into being" (Winnicott 1969) as a therapist.

Still, supervision does not necessarily lend itself to working through complex dynamics between supervisor and supervisee and that is what I lament, as the opportunity to work more closely with Dana was denied. In the end, I surrendered to Dana's termination in supervision. To date, she has not returned. I wonder if my request that she write her experience of our work isn't a seduction? Perhaps, but I believe I wanted her story in the hopes of developing a future opportunity for mutual surrender and an opportunity to express internal experience.

In looking back on the two clinical illustrations provided in this chapter, it is interesting to see they both deal with termination, a surrender to death. While this seems a dramatic association to Dana's leaving supervision, the finality of it may feel similar.

The Supervisee's Experience: Companion Paper
by Dana Lerner, CSW

MULTIPLE LAYERS OF EROTIC TRANSFERENCE IN PSYCHOANALYSIS AND SUPERVISION

This is the story of how Florence and I worked through an intense resistance in the treatment of a male patient I had worked with for the last three of my four years of analytic training. Treatment hit an impasse until I was able to deal with my own erotic and loving feelings for this patient and create an atmosphere where he could do the same. I turned to Florence only after two other supervisors failed to achieve a breakthrough. I will describe how I eventually broke through my resistance with my patient, and confronted my erotic feelings, which dominated my initial relationship with Chad.

As a first-year analytic candidate I had heard Florence discuss her work with erotic transference issues, yet I chose to seek supervision for my analytic control case with two male supervisors before contacting her. I assumed that a male supervisor could help me be more comfortable working with this patient. I wanted a man's point of view. My fantasy was that a male supervisor would put me more in touch with my countertransference and help me be more objective. What happened instead was that these experiences ended up frustrating me and, I believe, created a treatment impasse for both the patient and myself.

It is important to give specific attention to gender differences within the supervisory dyad, particularly keeping in mind both the conscious and unconscious manifestations of both individuals' subjective experiences. This means that a greater understanding of each person's belief about gender roles and identity is often material for discussion. If not addressed, this material can possibly create barriers or stalemates in cross-gender supervision. While attention to gender differences seems readily addressed in the analytic dyad, it is worth noting that, when cross-gender supervision is involved, both parties should be listening with a "third ear" for relevant material.

I recall vividly the moment, at the end of my first year of training, when I first met Chad in the waiting room of my office. It was one of those experiences that you recall as an analyst because it occurs so rarely. We shook hands and looked into each other's eyes and stared at each other in shock for a moment too long. It was like seeing someone you know very well out of the usual context, and you are momentarily startled. The attraction was immediate, intense, and I learned later, mutual. Physically, he was an attractive 35-year-old, dark-haired, green-eyed man, with a beautiful smile. Yet beyond his looks I remember thinking immediately to myself, "I like him." I sensed something powerful had happened.

Chad initially presented himself as an ideal patient. He was neat, well dressed, polite, and extremely earnest. It would have been very difficult not to like him. He had sought therapy only at the urging of his girlfriend, with whom he was having communication problems. He admitted that it was nearly impossible to speak openly and honestly to anyone about himself and was skeptical if therapy could help him. I was startled toward the end of one of our early sessions when he stated that he was relieved I was not wearing a dress, since he was somewhat distracted in our first session. I was caught completely off guard by this unexpected admission and overcome by anxiety, and could not respond to it. I fumbled for words and was obviously uncomfortable. A few sessions later he referred again to this incident and also added that he had seen my underwear. I am certain that this never occurred, yet found myself speechless and unable to pursue this further. My discomfort signaled him that this topic was off limits.

Although my anxiety overwhelmed me I confess to feeling validated that the attraction between us was mutual. Chad's comment about seeing my underwear felt very provocative and sexually charged. Acknowledging this put me in touch with a fear of being seen as seductive by my patient.

In our beginning sessions, when Chad was more direct with his sexually tinged comments, I was unable to explore with him and encourage him to tell more about his feelings of attraction to me. It would be years into his treatment before we were able to engage in an authentic dialogue concerning these feelings. Nonetheless, we both apparently felt sufficient comfort to enable the treatment to continue.

From a large family, Chad was secure in the fact that he was his mother's favorite. His childhood was extremely chaotic, complete with a remote, verbally abusive father and an intrusive, somewhat hysterical mother. Chad learned from an early age to focus all of his attention on others' needs as opposed to his own. His only positive feedback came from his mother when he gratified her narcissistic needs. This led to Chad's formulation of a false-self persona, which enabled him to function as a child in his family, but not as an adult in the outside world. It was this genetic dynamic that was the focus of his beginning transference. I interpreted his desperation and all-consuming focus on pleasing me as being similar to the way he related with all of the other important women in his life.

I remember discussing my erotic feelings about Chad with my first supervisor as honestly as I felt I could. At first he was very eager to listen and I hoped he would be able to help me solve my dilemma. Eventually sessions with this first male supervisor seemed also to contain elements of erotic transference between the two of us. This was extraordinarily difficult. I felt overwhelmed by all of this sexualization. I did not know what was mine, his, or the patient's. After confronting him with my impressions of what was occurring between us, he labeled these feelings a parallel process and we tried to discuss the emotions brought up in the supervision as a way to help me work with my patient. Unfortunately my supervisor and I were unable to sustain a dialogue that could enable me to speak more freely to my patient. I believe that my supervisor had become uncomfortable with the material I presented to him, and my intense transference reaction became an obstacle to learning rather than a tool. I was greatly disappointed, as it seemed that an invaluable opportunity had been missed.

During my second-year supervision on Chad with another male supervisor, I felt that I was in a battle. While acknowledging that my feelings were difficult to work with, this supervisor encouraged a more traditional interpersonal approach. He proposed my patient's erotic feelings were defensive, and that Chad was defending against his own anger. I was encouraged to focus on the patient's masochism. Each time I brought up my difficulty in addressing my erotic feelings within the sessions, he steered the discussion to one of power differentials and the patient's castration anxiety. While this made sense and was indeed accurate, I ended up feeling totally rejected in these supervisory sessions and therefore completely invisible. I suspect that this was how my patient was then feeling about me, that I literally could not see him. It was as though we were speaking two different languages and there was little understood between us. Neither my patient nor I were discussing our feelings, yet the desire in the room was palpable.

While it might not be fair to make a blanket statement about the way male supervisors might react to a female supervisee brimming with sexual and loving feelings for her male patient, a few questions invariably come to my mind. Might not both of these men have been unconsciously protecting my patient from what one might deem the "intrusive" mother? Did they themselves feel somehow threatened that I was able and willing to speak of my loving feelings for this patient? Was there a power struggle or battle of the sexes occurring? Was this another example of every woman's number one complaint against men, that they refuse to talk about their feelings? Or was I just overwhelmed by my erotic feelings and were they merely wondering, "What does this woman want?"

Perhaps my demands for an honest expression of feelings might have been forcing both of these male supervisors to examine aspects in their own lives that were uncomfortable. How might they or anyone have coped with letting themselves get swept up as I had?

These questions also describe the age-old dilemma destined to forever challenge analysts the world over: "Where does supervision end and analysis begin?" As much as both of my male supervisors were theoretically correct, I realize now that what I needed was to struggle through my erotic feelings with them. What they said made sense and one could not argue with either of these men or the theories espoused by them. Yet somehow I knew that this was not what would ultimately help me to work with my patient.

Perhaps with the individuals in both these supervisions I had become transformed into a different disavowed aspect of my patient in their presence. With my first supervisor I revealed all of my erotic yearnings, while with the second I felt stifled and not heard. Yet the enactments that had occurred in both these supervisions had not been addressed adequately because of what I believe was these supervisors' inability to disclose or examine the feelings induced in them. William Coburn (1997), in his article "The Vision in Supervision: Transference-Countertransference Dynamics and Disclosure in the Supervision Relationship," focuses on the importance of self-disclosure by supervisor and the supervisee. He writes about a sort of affective attunement that, if achieved in the supervisory session, can bring greater depth of meaning and understanding of the subjective experience of the patient. He suggests that supervisors make a point of promoting an open dialogue on the way "the supervision experience is impacting on the supervisee from a cognitive, affective, theoretical, and or practical standpoint" (p. 488).

I realized that the mutual lack of open dialogue in supervision had impeded the work and perhaps even further deepened resistances in my patient and myself. Discussing this patient in my own analysis, while helpful, was still not enough. I felt an important and harmful dichotomy in myself when expressing my emotions in my analysis yet editing and making excuses in my supervision. I had to find supervision with someone who would engage in this process with me or I would continue to be powerless and the dilemma would remain unresolved.

My feelings evoked tremendous guilt and shame. How could I feel so intensely about my patient? I felt estranged from the analytic community that I was struggling to join. Naturally when I was a new candidate in training I had expected feelings of insecurity and confusion but this continuing situation only added fuel to the fire. I found myself asking senior colleagues this question: "If a therapist sees a person on the street and finds him or her attractive, and the next day he or she shows up at your office as your new patient, is the attraction real or is it transference?" Unfortunately I was too focused on utilizing theory to try to explain my feelings, rather than using them as a treatment aid. The more I insisted on turning to theory (and I believe my male supervisors colluded with me on this), the more I kept coming up against a brick wall.

It was not until later, when I read Mitchell (1993), that the experiences and feelings with Chad at that point began to make more sense to me. Mitchell emphasizes "a sorting through and monitoring of the analyst's own self states with their patients" (p. 148). He encourages the analyst "to allow him- or herself to struggle to remain in those states even if they seem opaque" (p. 148). I believe that I was involved in a state of being that had been mutually co-created by myself and Chad. I realize now that he needed me to feel overwhelmed by my feelings for him, in order for me to truly grasp what he did not yet understand or have words for.

When Chad increased his sessions to begin psychoanalysis and moved to the couch, my feelings also increased and my desires grew stronger. I felt he began to silently overtake me, and at times I experienced a bursting of emotions for him. While my sexual feelings remained acute I began to notice increasing feelings of love. Music played in my head throughout our sessions and it ran the gamut from Led Zeppelin to Rachmaninoff. My feelings began to frighten me and I was afraid of losing control and even questioned whether I should stop working with him. Since Chad seemed unable to know or express his erotic feelings, I wondered if I had merely become the repository for both of our loving feelings and my cup was running over.

Something nonverbal was expressed that made us both feel wonderful when we were together. I often wondered if he was feeling this way too and not aware of it, or merely (like me) not speaking about it. Even as I look back and record this, it is difficult to articulate how deeply I was feeling, because there were no words for it.

I was becoming stimulated by anticipation even before he entered my office. I was even able to anticipate in advance what tone or flavor our sessions would have. I dreamt about him often. When I would see him after these dreams, I felt guilty, as though I were keeping secrets. With hindsight, I now feel my dreams furnished me with a tremendous amount of material about his dissociated desires. I would often feel astonished as he described a scenario in his own life that mirrored a particular aspect of my latest dream about him.

In sessions, I noticed how he repeated the same phrases over and over again, and how he had an acquired vocabulary of phrases and words as someone might if he or she were learning a second language. The listener understands what is being discussed and, logically it makes sense, but none of the depth of feeling gets translated. Looking back, each time I ran away from my erotic feelings for him, I was really taking him away from something authentic and genuine. He was once again not permitted to be spontaneous with anyone. Every thought was censored and edited before it was delivered. I had to locate the genuine, authentic experience in the treatment room with him, and my recognition and response to it was crucial. But clearly I was not sharing my own reactions with him. This was even more troublesome as I began to question if this was yet another reenactment of his own mother's inability to attune to him.

I struggled with the emotional and physical manifestations of the unspoken feelings in the room. I was even more hesitant to address the erotic transference, because I found myself fearing that his seduction of me might just be a mirroring of my own emotions. Also, I worried that if he truly understood or knew what I was experiencing; I might not be able to tolerate the humiliation. Still I felt he knew I enjoyed his non-verbal seduction and his attention, but my silence around this experience communicated that it was not up for discussion.

I was distressed. Although his life seemed better outside of his treatment, I thought I was failing to address a reality in the room and I felt entangled in this web of falseness. By the end of my second year of work with Chad, I was certain our sessions had reached an impasse. Chad must have thought something amiss too because he began sitting up and started staring at me in silence for long periods of time. Eventually he said he had been physically attracted to me from the very beginning and he had been struggling to suppress or eliminate those feelings, because he thought they were counterproductive. Still our work had created enough trust that he could now bring this out in the open. But at the same time, he wanted me to know that the attraction was now in the past and we had succeeded in finally developing a relationship not impeded by his sexual feelings for me. He felt elated that our relationship was no longer burdened by such distractions. He asked how I felt about his revelation and I avoided a direct response, choosing to fall back on interpretations I learned in training that maintained a blank-enough screen. I had once again missed an opportunity, something I hope would not happen now as I have since gathered more experience and courage to address uncomfortable erotic issues. As he left these sessions I noticed that he seemed exhilarated by his ability to be open with me, or triumph over me. He would often hum a little tune as he left and never failed to give me a smile as he left my office. I felt envious that he was able to get relief from his attempts to be more authentic with me. I also remember thinking that I did not believe the part about the sexual feelings being completely gone. In one of the sessions I asked him if he could tell me exactly where did these feelings go? He acknowledged that perhaps this was not completely true. Then he asked me if I was sexually attracted to him and as luck would have it (or so I thought then) the clock was on my side and I answered, "Our time is up."

It was at this time, the beginning of my fourth and final year of training, that I walked into Florence's office. I remember looking at her black leather analytic couch and telling her that I would like to be lying on it locked in an embrace with Chad. She smiled and asked me to tell her more about my fantasy and with this I felt immediately embraced by her. I remember breathing a huge sigh of relief. I no longer had to suppress my own feelings. I hoped I was with someone who would listen to and validate my thoughts.

Perhaps this relief freed me, because I felt permitted to speak candidly about my erotic emotions for Chad and his for me. I could see that Florence was more than willing to listen and expected and encouraged me to say more. Unlike my previous supervisors she actually wanted to focus on the feelings he evoked in me. With Florence's supervision my countertransference was now helping to inform me of my patient's experience, and of my reactions to him.

Mendell (1993) wrote, on the topic of cross-gender supervision, "some female candidates feel more comfortable revealing their counter-transference to a supportive male supervisor as this configuration can help them gain confidence in their work with a potentially overpowering male patient" (p. 272). However, Mendell found it more customary for female candidates to find that female supervisors can "empathize more fully with another woman, and that they can help them to look at their anxiety around problematic or shameful issues"(p. 272). I believe that in my treatment with Chad, that this latter view was true. In my fantasy a male supervisor would somehow give me strength but in actuality it was the empathy that I was searching for.

Florence's approach was in many ways different from the more interpersonal analytic stance in which I had been tutored up to that point. Rather than relying on interpretation of the patient's actions and the treatment enactments, she focused on exploring the patient's fantasies with him and my own with her. In Chapter 3 of this book, Florence refers to Kaftal's (1994) idea that in certain treatments interpretations might "dilute the transference prematurely," in essence putting an end to the patient's freedom to observe his feelings toward the therapist. Through his therapy thus far, Chad had come to understand that he had great difficulty expressing himself, recognizing that almost every thought or word, in the session or outside it, was not spontaneous. His greatest wish was to somehow escape these constraints and his self-imposed censorship. He thought he did not have the tools to do so. Florence helped to redirect my viewpoint and focus on the feelings I was containing, and to use these as incentives for honest expression. In other words, I could disclose my feelings to my patient as a way of moving his treatment forward.

I slowly began to describe my own experience to him rather than relying on those interpretations that seemed to be more cognitively focused and less emotionally related or intimate. I used what I was feeling in the session and formulated my own thoughts into honest expressions of my experience of what was happening between us. In one session I said, "It seems that there are times when it feels extremely intimate in here between us." When he became uncomfortable or tried to change the topic I wondered out loud if it was easier for him to run away from the intense feelings that were being stirred up for him rather than look at the emotional connection between us.

My hours with Florence helped broaden my language as an analyst. We discussed types of self-disclosure that would help me express myself to Chad in a manner that felt boundaried and safe. My vocabulary now included terms that felt comfortable and seemed to fit the moment. Most difficult for me were those times when I found him to be flirtatious, or I found myself feeling seduced by him. I began to comment to him that it felt at times as though we were on a date, and asked what his understanding was of what was going on between us. In doing so I was encouraging him to look at what was happening between us in the moment.

Initially he seemed a bit startled by some of my comments, but he gradually became more relaxed and eager to pursue this sort of dialogue. He became visibly moved and emotional during these conversations, and recognized that our sessions felt very different from his interactions with family and friends. That he was beginning to make that distinction gave hope that he was at last learning about himself through our talks. I was finally reaching a very private part of him.

I still felt real discomfort in always being the one initiating these conversations. This was confusing for two reasons. First, as discussed before, so much of Chad's life had been about pleasing others. I questioned whether his enthusiasm was merely another manifestation of this need. Might he be going along with my new approach simply to please and thus remain untrue to himself? Second, I struggled with my own feelings of seduction. As must be obvious at this point, my own countertransference played a large part in my difficulty with this material. I still worried that delving deeper would be for my own needs and not his. I had to acknowledge that his seductive ways were at times very enlivening for me.

Florence encouraged me to reveal to her certain aspects of my countertransference, which helped me recognize my own struggles as opposed to what was a co-creation between Chad and me. Yet I never felt pushed or prodded. I saw that, for the supervisor, this struggle to maintain the balance of supervision versus analysis was very delicate. What succeeded in our combined effort was that Florence let me decide how much to reveal. We were able to brainstorm ways of broaching topics with my patient that felt safe to me, and she always offered her support. When I could go no further with my own musing she provided hers.

A major obstacle I had to overcome was my own physical reaction to my patient. I would begin trembling, at times uncontrollably, during the sessions. By tracking when and why my symptoms emerged, Florence and I found they coincided with those moments I was holding back. Once Chad passed me in the hallway before our session and seemed purposely to bump me. Before he entered the room I felt myself begin to tremble and shake. I knew it would be difficult to point out that I thought this an aggressive or sexual gesture on his part. Or, if a session was full of loving and affectionate feelings not being addressed, I would often begin to tremble. I also realized that my trembling was more pronounced when Chad demanded I share more of my own feelings with him. These symptoms invariably vanished when I pushed through my own barrier and spoke out.

Florence's guidance allowed for my own spontaneous or creative side to emerge more comfortably with Chad. In one session I noticed that a button on my shirt had accidentally opened, leaving part of my skin exposed. Rather than panic or pretend to ignore it, I asked Chad to please close his eyes for a moment, and I proceeded to remedy the problem. Afterwards Chad asked me why I had made that request, and we spent time talking about his experience. This was the sort of interaction that I came to realize made for a richness in treatment; when the analyst allows him or herself to relax and let things happen, the possibilities for growth are endless.

I shared with Florence a dream I had, in which Chad and I were walking around a college campus, trying to find an office in which to hold a session. In the dream Chad seemed a bit agitated and he was unknowingly exposing his genitals. My feeling in the dream was one of extreme self-consciousness. Florence wondered what would happen if I shared my dream with him. Initially I balked at the suggestion. I thought immediately of Ferenczi. This would be a perfect way to end the fourth year of my analytic training. I too could be labeled insane by my colleagues as I pushed the self-disclosure envelope to new dimensions. In quite a few supervision sessions Florence and I explored the various possibilities that such an intervention might rouse in me and in Chad. I feared that I might be placing myself in a position of extreme vulnerability, and might tarnish the integrity of the treatment boundaries I was constantly struggling to clarify. I was worried that he might feel a need to interpret my dream in his usual attempt to please and submit.

Working with Florence allowed me to dance a little more dangerously in this dyad. After much thought, I decided to explore this, explaining to Chad that I wanted to share something personal but was uncertain if I should, and this was my way of asking his permission. Not surprisingly he encouraged me to do so, especially since I had been asking him to be even more honest with me in treatment. He responded that this should go both ways.

I told Chad of my dream about him and asked if he had any thoughts about how its contents might relate to his treatment. In an almost surreal role reversal, I found myself listening to him analyze my dream. He reveled in his new role as "my analyst." He commented that by my dreaming about him, I was bringing myself into the mix and he wondered which of my feelings and thoughts were informing this dream.

Chad was visibly moved by my decision to reveal this personal aspect of myself to him. We were heading in the right direction. It seemed that the more authentic and open I was able to be with him, the more he was able to respond in kind. My self-disclosure enabled him to realize he could have a meaningful relationship with someone in which he did not have to attend to his or her every thought.

Florence's supervision revealed yet another aspect of my resistance and difficulty with this treatment. I told her I was tired of being the one who always has to go first, using my subjectivity to elicit his. She asked what going first might mean for me, and helped me look at this in the context of my treatment with Chad. In discussing my countertransference I realized that it was unacceptable to go first because I was the woman and he was the man. As I had come from a male dominated background, there was something ego dystonic for me in assuming this position of power. Her inquiry touched a dissociated aspect of myself that could not allow an exploration of Chad's sexual fantasies because such powerful behavior was unconsciously unacceptable to me.

Florence also helped me reframe my dilemma by presenting it differently to Chad. Rather than just sitting with my feelings in the room with him, I studied them and let him know a certain part of my experience. Not my exact feelings, per se, but using my erotic feelings to inform my response. For example, I said, "I feel as though you want to tell me that you love me but you want me to say it to you first." He seemed at first surprised, and then he cried, admitting this was true. Florence and I realized that Chad was involving me in a manipulation that allowed him to dominate me by forcing me to do all of the work. He expressed the conflict in his desire to both control me and concurrently surrender to me so that I would be obliged to lead the way for him. Eventually it was my recognition of my own fear of going first (which I explored in supervision) that opened the way for a greater depth of experience.

After the session where the loving feelings between us were articulated, I became much more comfortable continuing with the dialogue we had both been avoiding. When opportunities arose to explore further the feelings between us, I could more easily speak about them. In one conversation, he said that he felt love always comes with conditions. I wondered out loud what conditions came with ours? These questions gave Chad an opportunity to examine the way our relationship had given him hope that he could have more in-depth, meaningful encounters with his girlfriend, friends, and family. It gave him a goal and something to strive toward. My openness modeled for him an interest in his own true feelings, and these sorts of inquiries helped him work toward establishing relationships outside of treatment where he could aim for a similar sort of intimacy.

Unfortunately as analysts we're not taught much about how to communicate love to our patients. Analytic training candidates are given very little if any exposure to this topic. In her article, "Terms of Endearment in Clinical Analysis," Fitzpatrick (1999) illustrates her struggle with this topic with a patient she felt lovingly toward. She pointed out to the patient that there seemed to be a rapport between them, and found that when her patient expressed his intimate feelings toward her she was able to validate him and respond in kind (p. 120). Most of the pertinent literature suggests that when these feelings are discussed in the treatment room, that the analyst chose his or her words carefully, always keeping in mind the need to be therapeutic. Aron (1996) posits that, while words matter, it is the analyst's way of speaking that is crucial. He acknowledges the wording, but also suggests that analysts pay attention to their "tone of voice and the emotional conviction with which they are speaking" (p. 129). It was Florence's validation of the feelings between Chad and me that enabled me to see them as authentic, and as something to be celebrated, not pushed aside. Examining the treatment in these terms I was freed up, as I no longer had to view myself as the seductress but rather a player in the mutual co-creation that had occurred. Chad and I were fortunate that our coming together triggered enormous growth for both of us.

Florence's presence and her ease with the erotic material aided my shifting beliefs about myself as an analyst, and perhaps as a woman as well. She represented a powerful mother who could accept and encourage my growth as a separate other. I began to identify with Florence as a strong woman. She was not frightened of going first and I was seeing that I needn't be either. This triangular configuration somehow allowed me to speak more freely to Chad, as it was she who led the way by speaking the words first to me.

Interestingly enough, Chad now felt, for the very first time, the freedom to express his conscious aggression toward women within the "safety" of the analytic space co-created between us. Some analysts would suggest that his sexual feelings had just been a resistance to this aggression all along, but I would disagree. Chad's sexual feelings were even more hidden than his awareness of his aggression. I continued to encourage him to fantasize, a luxury Chad had rarely allowed himself. His fantasies ran the gamut from loving encounters between us to scenarios where he would overtake me sexually and hurt me. Analysis of his feelings toward me helped us to understand the side of him that felt castrated and enraged. Subsequently he felt free to talk about his feelings of anger and disappointment toward me. My good little patient seemed to retreat into the distance. I had become a part-time bad object.

As supervision progressed I found myself wanting to identify with Florence and enjoy my newfound emotional freedom. However, I became acutely aware of new and frightening feelings. At times there was something almost overstimulating about merely being in Florence's presence.

While it was difficult to put into words, I felt that she was being seductive with me. Did Chad feel the same when coming to see me? Coincidentally as I was writing this paper, a woman I met recently in a supervision group commented, out of the blue, that she found me to be seductive. It led me to wonder more about what it is that people experience as sexual about another person. There is a considerable subjectivity about seduction and sexuality. One must think about the possibility that one might be totally unaware of the other's experience of us, which could be completely foreign to our own experience of our self.

I once came to our supervisory session wearing a tight-fitting black dress, which I deemed unsuitable for work. Somehow the topic of my dress came up and I remember Florence's comment that she would have no problem wearing something similar to a session. As I left our meeting I remember thinking "Who is this woman with her unusual desires and what the hell is going on here?" I wondered who she represented transferentially to me? Was she was becoming an overly seductive mother? Could I trust Florence to know what she was talking about in encouraging me to focus on my sexual and loving feelings in the treatment with Chad? I silently resolved to pay utmost attention to maintaining my own sense of self, and not be caught up completely in her concept of Chad's treatment. I distanced myself from her, enacting my fear, perhaps in a duplication of Chad's early reaction to his eroticism.

While writing this paper, I wondered what might have been my own unconscious motivation for wearing this particular dress to our session. Did I need to dress provocatively to enliven my own work? Or, was I attempting to seduce Florence as Chad did with me? Was this the only way to reach her, through some sort of stimulating interchange? Or was I enacting something I did not know about myself? Perhaps I was provoking Florence, a dare in a sense, to see if she would risk addressing the seductiveness in the room between the two of us. Maybe it was I who wasn't up for the dare even though I unconsciously provoked it.

My feelings toward Florence became very conflicted. She made me feel quite special and I fantasized that I was her favorite supervisee, and that she had found in me a protégée. It felt both exciting and burdensome. Then I realized something else. I was hesitating to bring into supervision potentially erotic material about my female patients, as I was concerned we would have to address directly the seduction occurring between us. I now realize I was unprepared to examine this with her. Ironically I began to feel more comfortable with my feelings for Chad and less with my feelings for her.

In one meeting in which we were discussing feelings of love for patients, Florence confided in me that it was difficult for her to feel love for her patients and that the sexual feelings were easier for her to be in touch with. I found myself almost boasting about the ways in which Chad and I were progressing in expressing our more intimate feelings for each other. Secretly, I enjoyed imagining that she was envious of me, and that made me feel powerful. Must love always contain aggression? In this case, it did. But my aggression was in defense of love and not vice versa. This was similar to Chad's aggression toward me in his treatment.

I began wanting to pull Chad away from Florence's supervision. She once asked if she could include some of our work in a paper she was preparing and I declined and asked her not to. My competitive feelings were at full throttle. Florence pointed out my possessiveness of him and wondered what this meant to me. Coincidentally, about that time Chad revealed that he had become engaged to be married. Did I already know that on some level, and was Florence Chad's other woman in the triangulation? Was my unconscious fear of losing him to another woman enacted in my reactions to Florence? I admit that strong feelings of abandonment were stirring in me as he approached his impending nuptials. In an act that seemed quite significant he married exactly to the day on the three-year anniversary of our work together. About that time, I left Florence and moved on to another supervisor, assuring her that I would be back at some point. I did not acknowledge the hurt I sensed she felt at my abrupt departure, but rather praised her for her invaluable help with Chad.

Preparing this paper forced me to examine my experiences with Florence and to confront the reasons I chose to leave. I felt the need to establish some sort of autonomy from her. I needed to know that I could separate from her, while retaining the wealth of knowledge she had bestowed and that I had gained. I needed to incorporate what I had learned about myself in my work with her, but also to spend time apart to understand what I was experiencing. I hoped we could separate for a time and remain together, just as Chad seemed to be asking of me.

I also realized that, at that time, I was not willing or able to speak to Florence honestly about my experiences with her. As I had grown more confident in my work with Chad the next logical step would have been to present other patients in more depth. I was fearful of what material might come up in our supervision around possible erotic transferences with female patients, which I was most reluctant to explore at that time. Homoerotics and homophobia have little space between them. Exploration of those treatment issues would leave Florence and me little choice but to delve more deeply into the erotic transference issues between us. When she inquired if this might be why I had to leave, my resistance became obvious in my response. Had she been more insistent, the outcome might have been different.

All of the elements of my decision to leave are not entirely clear to me. Did my growth as an analyst, added to my training experiences, move me to a state of independence and confidence such that only leaving would affirm my growth? If so, this was developmentally appropriate. My decision to terminate and not yet return remains definitely open ended. I surrendered myself to Chad; will I go back for more with Florence? This is uncharted territory, emotionally charged, the evolution of which is ongoing.

9

The Treatment of an Asexual Man

In Dostoevsky's *Crime and Punishment* (1866), a young man, Raskolnikov, a former student who is educated but impoverished, decides to murder an old female pawnbroker to save himself from a desperate financial situation. He justifies the murder by believing the pawnbroker to be old, bad-tempered, uneducated, selfish, deaf, and ill, and seeing her as ruining her younger stepsister's life by treating her as a scullion. Raskolnikov wants to kill the pawnbroker, leave the country, and spend the rest of his life engaged in self-righteous actions for the good of humanity. He believes such an attitude will atone for the crime of killing a worthless, evil, old woman. Raskolnikov rationalizes that punishment by law or by another is less forbidding than one's own desire for punishment.

After Raskolnikov murders the pawnbroker his state of mind is chaotic and confused from the shock of his crime. He becomes dissociated and splits off his murder, nearly forgetting it altogether. Dostoevsky leads the reader to experience Raskolnikov's subjectivity, which begins in a delirium of physical and emotional punishment motivated by guilt. Still, Raskolnikov's desire for the Napoleonic stance of "existing above the law" has led him to commit an even greater crime than the one he originally planned—that of killing the "good" stepsister, who happened to see the first murder.

The reader learns in Raskolnikov's confession to Sonya, a prostitute filled with a desperation to attain goodness, that Raskolnikov desires to be a compassionate protector of humanity and in doing so hopes to disregard moral law in his justification of murder. Sonya urges Raskolnikov to confess to the magistrate, which he eventually does, in an affectless manner lacking remorse. But Raskolnikov is never recognized by the magistrate as a suspect in the crime. This leads the reader and Raskolnikov to the punishment of surviving as a tortured soul unless he can atone through his notion of pious living.

In Freud's 1928 essay on Dostoevsky, which he wrote as an introduction for a published collection of early drafts for *The Brothers Karamazov*, he states, "Parricide [the act of] one who murders his father, mother or a close relative] according to a well-known view, is the principal and primal crime of humanity as well as of the individual" (p. 183). The desire to perform a violent death originates in ambivalent emotions involving guilt and identification. The young boy's hatred toward the father as rival (for mother) conflicts with the intolerability of this desire due to fear of castration.

At the beginning of the story, Raskolnikov voices his wish to commit parricide in first-person narrative, but as the story progresses Dostoevsky switches Raskolnikov's voice to third-person, in effect blurring the distinction between inner and outer world experience in Raskolnikov's mind. Dostoevsky leaves the reader unsettled in that we are not sure which voice we are listening to and when it changes in the story. In a sense the reader is left wondering, Who is experiencing what emotion? Who is containing what emotion and within whom did it originate?

THE CRIME

About nine years ago, one of Mario's colleagues insisted he begin therapy. Mario had spoken to him of a desire to commit suicide as a means of culminating his own punishment. He entered treatment with a female therapist who, within six months, moved to another city and referred him to me through her supervisor. I knew nothing about Mario and, after our first year of treatment, I knew very little more. He spent many of his sessions silently staring at the rug. It wasn't until my second and third year of treatment that I began to learn what Mario knew about himself.

In the first year of treatment, sessions began and ended with my questioning Mario or by providing interpretations about silence, mystery, secrets, aloneness, privacy, separation or attachment, dependence, intimacy, desire, dissociation—anything and everything. Still, the majority of each session was just spent sitting in silence. When I would ask why he came to therapy since he didn't talk, Mario replied that he had to, and I assumed he meant because his colleague had insisted. Mario never elaborated and never said more than just a very few words during a session. These comments did not originate with him, only in response to one of my questions—a question that I surmised he thought was appropriate to answer. In a sense I was like the magistrate in *Crime and Punishment* in that I was unsuspecting—both of the crime and the punishment.

Mario is nearly six feet tall and thin. His hair is worn shoulder-length. Most of the time he wears shorts, sometimes during the dead of winter, with loafers and no socks. He says he does not feel the cold—or the heat, either. He likes to wear button-down shirts that are buttoned up and set off with a collar pin—a rather priest-like fashion statement.

Seemingly out of character, Mario has a collection of some of the most expensive watches in the world, which he alternately wears. And he always wears a hat—a felt fedora in the winter and a straw fedora in the summer. In treatment, Mario crosses his legs in a manner similar to the way I do—at the knee, slanted, so that one leg rests on the side of the other. We are postured the same, across from each other, legs crossed and angled in the same direction, in the same mirrored manner. Mario rubs his hands throughout sessions. I have often wondered if he is wringing them in Lady Macbeth fashion, obsessively obliterating the crime from his hands. Mario's manner is stoic, emotionless, without facial expression, and I see him as Raskolnikov-like in his Napoleonic desire to surmount self-reproach. A frequent gesture, however, is his need to rub his eyes.

Mario is partially blind owing to a disease of the retina—a very rare defect, usually existing only in men, an inherited condition that varies in degrees of intensity, according to him. Mario has a severe case, identified at the hospital after his birth. One of the doctors who heard about his eye condition asked his family if she could use him and his father in a longitudinal study. Mario went through four or five eye operations to correct the retinas of both eyes. With age, the disease causes the retina to detach. A moderate jolt or impact to Mario's body or skull could also permanently detach the retina and leave him blind. His family stopped taking Mario to the medical researcher when he was in elementary school. He didn't know why their visits stopped, but he has always harbored a suspicion that he had committed some unknown crime and was being punished for it.

It was in the second and third year of treatment that I began to hear about Mario's childhood. One day after he entered the session, he put his hat on my couch and next to it placed the book he had been reading in the waiting room, face up. The book was *Ethan Frome*, by Edith Wharton, one of my favorites. I excitedly asked him where he was in reading the story. He told me he had read it multiple times, and I asked why. "Ethan Frome," Mario said without emotional inflection, "was a man who made a mistake. Ethan Frome spent his adult life in punishment for having allowed the wrong woman to love him. He couldn't escape his destiny. No one does."

Mario then told me his very favorite book was *Crime and Punishment*, and he said he admired Raskolnikov, who comes to realize he cannot escape his own destiny of punishment, just as Mario was destined to eternal punishment. Mario said his own destiny was to live a life without love or affection from another—he was never to feel love or give it. No one could love him. It was at this moment that I felt an aspect of the emotional emptiness Mario had consistently alluded to in his sessions, the hopelessness he spoke of in finding someone to love him or let him love them, the absence of desire expressed by a man who desired to desire.

In this same period of his treatment, Leonard, Mario's colleague, called to say that Mario was again suicidal. Leonard thought I didn't know. He knew Mario probably hadn't told me and he was right. On the phone, Leonard said he was probably Mario's only friend, and as such, they had occasional dinners together. He didn't know about anyone else existing in Mario's life. Leonard was married with two children and had little social time to give to Mario. After my questioning, or prying, depending on the perspective, Mario said he thought Leonard was like a father to him. He loved him like a father . . . he thought . . . even though he was sure he didn't really know about feeling love.

I have always wondered if there were any sexual feelings in Mario's relationship with Leonard, and Mario looked at me as though I was crazy when I asked him. His recuperation period from my question took many months of silence. Perhaps it wasn't recuperation, it may have been punishment—but for whom? I still suspect there may have been sexual feelings that Leonard felt for Mario, since in one narrative Mario said Leonard once attempted to hold him in an embrace. Mario refused the offer, believing it to be useless. In a sense, he issued his regrets for an unperformed function.

Mario grew up in the South. His father and mother are both college educated. His father has been successful in business, his mother remains a homemaker, and his only sibling, an older sister, is now married, has a child, and lives in another state.

One day soon after Leonard called me, he insisted that Mario tell me his history. What Mario took from Leonard's demand was that he was to list a series of childhood events, which he did without emotional inflection. When Mario was 5, he had been playing and was unaware that he had done something to anger his mother. She began reprimanding him and her anger seemed to feed itself until she pushed Mario's head through the plate-glass window, shattering the window. Head wounds typically bleed a great deal. She became enraged that Mario was bleeding and sent him to his room. Hours later, after a full day at the office, Mario's father came home and took him to the hospital for stitches. There was no evidence of any discord between Mario's parents on this event; instead they seem to have colluded in their mutual dislike and treatment of him.

The next event was also recited without emotion: Mario had angered his mother for a reason he didn't know. He thinks it was because he was playing with his sister or because he was different from his sister—he thought his mother didn't like boys, only girls like herself. In an event that was repeated many times, Mario was forced to put on his sister's dress. One time he was tied to a tree in the backyard wearing the dress, another time he was tied up in the basement wearing the dress. Once he was left in a darkened basement, tied up for hours. He learned that if he kept silent, out of his mother's view, he was punished less. Punishment was his destiny. I asked, "Was the capacity to survive also your destiny?" He didn't answer. I then asked what he felt during and after these experiences with his family, he answered that he felt nothing and thought nothing about the events. He knew the events made people upset when he related them. I asked if he thought I was upset on hearing these stories and he thought I was since I had asked if he thought I was upset. He said he didn't know what I was experiencing, he couldn't tell, he couldn't determine or decipher my facial expressions. I thought I looked like Bela Lugosi as I fantasized about pouncing on his mother and swinging her about the room by her ankles and bashing her head into furniture. How could he miss my emotion? I then realized that while I had a wish for him to have a certain emotional experience, he seemed to express an unconscious wish that *I* have a certain experience (a projective identification), so that he didn't have to feel it. Mario's friends and I were unconsciously performing a function for him, that of feeling what he was too frightened to experience again—the emotional agony of remembered physical pain from childhood. He said he regretted not feeling, as though he was again politely refusing an invitation to an event. Still, I realized I now had company; Mario had friends.

I had never heard about any friends previously. Mario said he had told his friends about his childhood when he was in college. His friends were his old roommates. He had been at a small college on the East Coast. "Are your college friends still friends?" I asked. "Two of them," he answered, "but Jason lives in California and Riley lives near my family." Then Mario volunteered something: He had been accepted at Harvard, but his family wouldn't let him attend, saying finances prohibited it. In a matter-of-fact manner, Mario said he knew that was a lie. His father made a lot of money and still does. They wouldn't let Mario take out a loan, nor would they do so. He wasn't angry about it then or now, his answer to my questions on this was that it was what it was . . . just fact. His reference to anger reminded me that he hadn't seen my anger when he discussed his mother's treatment of him. I asked about the absence of emotion on his face and that he seemed unable to decipher emotion on another's face. Mario responded that he just couldn't see facial expression, that his eyesight excluded that possibility. He can only see what is a few inches away; everything else is blurred. He could see shapes, large shapes and colors, but no definition. He said he couldn't make out my eyes, my mouth—my expression was unavailable to him. Mario told me that he could never really see me, my black clothing blended into the black leather of my chair. He could see my skin, but it was as though my face and arms floated about on the black chair, as though I was the chair or the chair itself had facial features. I felt devastated because so much was absent in our sessions. In anguish I asked him what the danger was to his eyesight when his mother had beaten him about the head when he was young. Without emotion, Mario answered that she could have blinded him. I assume Mario did not see that I started crying and was unable to stop—projective identification feels real to the container of the other's split-off or dissociated emotion. I told him I was very upset, and he understood, saying his friends always had a similar reaction to his mother's behavior. Every so often, these sessions punctuated the treatment that, for the most part consisted of his struggle to remain affectively absent.

About four or five years into treatment, Mario told me he had a new address. It seemed that for the last few years he'd been living in a very crowded apartment with four roommates he didn't really know. He had gotten a promotion at work and could afford a better place. When asked why he had never told me about his living situation, he said it didn't seem to matter. After questioning what that meant, he said, it didn't matter to him where he lived or with whom, why should it matter to me? I tried to analyze why he thought it wouldn't matter to me, I made transference interpretations, genetic interpretations, questioned him further, asked about everything I could think of and was left with, "Where I live doesn't matter to me." In frustration tinged with anger, I told him it mattered to me. Even if he didn't matter to himself, could he at least consider—even if he didn't understand why—that he mattered to me. He looked bewildered and asked me why my voice sounded strange and tight. I told him I was hurt and angry, he'd been with me for years now, he didn't know that he mattered to me, and obviously, I didn't matter *at all* to him. Then, in a moment, I felt whorish, as though he was abusing my body in order to experience his emotion, once too often—and I was (emotionally) paying for it, as well. I was like Sonya, the prostitute in *Crime and Punishment*, to his Raskolnikov. I said he was punishing me for the crime of caring for him. My desire to create desire in him was leaving me feeling abused. I knew my longing for attachment to him was an emotional creation in my body of his wish for attachment to me. My body housed his dissociation from his own body. I wondered at the time what my emotional reference to feeling whorish meant in our work together, what was my countertransference? I decided to keep my desire to know the origins of my sexualized thought silent, in hopes of eliminating the punishment of his being emotionally absent in the following sessions. I felt I was living in a chasm filled with his regret—between cliffed moments that hang sorrow with remorse, and abandonment. I fantasized the black Cliffs of Moher in Ireland, cliffs that fall straight down to the white sea foam, the black cliffs eliminating all movement of the sea.

When he returned to the following session he sat silently for a moment, stroking the leather on the chair. Then, without prompting, he told me he had just purchased the same chair for his new apartment. He'd looked all around the city to find the exact chair because he liked it and felt comfortable in it and wanted one for himself. I understood this as transference and asked if taking the chair into his apartment was a metaphor for taking me in, emotionally. He said he didn't really understand my question and I silently mused about sexual metaphor and wondered whose sex was absent—his or mine. I stayed with his comment, however, and asked if he had bought anything else for the apartment. He had, and in this session he volunteered information on everything, including the iron bed with sheer netting draped over it. I felt elated and he said he felt nothing except he knew I wanted to know.

During the next very-many sessions, Mario returned to his silence and nothing I could say altered that for a time. Finally, during one session after I realized I had been musing about his living room in a countertransference moment, I decided to use my subjectivity to elicit his and told him how I decorated my own living room. I hoped my fantasy would create a door to his fantasy apartment or to his inner world. Would my risk of self-disclosure elicit his? I told him about the furniture, the rugs, the wall color, the tables, the candles, and then mentioned I collected antique French posters from the 1930s of female cabaret singers—big posters, five feet tall, six of them, all over the apartment. Mario sat silent and then looked quizzical and smiled. He said he had a collection of antique cels from animated cartoons. He had one-of-a-kind cels, originals, expensive ones, hung all over the apartment. Was this response an insight to his identification with cartoon cels—surface without depth? In this narrative, he added that a friend of his had come over and they'd hung his cartoon cels together.

This was a surprise—I didn't know Mario had new friends in town. I kept my questions and my excitement to myself, as he elaborated and told about sipping martinis out of his new, special martini glasses with blue stems, which he had found at an antique fair. I mused aloud that some thought or emotion seemed to let him talk about himself. "Why does it matter?" he asked. "It doesn't matter that I want to know you?" I said. He responded negatively and I told him that since it didn't matter, there shouldn't be any reason why he couldn't tell me everything. I again felt as though I were playing the magistrate in *Crime and Punishment* to Mario's Raskolnikov in that I was unaware of events that had taken place but was taking down data all the same in hopes of learning more.

It was as though Mario had decided to play cat and mouse with me, giving me a few clues to the crime he was about to confess. Mario then told about his friendship with Leonard, restating his wish for Leonard to be his "father." He felt parented by Leonard, who mentored him at the office. It seemed, however, that Leonard was emotionally removing himself from Mario, complaining that he was making too many demands on him. Mario wanted Leonard to socialize more with him and when Leonard declined, Mario considered this a confirmation that he was not worth desiring. When I asked what Mario meant by desire in this circumstance, he clarified that desire meant being in relation to another. I asked if desire was ever associated to sexuality in his life, thinking again that Leonard (or maybe Mario) had felt some sexuality toward the other, and Mario replied that he was without sexuality.

Mario then told about never feeling sexual; he never felt aroused, and did not understand the feeling when he saw it in the movies or when he read about sexuality in books. He tended to read classic literature in order to escape references to sexuality and liked movies from the 1940s when sexuality was less present on screen. He said that he had gone many years without being touched physically by another person. His friends did not hold him and he never reached out physically to anyone. In the next session, Mario brought in a video from his private collection; a Bette Davis film entitled *Now Voyager* (1942). He asked if I would watch it and I did. In the movie, the heroine, played by Bette Davis, who we first see as an unattractive innocent woman berated and kept isolated by her dominant and verbally abusive mother, escapes her mother's mistreatment by entering a psychiatric rest home run by a male psychiatrist. In the rest home, Bette meets a young girl, and they identify with each other. Through a mutual relationship of tenderness and caring they achieve, in their own way, a personal sense of cure. The psychiatrist then encourages Bette to solidify her newly found emotional health by taking a cruise, where she meets a man who loves her and whom she loves in return. I asked if Mario understood Bette's relationship to the psychiatrist as similar to his with me, and he saw no connection. Was there any association to Bette's relationship with the man she falls in love with, I asked, could some aspect of their relationship relate to ours? Mario said there was nothing similar.

THE PUNISHMENT

Mario feels that as a child he was punished for being undesirable, punished for being a child his parents did not love, punished for being male—for being born. He says he deserved his parents' treatment because he must have done something wrong, committed some crime that his parents knew about, although he was unaware of his exact crime. His parents took care of his punishment during his childhood. Now, as an adult, even though he had no adult desires, he found a new punishment for existing—his therapy. I am his jailer, in essence. My questions pierce him with anguish because each query means he has missed a piece of life, an experience, an emotion he should have known to have attained, or known about, or anticipated. I can keep questioning him and inflict great pain or sit silently creating a less intensive suffering. Mario is absent or missing in what or how he should be in life. I wonder aloud in his sessions about which one of us is being punished by the other; we both feel beaten in relation, we are both trapped by the other's existence. He is left to feel absence in my presence and I am left containing all emotion for us both. We are both powerless in the presence of the other, yet we meet driven by our own desires—his to not escape his destiny, and mine *to* help him escape his destiny. I regret that my desire has not yet created desire in him, and I believe he regrets that my attempts have failed so far, as well.

Recently, an episode occurred that has great meaning to me and "a little" meaning to Mario, according to him. Mario was sought out for a good position in another company that paid well and had management opportunities. He was to supervise a group of ten employees on a team that he would head. His salary was tripled, he was given a large office, and international travel as a consultant. He took the job, feeling he needed to get away from Leonard whose presence felt more and more punishing to him. Still, he thought leaving the company would also bring punishment because it would create a greater isolation.

On the day Mario was leaving his old company, someone in the office threw him a surprise going-away party. It was a large event—nearly fifty people attended, and Mario was faced with their lament that he was leaving them. They would miss him. A few of the women cried and everyone touched him as they shook his hand, congratulating him on his good, well-deserved fortune.

When Mario related this event in session, he sobbed, believing he had made a mistake in taking the new job, that he had made a mistake in judging his co-workers in their not caring about his work, about their not rejecting his companionship. He thought he'd missed out on being social with them, on being more available, on helping them. As he cried throughout the session, I found myself equally as tearful and told him that people actually did care for him, and then I said he seemed to only partially understand what had emotionally transpired at his good-bye party. He agreed, he didn't think he had the emotional ability to understand what his friends felt for him. As I saw him sob in this session I was gripped with fear watching him rub his eyes trying to rid them of tears—I feared he would injure his eyes, maybe blind himself, literally, because he was emotional. Now we were both afraid of his feelings and both anticipated loss in our different fantasies of his future.

AFTER WORDS

I regret that there is no ending to this particular clinical illustration, no story ending, no summation of how treatment works with this type of patient, only a listing of a very few events over very many years. Perhaps in Mario's dissociation, the treatment is also dissociated in my understanding of it, a continuing projective identification process. Still, he continues to come to sessions, his outside life is much better over the years, he has friends that I know about, and I am fond of him—which I attribute to him. Yet, I wanted to tell this story because it is about a patient who is beyond clinical understanding. I believe we all have had such an experience in our work, maybe with patients who are similar to Mario. Such patients regret their lives, regret events that happened, regret who they've become, regret what they feel they've missed, and regret the sorrow they feel when in relation with another caring person. In Dostoevsky's *Crime and Punishment*, Raskolnikov expresses the tortured struggle between the experience of the self in relation to a punishing external world. Eventually, with the help of a redeeming prosecutor, Raskolnikov is able to fight emotionally for freedom in his mental life, and at the end of the story, when he confesses his crime to the magistrate, he begins to feel relief from his oppression.

Writing about Mario was risky. It was not so much the risk of relating inexperience in technique, as some readers may judge, but the risk of repeatedly allowing Mario's feelings to present themselves through my experience, in the beginning of this story. And later, as the story progressed—in reversed Dostoevsky form, with third-person narrative becoming first-person—realizing that Mario was only able to claim his own feelings when he felt forced to relate to people who cared about him. In this clinical illustration, projective identification created therapeutic action, and containing Mario's emotions within me has eventually led to his own expression of what he feels. As Dostoevsky (1866) tells us:

He did not open . . . [the book] now, but one thought burned within him: Her faith, her feelings, may not mine become like them? Sonya was very agitated during all the day, and at night was ill again. But she was so happy that nothing could mar her joy. Seven years—only seven years! At the commencement of their happiness they were ready to look upon these seven years as seven days. They did not know that a new life is not given for nothing; that it has to be paid dearly for, and only acquired by much patience and suffering, and great future efforts.

But now a new history commences: a story of the gradual renewing of a man, of his slow progressive regeneration, and change from one world to another—an introduction to the hitherto unknown realities of life. This may well form the theme of a new tale; the one we wished to offer the reader is ended. [pp. 401–402]

References

Abraham, K. (1919). A particular form of neurotic resistance against the psychoanalytic method. In *Selected Papers of Karl Abraham, M.D.*, pp. 303–311. London: Hogarth.

Agger, E. (1988). Psychoanalytic perspectives on sibling relationships. *Psychoanalytic Inquiry* 8:3–30.

Apter E. (1991). *Feminizing the Fetish: Psychoanalysis and Narrative Obsession in Turn-of-the-Century France.* Ithaca, NY: Cornell University Press.

Aron, L. (1991). The patient's experience of the analyst's subjectivity. *Psychoanalytic Dialogues* 1:29–51.

——— (1996). *A Meeting of Minds: Mutuality in Psychoanalysis.* Hillsdale, NJ: Analytic Press.

Aron, L., and Anderson, J. (1998). The clinical body and the reflexive mind. In *Relational Perspectives on the Body*, vol. 12, pp. 3–38. Hillsdale, NJ: Analytic Press.

Aron, L., and Harris, A. eds. (1993). *The Legacy of Sandor Ferenczi.* Hillsdale, NJ: Analytic Press.

Bach, S. (1985). *Narcissistic States and the Therapeutic Process.* New York: Jason Aronson.

——— (1991). On sadomasochist object relations. In *Perversions and Near-Perversions in Clinical Practice: New Psychoanalytic Perspectives*, ed. G. I. Fogel and W. A. Myers. New Haven: Yale University Press.

——— (1994). *The Language of Perversion and The Language of Love*. Northvale, NJ: Jason Aronson.

Bak, R. (1953). Fetishism. *Journal of the American Psychoanalytic Association* 1:285–298.

——— (1956). Aggression and perversion. In *Perversions: Psychodynamics and Therapy*, ed. S. Lorand, pp. 23–240. New York: Random House.

——— (1968). The phallic woman: the ubiquitous fantasy in perversions. *Psychoanalytic Study of the Child* 23:15–36. New York: International Universities Press.

Benjamin, J. (1988). *The Bonds of Love: Psychoanalysis, Feminism, and the Problem of Domination*. New York: Pantheon.

——— (1991). Father and daughter: identification with difference: a contribution to gender heterodoxy. *Psychoanalytic Dialogues* 1:277–299.

——— (1995). *Like Subjects, Love Objects*. New Haven: Yale University Press.

——— (1996). In defense of gender ambiguity. *Gender and Psychoanalysis* 1:27–44.

Bergler, E. (1949). *The Basic Neurosis, Oral Regression and Psychic Masochism*. New York: Grune & Stratton.

Bergmann, M. (1994). The challenge of erotized transference to psychoanalytic technique. *Psychoanalytic Inquiry* 14:499–518.

Berliner, B. (1958). The role of object relations in moral masochism. *Psychoanalytic Quarterly* 27:38–56.

Bernstein, I. (1957). The role of narcissism in moral masochism. *Psychoanalytic Quarterly* 26:358–377.

Bibring-Lehner, G. (1936). A contribution to the subject of transference resistance. *International Journal of Psycho-Analysis* 17:181–189.

Blum, H. (1973). The concept of erotized transference. *Journal of the American Psychoanalytic Association* 21:61–76.

——— (1994). Discussion on the erotic transference: Contemporary perspectives. *Psychoanalytic Inquiry* 14:622–635.

Bollas, C. (1986). The transformational object. In *The British School of Psychoanalysis: The Independent Tradition*, ed. G. Kohon, pp. 83–100. New Haven: Yale University Press.

——— (1989). *Forces of Destiny: Psychoanalysis and Human Idiom*. London: Free Association Books.

——— (1994). Aspects of the erotic transference. *Psychoanalytic Inquiry* 14:572–590.

Brenman, M. (1952). On teasing and being teased: and the problem of "moral masochism." *Psychoanalytic Study of the Child* 7:264–285. New York: International Universities Press.

Brenner, C. (1959). The masochistic character: genesis and treatment. *Journal of the American Psychoanalytic Association* 7:197–226.

Butler, J. (1990). Gender trouble, feminist theory, and psychoanalytic discourse. In *Feminism/Postmodernism*, ed. L. Nicholson, pp. 324–340. New York: Routledge.

——— (1995). Melancholy gender—refused identification. *Psychoanalytic Dialogues* 5:165–180.

Bychowski, G. (1959). Some aspects of masochistic involvement. *Journal of the American Psychoanalytic Association* 7:248–273.

Canestri, J. (1993). A cry of fire: some considerations on transference love. In *On Freud's "Observations on Transference Love,"* ed. E. S. Person, A. Hagelin, and P. Fonagy, pp. 146–164. New Haven:Yale University Press.

Carpy, D. V. (1989). Tolerating the countertransference: a mutative process. *International Journal of Psycho-Analysis* 70:287–294.

Coates, S. W. (1997). Is it time to jettison the concept of developmental lines? Commentary on de Marnette's paper "Bodies and Words." *Gender and Psychoanalysis* 2:35–54.

Coates, S. W., Friedman, R., and Wolfe, S. (1991). The etiology of boyhood gender disorder. *Psychoanalytic Dialogues* 1:481–523.

Coates, S. W., and Wolfe, S. (1995). Gender identity and disorder in boys: the interface of constitution and early experience. *Psychoanalytic Inquiry* 15:6–38.

Coburn, W. (1997). The vision in supervision: transference–countertransference dynamics and disclosure in the supervision relationship. *Bulletin of the Menninger Clinic* 61(4):481–494.

Coen, S. J. (1996). Love between therapist and patient: a review. *American Journal of Psychotherapy* 50:14–27.

Cooper, A. (1983). *Psychoanalytic Inquiry and New Knowledge: Reflections on Self Psychology*, ed. J. Lichtenberg and S. Kaplan. Hillsdale, NJ: Analytic Press.

———— (1988). The narcissistic-masochistic character. In *Masochism: Current Psychoanalytic Perspectives*, ed. R. A. Glick and D. I. Meyers, pp. 117–138. Hillsdale, NJ: Analytic Press.

Davies, J. M. (1994). Love in the afternoon: a relational reconsideration of desire and dread in the countertransference. *Psychoanalytic Dialogues* 4:153–170.

Davies, J. M., and Frawley, M. G. (1994). *Treating the Adult Survivor of Childhood Sexual Abuse: A Psychoanalytic Perspective*. New York: Basic Books.

de Beauvoir, S. (1952). *The Second Sex*. New York: Vintage Books.

Deri, S. K. (1984). *Symbolization and Creativity*. New York: International Universities Press.

Des Rosiers, P. (1993). Separation-individuation issues in sister transference. *Journal of the American Academy of Psychoanalysis* 21:273–289.

de St. Jorre, J. (1994). The unmasking of O. *The New Yorker*, August 1, pp. 42–49.

Dimen, M. (1997). *Bodies, acts and sex: thinking through the relational*. Paper presented at the First Annual Lecture Series, "Contemporary Approaches to Gender and Sexuality," Psychoanalytic Psychotherapy Study Center, New York, September 26.

Dostoevsky, F. (1866). *Crime and Punishment*. Hertfordshire, England: Wordsworth Editions Ltd., 1993.

Dupont, J. (1988). Ferenczi's madness. *Contemporary Psychoanalysis* 24:250–261.

Ehrenberg, D. B. (1992). On the question of analyzability. *Contemporary Psychoanalysis* 28:16–31.

———— (1995). Self-disclosure: Therapeutic tool or indulgence? *Contemporary Psychoanalysis* 31:213–228.

———— (1996). On the analyst's emotional availability and vulnerability. *Contemporary Psychoanalysis* 32:275–286.

Eickoff, F. W. (1993). A reading of "Transference Love." In *On Freud's "Observations on Transference Love,"* ed. E. S. Person, A. Hagelin, and P. Fonagy, p. 36. New Haven: Yale University Press.

Eidelberg, L. (1959). Humiliation in masochism. *Journal of the American Psychoanalytic Association* 7:274–283.

Eisenbud, R. J. (1967). Masochism revisited. *Psychoanalytic Review* 54:561–582.

Elise, D. (1991). When sexual and romantic feelings permeate the therapeutic relationship. In *Gays, Lesbians and Their Therapists,* ed. C. Silverstein, pp. 52–61. New York: Norton.

Elkind, S. N. (1992). *Resolving Impasses in Therapeutic Relationships.* New York: Guilford.

Epstein, L., and Feiner, A., eds. (1979). *Countertransference: The Therapist's Contribution to the Therapeutic Situation.* New York: Jason Aronson.

Fast, I. (1990). Aspects of early gender development: toward a reformulation. *Psychoanalytic Psychology* 7:105–118.

Fenichel, O. (1941). *Problems of Psychoanalytic Technique.* New York: Psychoanalytic Quarterly Press.

———— (1945). *The Psychoanalytic Theory of Neurosis.* New York: Norton.

Ferenczi, S. (1913). To whom does one relate one's dreams? In *Further Contributions to the Theory and Technique of Psychoanalysis,* ed. J. Richman, trans. J. Suttie, pp. 213–239. London: Karnac.

———— (1931). Child analysis in the analysis of adults. In *Final Contributions to the Problems and Methods of Psychoanalysis,* ed. M. Balint, trans. E. Mosbacher, pp. 126–142. London: Karnac.

———— (1932). *The Clinical Diary of Sandor Ferenczi.* Cambridge, MA: Harvard University Press.

———— (1933). Confusion of tongues between adult and child. In *Final Contributions to the Problems and Methods of Psychoanalysis,* ed. M. Balint, trans. E. Mosbacher, pp. 156–167. London: Karnac.

Fitzpatrick, K. (1999). Terms of endearment in clinical analysis. *Psychoanalytic Quarterly* 68:119–125.

Flugel, J. C. (1930). *The Psychology of Clothes.* London: Hogarth.

Fonagy, P., and Target, M. (1985). Understanding the violent patient: the use of the body and the role of the father. *International Journal of Psychoanalysis* 76:487–501.

———— (1996). Playing with reality: I. Theory of mind and the normal development of psychic reality. *International Journal of Psychoanalysis* 77:217–233.

———— (1998). Mentalization and changing aims in child psychoanalysis. *Psychoanalytic Dialogues* 8:87–114.

Frank, K. A. (1997). The role of the analyst's inadvertent self-revelations. *Psychoanalytic Dialogues* 7:281–314.

Freud, S. (1905a). Three essays on the theory of sexuality. *Standard Edition* 7:125–243.

———— (1905b). Fragment of an analysis of a case of hysteria. *Standard Edition* 7:7–124.

———— (1907). Delusions and dreams in Jensen's *Gradiva*. *Standard Edition* 9:3–93.

———— (1910). A special type of choice of object made by men. *Standard Edition* 11:163–176.

———— (1912). The dynamics of transference. *Standard Edition* 12:97–109.

———— (1914). On narcissism: an introduction. *Standard Edition* 14:73–104.

———— (1915a). Observations on transference love. *Standard Edition* 12:157–171.

———— (1915b). Instincts and their vicissitudes. *Standard Edition* 14:117–140.

———— (1918). From the history of an infantile neurosis. *Standard Edition* 17:7–104.

———— (1920). The psychogenesis of a case of homosexuality in a woman. *Standard Edition* 18:145–172.

———— (1921). Group psychology and the analysis of the ego. *Standard Edition* 18:69–144.

———— (1923). The ego and the id. *Standard Edition* 19:13–68.

———— (1924). The economic problem of masochism. *Standard Edition* 19:159–170.

———— (1926). Inhibitions, symptoms, and anxiety. *Standard Edition* 20:77–175.

———— (1927). Fetishism. *Standard Edition* 21:149–158.

———— (1928). Dostoevsky and parricide. *Standard Edition* 21:175–198.

———— (1932). Letter to Stefan Zweig. 2 June. In *Freud: Biologist of the Mind*, ed. F. Sulloway, p. 80. New York: Basic Books, 1979.

———— (1937). Analysis terminable and interminable. *Standard Edition* 23:211–253.

———— (1938). Splitting of the ego in the process of defense. *Standard Edition* 23:275–278.

Frommer, M. S. (1995). Countertransference obscurity in the psychoanalytic treatment of homosexual patients. In *Disorienting Sexuality: Psychoanalytic Reappraisals of Sexual Identities*, ed. T. Domenici and R. C. Lesser, pp. 65–82. New York: Routledge.

Gabbard, G. O. (1994). Sexual excitement and countertransference love in the analyst. *Journal of the American Psychoanalytic Association* 42:1083–1106.

Ghent, E. (1990). Masochism, submission, surrender: masochism as a perversion of surrender. *Contemporary Psychoanalysis* 26:108–136.

———— (1992). Foreword. In *Relational Perspectives in Psychoanalysis*, ed. N. J. Skolnick and S. C. Warshaw, pp. xii–xxii. Hillsdale, NJ: Analytic Press.

Gill, M. M. (1993). One-person and two-person perspectives: Freud's "Observations on transference-love." In *On Freud's "Observations on Transference-Love*," ed. E. S. Person, A. Hagelin, P. Fonagy, pp.114–129. New Haven: Yale University Press.

Gillespie, W. (1940). A contribution to the study of fetishism. *International Journal of Psycho-Analysis* 21:401–415.

Gitelson, M. (1952). The emotional position of the analyst in the psychoanalytic situation. *International Journal of Psycho-Analysis* 33:1–10.

Glick, R. A., and Meyers, D. I. (1988). *Masochism: Current Psychoanalytic Perspectives*. Hillsdale, NJ: Analytic Press.

Glover, E. (1932a). On the etiology of drug-addiction. In *On the Early Development of the Mind*, pp. 187–215. New York: International Universities Press.

———— (1932b). Perversion-formation and reality-sense. In *On the Early Development of the Mind*, pp. 216–234. New York: International Universities Press.

———— (1955). *The Technique of Psycho-Analysis*. New York: International Universities Press.

Goldberg, A. (1975). A fresh look at perverse behavior. *International Journal of Psycho-Analysis* 56:335–342.

——— (1988). *A Fresh Look at Psychoanalysis*. Hillsdale, NJ: Analytic Press.

Goldberger, M., and Evans Holmes, D. E. (1985). On transference manifestations in male patients with female analysts. *International Journal of Psycho-Analysis* 66:295–309.

——— (1993). Transferences in male patients with female analysts: an update. *Psychoanalytic Inquiry* 13:173–191.

Gould, E. (1994). A case of erotized transference in a male patient: formations and transformations. *Psychoanalytic Inquiry* 14:558–571.

Graham, I. (1988). The sibling object and its transferences: alternate organizer of the middle field. *Psychoanalytic Inquiry* 8:88–107.

Greenacre, P. (1960). Further notes on fetishism. In *Emotional Growth*, pp. 182–198. New York: International Universities Press.

——— (1979). Fetishism. In *Sexual Deviation*, ed. J. Rosen, pp. 79–108. New York: Oxford University Press.

Greenberg, J. (1991). *Oedipus and Beyond: A Clinical Theory*. Cambridge, MA: Harvard University Press.

Greenson, R. R. (1960). Empathy and its vicissitudes. *International Journal of Psycho-Analysis* 41:418–424.

——— (1968). Dis-identifying from mother: its special importance for the boy. *International Journal of Psycho-Analysis* 49:370–374.

——— (1978). *Explorations in Psychoanalysis*. New York: International Universities Press.

Grinberg, L. (1962). On a specific aspect of countertransference due to the patient's projective identification. *International Journal of Psycho-Analysis* 43:436–440.

Grunberger, B. (1964). Outline for a study of narcissism in female sexuality. In *Female Sexuality: New Psychoanalytic Views*, ed. J. Chasseguet-Smirgel, pp. 68–83. London: Maresfield Library.

——— (1971). *Narcissism: Psychoanalytic Essays*. New York: International Universities Press.

Hamilton, G. N. (1990). The containing function and the analyst's projective identification. *American Journal of Psychoanalysis* 71:445–453.

Harris, A. (1997). Aggression, envy, and ambition: circulating tensions in women's psychic life. *Gender and Psychoanalysis* 2:291–326.

Hartmann, H. (1958). *Ego Psychology and the Problem of Adaptation*. New York: International Universities Press.

Heimann, P. (1950). On countertransference. *International Journal of Psycho-Analysis* 31:81–84.

Hirsch, I. (1986). Mature love in the countertransference. In *Love*, ed. J. F. Lasky and H. W. Silverman, pp. 200–212. New York: New York University Press.

——— (1994). Countertransference love and theoretical model. *Psychoanalytic Dialogues* 4:171–194.

——— (1996). Observing-participation, mutual enactment, and the new classical models. *Contemporary Psychoanalysis* 32:359–384.

Hoffer, A. (1993). Is love in the analytic relationship "real?" *Psychoanalytic Inquiry* 13:343–356.

Hoffman, I. A. (1992). Some practical implications of a social-constructivist view of the psychoanalytic situation. *Psychoanalytic Dialogues* 2:287–304.

Horney, K. (1935). The problem of feminine masochism. *Psychoanalytic Review* 22:241–257.

——— (1936). The problem of the negative therapeutic reaction. *Psychoanalytic Quarterly* 5:29–44.

Isay, R. A. (1996). *Becoming Gay: The Journey to Self-Acceptance*. New York: Pantheon.

James, W. (1896). The will to believe. In *The Essential Writing*, ed. B. W. Wilshire, pp. 309–325. Albany, NY: State University of New York Press.

Jones, E. (1953). *The Life and Work of Sigmund Freud, Vol. 1: The Formative Years and the Great Discoveries*. New York: Basic Books.

Kaftal, E. (1983). Self psychology and psychological interrelatedness. *Contemporary Psychotherapy Review* 1:20–46.

——— (1991). *The surprising patient*. Paper presented at APA Conference, Philadelphia, PA, April.

——— (1994). *Some obstacles to the heterosexual analyst's introspection*. Paper presented at the 14th Annual Division 39 Spring Meeting of the American Psychological Association, Washington, DC, April.

——— (1995). *Therapeutic action, narrative and uncertainty*. Presentation at APA Conference. Philadelphia, PA, April.

———— (1997). Untying the relational knot. *Psychoanalytic Dialogues* 7:341–346.

Kaplan, L. J. (1991a). Women masquerading as women. In *Perversions and Near-Perversions in Clinical Practice: New Psychoanalytic Perspectives.* ed. G. I. Fogel and W. A. Myers, pp. 127–152. Hillsdale, NJ: Analytic Press.

———— (1991b). *Female Perversions: The Temptations of Emma Bovary.* New York: Doubleday.

Karme, L. (1993). Male patients and female analysts: erotic and other psychoanalytic encounters. *Psychoanalytic Inquiry* 13:192–205.

Keiser, S. (1949). The fear of sexual passivity in the masochist. *International Journal of Psycho-Analysis* 30:162–171.

Kelly, M. (1985). *Post-Partum Document.* London: Routledge & Kegan Paul.

Kernberg, O. (1965). Notes on countertransference. *Journal of the American Psychoanalytic Association* 13:38–56.

———— (1992). Love in the analytic setting. *Journal of the American Psychoanalytic Association* 42:1137–1157.

Kernberg, P. A., and Richards, A. K. (1988). Siblings of preadolescents: their role in development. *Psychoanalytic Inquiry* 8:51–65.

Khan, M. (1979). *Alienation in Perversions.* New York: International Universities Press.

Klein, M. (1946). Notes on some schizoid mechanisms. *International Journal of Psycho-Analysis* 33:430–438.

———— (1957). *Envy and Gratitude.* New York: Basic Books.

Kohut, H. (1959). Introspection, empathy and psychoanalysis. In *The Search for the Self,* vol. 1, ed. P. Ornstein, pp. 205–232. New York: International Universities Press.

———— (1968). The psychoanalytic treatment of narcissistic personality disorders. *Psychoanalytic Study of the Child* 23:86–113. New York: International Universities Press.

———— (1971). *The Analysis of the Self.* New York: International Universities Press.

———— (1977). *The Restoration of the Self.* New York: International Universities Press.

————— (1984). *How Does Analysis Cure?* Chicago: University of Chicago Press.

Kohut, T. (1994). Paper presented at the Annual Self Psychology Conference, Toronto, Canada, October.

Kulish, N., and Mayman, M. (1993). Gender-linked determinants of transference and countertransference in psychoanalytic psychotherapy. *Psychoanalytic Inquiry* 13:286–305.

Kumin, I. (1985). Erotic horror: desire and resistance in the psychoanalytic situation. *International Journal of Psychoanalytic Psychotherapy* 11:3–20.

Laplanche, J. and Pontalis, J. B. (1973). *The Language of Psychoanalysis.* New York: Norton.

Lesser, R. M. (1978). Sibling transference and countertransference. *Journal of the American Academy of Psychoanalysis* 9:37–49.

Lester, E. P. (1985). The female analyst and the erotized transference. *International Journal of Psycho-Analysis* 66:283–293.

————— (1993). Boundaries and gender: their interplay in the analytic situation. *Psychoanalytic Inquiry* 13:153–172.

Levenson, E. A. (1992). Mistakes, errors and oversights. *Contemporary Psychoanalysis* 28:555–571.

Lewin, B. (1950). *Psychoanalysis of Elation.* New York: Norton.

Loewenstein, R. (1945). A special form of self-punishment. *Psychoanalytic Quarterly* 14:46–61.

————— (1957). A contribution to the psychoanalytic theory of masochism. *Journal of the American Psychoanalytic Association* 5:197–234.

Marcus, B. F. (1993). Vicissitudes of gender identity in the female therapist/male patient dyad. *Psychoanalytic Inquiry* 13:258–269.

Maroda, K. J. (1999). *Seduction, Surrender, and Transformation: Emotional Engagement in the Analytic Process.* Hillsdale, NJ: Analytic Press.

McDougall, J. (1986). Eve's reflection: on the homosexual components of female sexuality. In *Between Analyst and Patient*, ed. H. Meyers, Hillsdale, NJ: Analytic Press.

————— (1995). *The Many Faces of Eros.* New York: Norton.

McWilliams, N. (1996). Therapy across the sexual orientation boundary: reflections of a heterosexual female analyst on working with lesbian, gay, and bisexual patients. *Gender and Psychoanalysis* 1:203–222.

Meissner, W. W. (1998). The self and the body, III: the body image in clinical perspective. *Psychoanalysis and Contemporary Thought* 21:113–146.

Menaker, E. (1953). Masochism: a defense reaction of the ego. *Psychoanalytic Quarterly* 22:205–225.

Mendell, D. (1993). Supervising female therapists: a comparison of dynamics while treating male and female patients. *Psychoanalytic Inquiry* 13(2):270–285.

Menninger, K. (1958). *Theory of Psychoanalytic Technique.* New York: Basic Books.

Middlebrook, D. W. (1998). *Suits Me.* New York: Houghton-Mifflin.

Miller, S. B. (1993). Disgust reactions: their determinants and manifestations in treatment. *Journal of Contemporary Psychoanalysis* 29:711–735.

Milner, M. (1969). *The Hands of the Living God: An Account of a Psycho-Analytic Treatment.* New York: International Universities Press.

——— (1988). *The Suppressed Madness of Sane Men.* London: Tavistock.

Mitchell, S. A. (1988). *Relational Concepts in Psychoanalysis: An Integration.* Cambridge, MA: Harvard University Press.

——— (1993). *Hope and Dread in Psychoanalysis.* New York: Basic Books.

——— (1997). *Influence and Autonomy in Psychoanalysis.* Hillsdale, NJ: Analytic Press.

Morrison, A. P. (1999). Walking taller, though still wounded: discussion of "Wounded but still walking: One man's effort to move out of shame." *Psychoanalytic Inquiry* 19:320–331.

Nacht, S. (1938). Introduction. In *Essential Papers on Masochism,* ed. M. Hanly, pp. 18–34. New York: New York University Press.

Noyes, J. K. (1997). *The Mastery of Submission: Inventions of Masochism.* Ithaca, NY: Cornell University Press.

Nydes, J. (1963). The magical experience of the masturbation fantasy. *American Journal of Psychotherapy* 4:303–310.

O'Connor, N., and Ryan, J. (1993). *Wild Desires and Mistaken Identities.* New York: Columbia University Press.

Ogden, T. H. (1982). *Projective Identification and Psychotherapeutic Technique*. New York: Jason Aronson.

———— (1989). *The Primitive Edge of Experience*. Northvale, NJ: Jason Aronson.

———— (1990). *The Matrix of the Mind: Object Relations and the Psychoanalytic Dialogue*. Northvale, NJ: Jason Aronson.

Olinick, S. L. (1964). The negative therapeutic reaction. *International Journal of Psycho-Analysis* 45:540–548.

Orange D. M., and Stolorow, R. D. (1998). Self-disclosure from the perspective of intersubjectivity theory. *Psychoanalytic Inquiry* 18:530–537.

Parens, H. (1988). Siblings in early childhood: some direct observational findings. *Psychoanalytic Inquiry* 8:31–50.

Person, E. S. (1985). The erotic transference in women and men: differences and consequences. *Journal of the American Academy of Psychoanalysis* 11:159–180.

———— (1993). Introduction. In *On Freud's "Observations on Transference-Love,"* ed. E. S. Person, A. Hagelin, and P. Fonagy, pp. 1–14. New Haven: Yale University Press.

Person, E. S., and Ovesey, I. (1983). Psychoanalytic theories of gender identity. *Journal of the American Academy of Psychoanalysis* 11:203–226.

Philipson, I. J. (1993). *On the Shoulders of Women*. New York: Guilford.

Phillips, A. (1993). *On Kissing, Tickling, and Being Bored: Psychoanalytic Essays on the Unexamined Life*. Cambridge, MA: Harvard University Press.

———— (1994). *On Flirtation*. Cambridge, MA: Harvard University Press.

Racker, H. (1968). *Transference and Countertransference*. New York: International Universities Press.

Rank, O. (1922). Perversion and neurosis. *International Journal of Psycho-Analysis* 4:270–292.

Rappaport, E. (1956). The management of an erotized transference. *Psychoanalytic Quarterly* 26:515–529.

———— (1959). The first dream in an erotized transference. *International Journal of Psycho-Analysis* 40:240–245.

Réage, P. (1965). *Story of O*. New York: Blue Moon Books, 1993.

Reed, G. S. (1996). The analyst's interpretation as fetish. *Journal of the American Psychoanalytic Association* 45:1153–1181.

Reich, A. (1951). On counter-transference. *International Journal of Psycho-Analysis* 32:25–31.

Reich, W. (1933). *Character Analysis*. New York: Orgone Institute Press.

Reik, T. (1941). *Masochism in Modern Man*. New York: Farrar & Straus.

Richards, A. K. (1990). Female fetishes and female perversions: Hermine Hug-Hellmuth's "A Case of Female Foot or More Properly Boot Fetishism" reconsidered. *Psychoanalytic Review* 77:11–23.

―――― (1996). Ladies of fashion: pleasure, perversion, or paraphilia. *International Journal of Psycho-Analysis* 77:337–351.

Ringstrom, P. A. (1998). Therapeutic impasses in contemporary psychoanalytic treatment: revisiting the double bind hypothesis. *Psychoanalytic Dialogues* 8:297–315.

Riviere, J. (1929). Womanliness as a masquerade. In *Formations of Fantasy*, ed. V. Burgin, J. Donald, and C. Kaplan, pp. 35–44. London: Methuen.

Rosenfeld, H. (1985). *Presentations of Gender*. New Haven: Yale University Press.

―――― (1987). *Impasse and Interpretation: Therapeutic and Anti-Therapeutic Factors in the Psychoanalytic Treatment of Psychotic, Borderline, and Neurotic Patients*. London: Tavistock/Routledge.

Rosiello, F. (1993). The interplay of masochism and narcissism in the treatment of two prostitutes. *Contemporary Psychotherapy Review* 8:28–40.

―――― (1995). Passions in the selfobject transference of an AIDS group psychotherapy. *Group Analysis* 28:72–86.

Rosner, S. (1985). On the place of siblings in psychoanalysis. *Psychoanalytic Review* 72:457–477.

Russ, H. (1993). Erotic transference through countertransference: the female therapist and the male patient. *Psychoanalytic Psychology* 10:393–406.

Sachs, H. (1923). Zur Gneses der Perversionen. *International Journal of Psycho-Analysis* 9:173.

Schafer, R. (1959). Generative empathy in the treatment situation. *Psychoanalytic Quarterly* 28:347–373.

Schilder, P. (1935). *The Image and Appearance of the Human Body: Studies in the Constructive Energies of the Psyche.* New York: Wiley.

Searles, H. (1959). Oedipal love in the countertransference. In *Collected Papers on Schizophrenia and Related Topics*, pp. 284–303. New York: International Universities Press.

———— (1965). Introduction. In *Collected Papers on Schizophrenia and Related Topics*, pp. 19–38. New York: International Universities Press.

Siegel, E. V. (1988). *Female Homosexuality: Choice Without Volition.* Hillsdale, NJ: Analytic Press.

Socarides, C. (1958). The function of moral masochism: with special reference to the defense processes. *International Journal of Psycho-Analysis* 39:587–597.

Stern, D. (1997). *Unformulated Experience: From Dissociation to Imagination in Psychoanalysis.* Hillsdale, NJ: Analytic Press.

Stoller, R.J. (1968). *Sex and Gender.* New York: Jason Aronson.

———— (1975). *Sex and Gender II.* New York: Jason Aronson.

Stolorow, R. D. (1975). The narcissistic function of masochism and sadism. *International Journal of Psycho-Analysis* 56:441–448.

———— (1984). Aggression in the psychoanalytic situation: an intersubjective viewpoint. *Contemporary Psychoanalysis* 20:643–651.

———— (1986). Critical reflections on the theory of self psychology: an inside view. *Psychoanalytic Inquiry* 6:387–402.

Stolorow, R. D., and Atwood, G. E. (1984). *Structures of Subjectivity: Explorations in Psychoanalytic Phenomenology.* Hillsdale, NJ: Analytic Press.

———— (1992). *Contexts of Being: The Intersubjective Foundations of Psychological Life.* Hillsdale, NJ: Analytic Press.

Stolorow, R. D., Atwood, G. E., and Brandchaft, B., eds. (1987). *Psychoanalytic Treatment: An Intersubjective Approach.* Hillsdale, NJ: Analytic Press.

———— (1994). *The Intersubjective Perspective.* Northvale, NJ: Jason Aronson.

Stolorow, R. D., and Lachmann, F. (1979). *Faces in a Cloud: Subjectivity in Personality Theory.* New York: Jason Aronson.

——— (1980). *Psychoanalysis of Developmental Arrests*. Madison, CT: International Universities Press.

Stolorow, R. D., and Trop, J. L. (1992). Varieties of therapeutic impasse. In *Contexts of Being: The Intersubjective Foundations of Psychological Life*, ed. R. D. Stolorow and G. E. Atwood, pp. 103–122. Hillsdale, NJ: Analytic Press.

Sullivan, H. S. (1953). *The Interpersonal Theory of Psychiatry*. New York: Norton.

Swartz, J. (1967). The erotized transference and other transference problems. *Psychoanalytic Forum* 3:307–318.

Tansey, J. J. (1994). Sexual attraction and phobic dread in countertransference. *Psychoanalytic Dialogues* 4:139–152.

Target, M., and Fonagy, P. (1996). Playing with reality: II. The development of psychic reality from a theoretical perspective. *International Journal of Psycho-Analysis* 77:459–479.

Taylor, J. (1998). *Paper Tangos*. Durham, NC: Duke University Press.

Thompson, C. (1956). The role of the analyst's personality. In *Essential Papers on Countertransference*, ed. B. Wolstein, pp. 120–130. New York: New York University Press.

Tosone, C., and Aiello, T., eds. (1999). *Love and Attachment: Contemporary Issues and Treatment Considerations*. Northvale, NJ: Jason Aronson.

Tower, L. E. (1956). Countertransference. *Journal of the American Psychoanalytic Association* 4:331–336.

Trop, J. L. (1988). Erotic and eroticized transference: a self psychology perspective. *Psychoanalytic Psychology* 5:269–284.

Volkan, V. D., and Ast, G. (1997). *Siblings in the Unconscious and Psychopathology*. Madison, CT: International Universities Press.

Welles, J. K., and Wrye, H. K. (1991). Maternal erotic countertransference. *International Journal of Psycho-Analysis* 72:93–106.

Winnicott, D. W. (1949). Mind and its relation to the psyche-soma. In *Through Paediatrics to Psycho-Analysis*, pp. 243–254. New York: Basic Books.

——— (1958). The capacity to be alone. In *The Maturational Processes and the Facilitating Environment*, ed. M. Khan, pp. 29–36. Madison, CT: International Universities Press.

——— (1960). The theory of the parent–infant relationship. In *The Maturational Processes and the Facilitating Environment*, ed. M. Khan, pp. 37–55. Madison, CT: International Universities Press.

——— (1969). The use of an object and relating through identifications. In *Playing and Reality*, pp. 86–94. London: Tavistock, 1971.

——— (1971). *Playing and Reality*. London: Tavistock.

Wolf, E. S. (1988). *Treating the Self: Elements of Clinical Self Psychology*. New York: Guilford.

——— (1994). Narcissistic lust and other vicissitudes of sexuality. *Psychoanalytic Inquiry* 14:519–534.

Wrye, H. K. (1993). Erotic terror: male patients' horror of the early maternal erotic transference. *Psychoanalytic Inquiry* 13:240–257.

Wrye, H. K., and Welles, J. K. (1994). *The Narration of Desire: Erotic Transferences and Countertransferences*. Hillsdale, NJ: Analytic Press.

Wurmser, L. (1999). Trauma, shame conflicts, and affect regression: discussion of "Wounded but Still Walking." *Psychoanalytic Inquiry* 19:309–319.

Index

ABOUT THE AUTHOR

Florence Rosiello, Ph.D., is a graduate of the doctoral program at New York University School of Social Work. She is faculty and supervisor at the Institute for Contemporary Psychotherapy, where she received a certificate in psychoanalysis, as well as faculty and supervisor at Psychoanalytic Psychotherapy Study Center and the New York Institute for Psychoanalytic Self Psychology. Author of psychoanalytic journal articles on the erotic transference/countertransference, Dr. Rosiello was Editor of *Contemporary Psychotherapy Review* and Editor-in-Chief of *Newsletter for the Committee on Psychoanalysis*. She is in private practice in psychoanalysis and psychotherapy in New York City.